YOU ARE HERE.

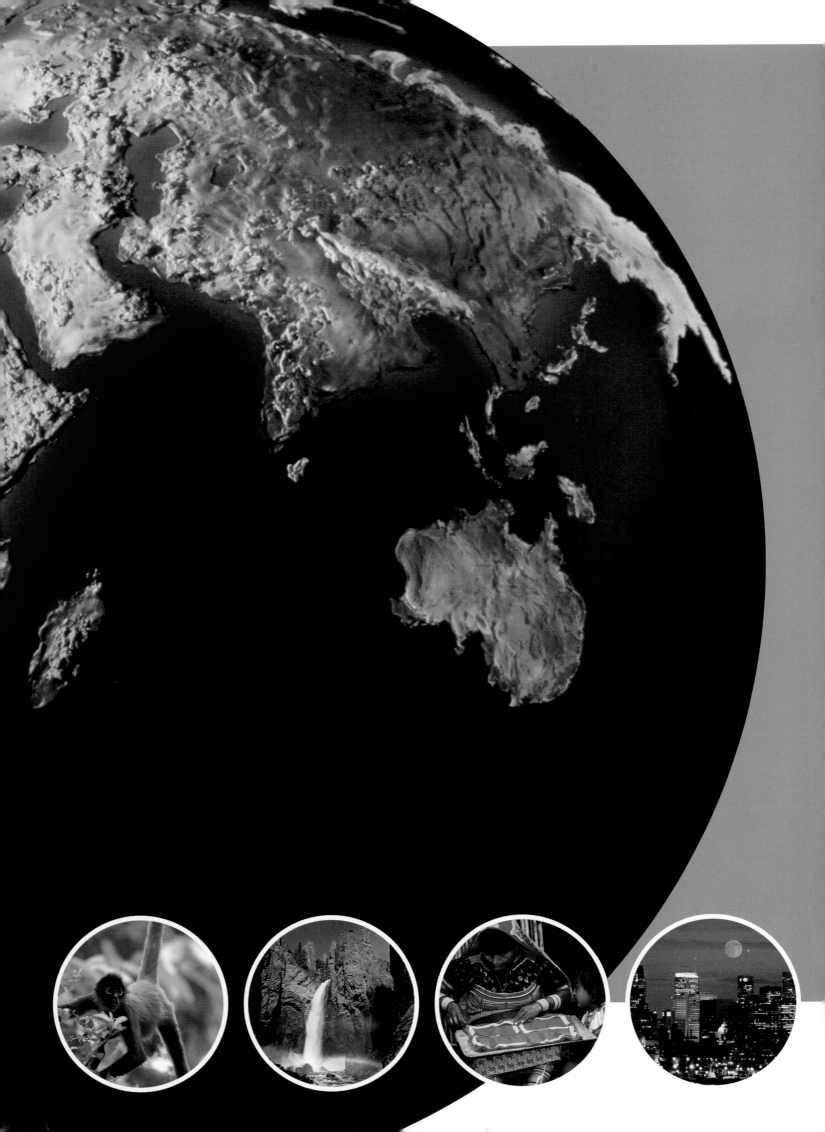

NATIONAL GEOGRAPHIC

WORLD ATLAS

FOR YOUNG EXPLORERS

THIRD EDITION

NATIONAL GEOGRAPHIC   WASHINGTON, DC

TABLE OF CONTENTS

North America: Grand Canyon, page 64

South America: Llama, page 81

Europe: Colosseum, pages 96–97

Antarctica: Penguins, pages 162–163

Australia, New Zealand, & Oceania: Maori man, page 152

Africa: Mother and child, page 137

HOW TO USE THIS ATLAS

This atlas is a window on your planet. Through it you can explore the world. To learn about maps, use the first section, Understanding Maps. Some basic facts about Earth as a planet are included in the section called Planet Earth. The Physical World includes world maps that focus on different aspects of nature, the environment, and the oceans. The Political World contains world maps about how humans live on the planet. After that, the maps, photographs, and essays are arranged by continent and region. You can look up specific places or just browse. Remember, it's your planet—learn it, love it, explore it!

WEB LINKS

Throughout the book you'll find black-and-yellow Web link icons for photos, videos, sounds, and games. You can get to all of these links through one URL: www.nationalgeographic.com/kids-world-atlas. This link takes you to the Web site specially designed to go with this atlas. Bookmark it, and use it often. See pages 8–9 for how to use the Web site.

STATS & FACTS

At the left-hand edge of each continent opener and regional page is a bar that includes basic information about the subject. This feature is a great first stop if you're writing a report.

CHARTS & GRAPHS

Each region includes a chart or graph that shows information visually.

"YOU ARE HERE"

Locator globes help you see where one area is in relation to others. On regional pages (shown here), the area covered by the main map is yellow on the globe, and its continent is green. On pages with continent maps, the locator globe shows the whole continent in yellow. The surrounding land is brown.

124 | SOUTHWEST ASIA

THE CONTINENT:
ASIA

SOUTHWEST ASIA

This region, made up largely of deserts and mountains, includes the countries of the Arabian Peninsula and those that border the Persian Gulf. Islam is the dominant religion in each, and the two holiest places for Muslims—Mecca and Medina—are here. Arabic is the principal language everywhere but Iran, where most people speak Farsi. While water has been the most important natural resource here for millennia, global attention has focused in recent decades on the region's oil wealth. With the majority of the world's reserves found here, oil has brought outside influences and military conflict. Long a cradle of civilization, Southwest Asia continues to hold the world's gaze.

THE BASICS

STATS

Largest country
Saudi Arabia 726,985 sq mi (1,960,582 sq km)

Smallest
Bahrain 277 sq mi (717 sq km)

Most populous country
Iran 70,300,000

Least populous country
Bahrain 700,000

Predominant languages
Arabic, Farsi (modern-day Persian)

Predominant religion
Islam

Highest GDP per capita
Qatar $56,312

Lowest GDP per capita
Yemen $849

Highest life expectancy
Kuwait 78 years

Highest literacy rate
Bahrain, Qatar
89%

GEO WHIZ

Rub' al Khali (Empty Quarter), the world's largest sand desert, covers 225,000 square miles (583,000 sq km), an area larger than France.

More than 4,000 years ago, the Sumerians built the first cities in the world on the plain between the Tigris and Euphrates Rivers in what is now Iraq.

The ancient Romans called Yemen "Arabia Felix," meaning "Happy Arabia."

Five times a day, every day, Muslims all over the world face the city of Mecca, in Saudi Arabia, to pray. Mecca is the birthplace of the prophet Muhammad, the founder of Islam.

Iran drilled the first oil wells in the region in 1908.

Causeways connect Bahrain Island—the largest of the 36 islands that make up the country of Bahrain—to two others and to the mainland of Saudi Arabia.

REGIONAL OIL RESERVES

Saudi Arabia 281.8 billion barrels
Iraq 112.5 billion barrels
United Arab Emirates 97.8 billion barrels
Kuwait 96.5 billion barrels
Iran 89.7 billion barrels
Qatar 15.2 billion barrels
Oman 5.5 billion barrels
Yemen 3 billion barrels
Bahrain 0.1 billion barrels

Figures are for all reserves.

Saudi Arabia leads the region and the world in oil reserves and production, but four other countries in Southwest Asia also rank near the top.

⇧ GIRL TALK. Young Iranian girls get together at a film festival in Tehran. The scarves they are wearing are part of the Islamic dress code hijab, which says that women and girls must cover their heads and dress modestly.

⇧ HE'S GOT THE BEAT. This Omani drummer plays at a dance in the Arabian Sea port of Qurayyat. Though modernized in many ways, Oman works hard to preserve its traditional culture.

⇦ DIFFERENT WORLDS. A contrast between horse and horsepower, this roadside meeting in Qatar also displays both traditional Arab and Western clothing styles. This Persian Gulf country preserves a rich history of Arabian horse breeding and continues to produce champions.

ABOUT THE CONTINENT

THE CONTINENT:
ASIA

more about
ASIA

WHERE THE PICTURES ARE

ABOUT THE CONTINENT

THE CONTINENT:
ASIA

WHERE ARE THE PICTURES?

If you want to know where a picture in the regional sections of this atlas was taken, look for the map in the photo essay. Find the label that describes the picture you're curious about, and follow the line to its location.

Maps use symbols to stand for many political and physical features. At right is the key to the symbols used in this atlas. If you are wondering what you're looking at on a map, check here.

INDEX AND GRID

Look through the index for the place-name you want. Next to it is a page number, a letter, and another number. Go to the page. Draw imaginary lines from the letter along the side of the map and the number along the top. Your place will be close to where the lines meet.

Río Muni (region),
  Equatorial Guinea
  145 F2
Rivera, Uruguay **89** D4
Riverside, California
  70 E2
Riviera (region), Europe
  92 F3
Rivne, Ukraine **103** D6
Riyadh, Saudi Arabia
  125 E4

COLOR BARS

Every section of this atlas has its own color. Look for the color on the Contents pages and across the top of every page in the atlas. Within that color bar, you'll see the name of the section and the title for each topic or map. These color bars are a handy way to find the section you want.

North America
South America
Europe
Asia
Africa
Australia, New Zealand, & Oceania
Antarctica

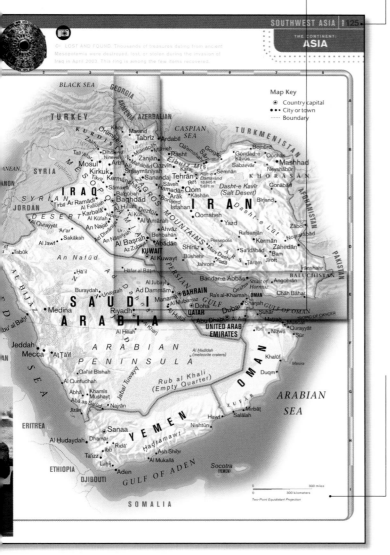

SOUTHWEST ASIA | 125

THE CONTINENT:
ASIA

BAR SCALE

If you want to find out how far it is from one place on a map to another, use the scale. A bar scale appears on every map. It shows how distance on paper relates to distance in the real world.

MAP KEY

• • • City / Town	791 ft. / 241 m +	Mountain peak with elevation above sea level	⤙ Waterfall	Dry / Salt Lake
⊛ Country capital			⊐ Dam	Glacier
⊙ State / Provincial capital	-282 ft. / -86 m	Low point with elevation below sea level	Canal	Swamp
◆ Small country	⋯⋯	Defined boundary	Ice Shelf	Sand
∴ Ruin	⋯ ⋯	Undefined boundary	Reef	Tundra
■ Point of Interest	⋯⋯	Claimed boundary	Lake	Lava
	⌇	River	Intermittent Lake	Below sea level

HOW TO USE THE ATLAS WEB SITE

As you can see by flipping through it, this atlas is chock full. There are photographs, statistics, quick facts and—most of all—lots of detailed maps and charts. And the companion Web site adds even more. You can watch videos of animals in their natural surroundings, listen to animal sounds and to music from many different cultures, find lots of country information, download pictures and maps for your school reports, play games that allow you to explore the world interactively, and even send e-postcards to your friends. The Web site extends specific subjects in the atlas and also helps you explore on your own, taking you deep into the resources of National Geographic and beyond. Throughout the book you will find these icons.

PHOTOS   VIDEO   AUDIO   GAMES

Some icons are placed near pictures. Others are with text. Each icon tells you that you can find more on that subject on the Web site. To follow any icon link, go to www.nationalgeographic.com/kids-world-atlas.

⇩START HERE. There are three ways to find what you are looking for from the Home Page:

1. BY ATLAS PAGE NUMBER
2. BY TOPIC
3. BY ICON

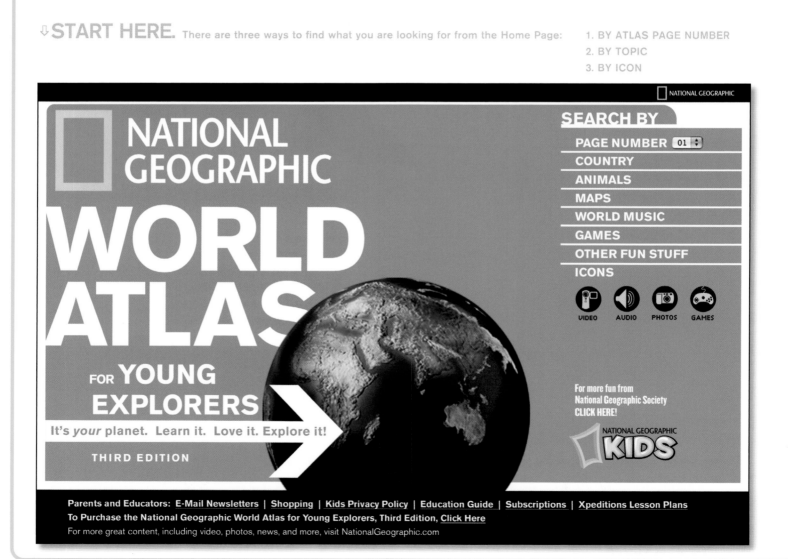

www.nationalgeographic.com/kids-world-atlas

1. SEARCH BY ATLAS PAGE NUMBER

⇦PAGE NUMBER PULL-DOWN MENU. If you find an icon in the atlas and want to go directly to that link, use the page number pull-down menu. Just drag and click.

2. SEARCH BY TOPIC

⇨LIST OF TOPICS. If you want to explore a specific topic, click on the entry in the topic list. This list is your portal to vast quantities of National Geographic information, photos, videos, games, and more, all arranged by subject. Say you're interested in Animals. One click takes you to the Animals choice page (below).

⇩ CREATURE FEATURES. Click to go to the National Geographic Kids' animal site. Click on an animal, and you will find a full feature about it, including photos, video, a range map, and other fun info.

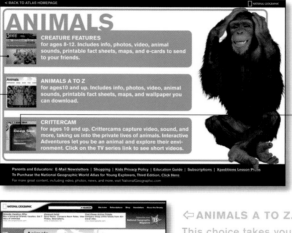

⇩ CRITTERCAM. Scientists put video cameras on animals to learn about the animal from its point of view. Click to see those videos, learn about the project, play games such as exploring the virtual world of a seal, and more.

⇦ANIMALS A TO Z. This choice takes you to the animal site for adults and older kids. Use the list of animals in the upper right-hand corner of the page. Clicking on an animal there takes you to the profile of that animal.

3. SEARCH BY ICON

⇦ SELECT ONE OF FOUR ICONS. If you want to find all the videos referenced in the atlas, or all of the audios, photos, or games, click on one of the icons. A list of page numbers will drop down. Choose from the list, and you're there! Clicking on King Tut takes you to several King Tut videos.

EXPLORING YOUR WORLD

Earth is a big place. Even from space you can't see it all at one time. But with a map, you can see the whole world or just a part of it. Thanks to the Internet, you can download programs that allow you to experience Earth from space, pick a place you want to explore, and zoom closer and closer until you are "standing" among its buildings! These screenshots (right) take you from space to Chicago at the click of a mouse. You can even find a satellite view of your house (see below).

Compare the computer enhanced satellite images with the maps on the opposite page, and you will see how the same places can be shown in very different ways. You will want to explore all of them to really get to know your world.

FIND YOUR HOUSE

This image from SkylineGlobe shows National Geographic offices in Washington, D.C. To see your house, go to www.skylineglobe.com, one of several Web sites that allows you to view satellite imagery of the world.

Images from SkylineGlobe
(www.skylineglobe.com)

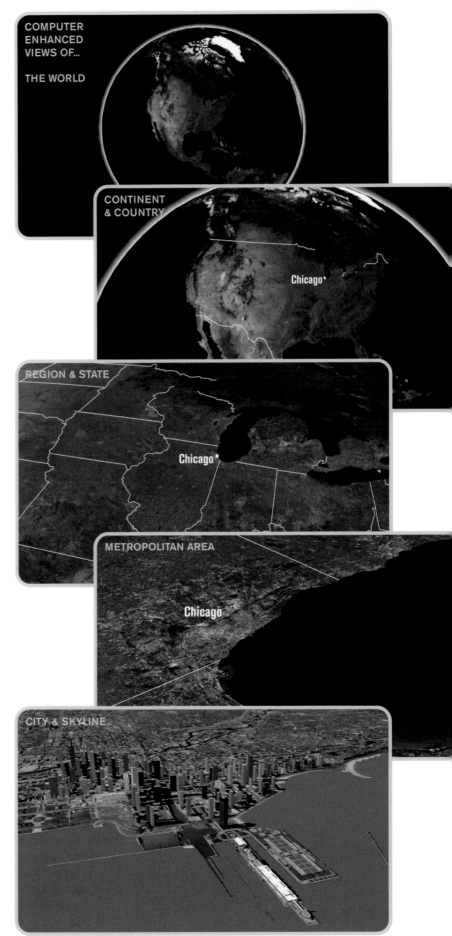

COMPUTER ENHANCED VIEWS OF...

THE WORLD

CONTINENT & COUNTRY

Chicago

REGION & STATE

Chicago

METROPOLITAN AREA

Chicago

CITY & SKYLINE

⇦ STATE MAP. This political map allows a close look at the state of Illinois in the midwestern region of the United States. This large-scale map shows only a small part of Earth's surface, but it includes such details as boundaries, physical features, and selected cities. This map is good for examining relationships within the state.

⇨ COUNTRY MAP, WORLD MAP. As the scale of a map becomes smaller, you can see more of Earth but in less detail. The map of the United States (above) has a smaller scale than the state map (top). This means you can see the entire country and the location of Illinois relative to other states, but you can no longer see as many details within the state. The world map (right) has an even smaller scale. How is this map different from the other two? Its all a mtter of scale!

KINDS OF MAPS

Maps are special tools that geographers use to tell a story about Earth. Some maps show physical features, such as mountains or vegetation. Maps also show climates or natural hazards and other things we cannot easily see. Other maps illustrate different human features on Earth—political boundaries, urban centers, and economic systems.

Maps are not perfect. A globe is a scale model of Earth with accurate relative sizes and locations. Because maps are flat, they involve distortions of size, shape, and direction. Also, cartographers—people who create maps—make choices about what information to include. Because of this, it is important to study many different types of maps to learn the complete story of Earth.

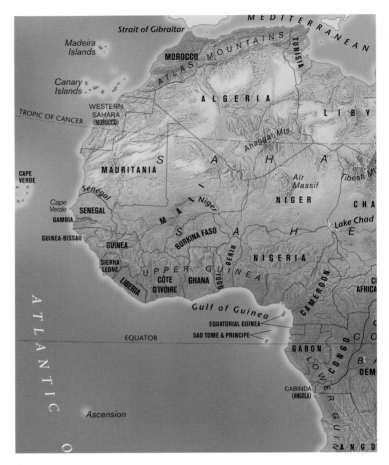

⬆ PHYSICAL MAPS. Earth's natural features—landforms, water bodies, and vegetation—are shown on physical maps. The map above uses color and shading to illustrate mountains, lakes, rivers, and deserts of western Africa. Country names and borders are added for reference, but they are not natural features.

⬅ MAP PROJECTIONS. To create a map, cartographers transfer an image of the round Earth to a flat surface, a process called projection. All projections involve distortion. For example, an interrupted projection (top map) shows accurate shapes and relative sizes of land areas, but oceans have gaps. Other types of projections are cylindrical, conic, or azimuthal—each with certain advantages, but all with some distortion.

MAKING MAPS

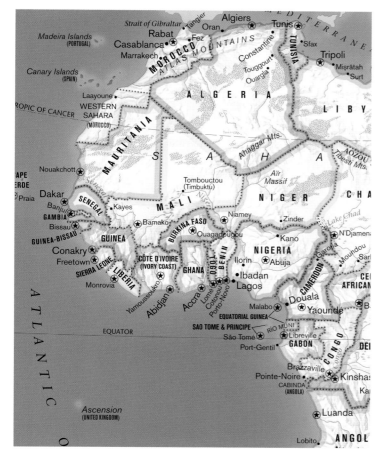

⇧ POLITICAL MAPS. These maps represent human characteristics of the landscape, such as boundaries, cities, and place-names. Natural features are added only for reference. On the map above, capital cities are represented with a star inside a circle, while other cities are located with black dots.

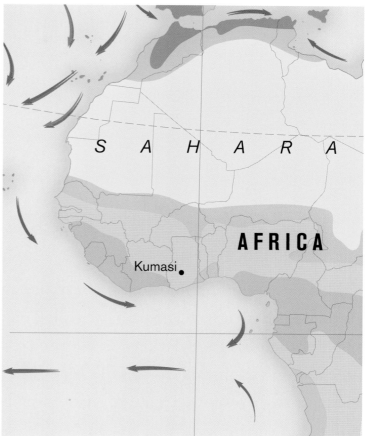

⇧ THEMATIC MAPS. Patterns related to a particular topic, or theme, such as population distribution, appear on these maps. The map above displays the region's climate zones, which range from tropical wet (bright green) to tropical wet and dry (light green) to semiarid (dark yellow) to arid or desert (light yellow).

Long ago, cartographers worked with pen and ink, carefully hand-crafting maps based on explorers' observations and diaries. Today, map-making is a high-tech business. Cartographers use Earth data stored in "layers" in a Geographic Information System (GIS) and special computer programs to create maps that can be easily updated as new information becomes available. The cartographers at left are changing country labels on a map of the Balkans.

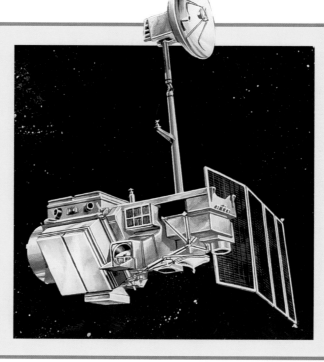

Satellites in orbit around Earth act as eyes in the sky, recording data about the planet's land and ocean areas. The data is converted to numbers that are transmitted back to special computers, which are programmed to interpret the data. They record it in a form that cartographers can use to create maps.

HOW TO READ A MAP

Every map has a story to tell, but first you have to know how to read the map.

Maps are useful for finding places because every place on Earth has a special address called absolute location. Imaginary lines, called latitude and longitude, create a grid that makes finding places easy since these lines cross at the same spot every time. In addition, special tools, called Global Positioning Systems (GPS), communicate with orbiting satellites to determine absolute location.

Maps are useful for determining distance and direction. Maps have a scale, often a bar scale or a verbal scale, that shows the relationship between distance on the map and distance on Earth. Maps often have a compass rose to show direction. Many people think north is at the top of a map, but this is not always true. The compass rose indicates north for each map.

Maps represent other information by using a language of symbols. Knowing how to read these symbols provides access to a wide range of information. To find out what each symbol means, you must use the map key. Think of the map key as your secret decoder, identifying information represented by each symbol on the map.

⇨ ABSOLUTE LOCATION. The imaginary grid composed of lines of latitude and longitude helps us locate places on a map. Suppose you are playing a game of global scavenger hunt. The clue says the prize is hidden at absolute location 30°S, 60°W. You know that the first number is south of the Equator, and the second is west of the prime meridian. On the map at left, find the line of latitude labeled 30°S. Now find the line of longitude labeled 60°W. Trace these lines with your fingers until they meet. Identify this spot. The prize must be located in central Argentina (see arrow, right).

⇨ LATITUDE AND LONGITUDE. Latitude and longitude lines help us determine locations on Earth. Lines of latitude run west to east, parallel to the Equator (below, left). These lines measure distance in degrees north or south, from the Equator (0° latitude) to the North Pole (90°N) or to the South Pole (90°S). One degree of latitude is approximately 70 statute miles (113 km).

Lines of longitude run north to south, meeting at the Poles (below, right). These lines measure distance in degrees east or west from 0° longitude (prime meridian) to 180° longitude. The prime meridian runs through Greenwich, England.

Latitude

Longitude

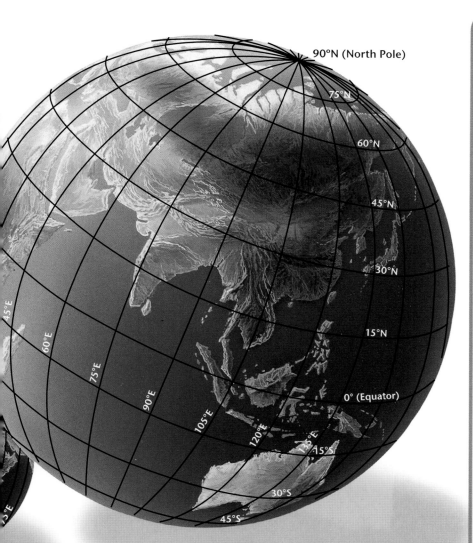

90°N (North Pole)
75°N
60°N
45°N
30°N
15°N
0° (Equator)
15°S
30°S
45°S

45°E
60°E
75°E
90°E
105°E
120°E
135°E

SYMBOLS

There are three main types of map symbols: points, lines, and areas. Points, which can be either dots or small icons, represent the location or the number of things, such as schools, cities, or landmarks. Lines are used to show boundaries, roads, or rivers and can vary in color or thickness. Area symbols use patterns or color to show regions, such as a sandy area or a neighborhood.

POINT
A point symbol, a black dot, indicates a city, such as Omdurman.

LINE
Sudan's country boundary appears as a line symbol: a dotted line with a colored edge.

AREA
Sandy places, such as parts of the Saharan Desert, are shown by a tan, speckled area.

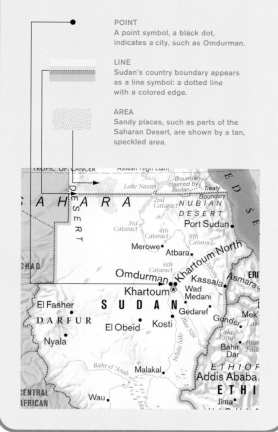

SCALE & DIRECTION

The scale on a map is shown as a fraction, as words, or as a line or bar. It relates distance on the map to distance in the real world. Sometimes the scale identifies the type of map projection. Maps may include an arrow or compass rose to indicate north on the map. Maps in this atlas are oriented north, so they do not use a north indicator.

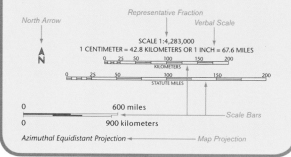

North Arrow
Representative Fraction
Verbal Scale

SCALE 1:4,283,000
1 CENTIMETER = 42.8 KILOMETERS OR 1 INCH = 67.6 MILES

N

0 25 50   100   150   200
KILOMETERS

0 25   50   100   150   200
STATUTE MILES

0   600 miles
0   900 kilometers

Scale Bars

Azimuthal Equidistant Projection ◄ ─── ─── Map Projection

⇨ **APPLYING WHAT YOU'VE LEARNED.**
Now that you know how to read a map, can you find places on the maps in this atlas? What about Sapporo in the eastern Asian country of Japan? The index at the back of this atlas tells you that Sapporo is on "page **121** B10." Along the edges of the map are letters and numbers. Place one finger on the B at the side and another finger on the 10 at the top. Now trace straight across from the B and down from the 10. Sapporo is where your fingers meet!

EARTH IN SPACE

Earth, the planet we call home, is part of a cosmic family called the solar system. It is one of the planets that revolve around a giant solar nuclear reactor that we call the Sun.

The extreme heat and pressure on the Sun cause atoms of hydrogen to combine in a process called fusion, producing new atoms of helium and releasing tremendous amounts of energy. The Sun is the essential source of energy that makes life on Earth possible. It also provides us with light and warmth.

Time on Earth is defined by our relationship to the Sun. It takes Earth, following a path called an orbit, approximately 365 days—one year—to make one full revolution around the Sun. As Earth makes its way around the Sun, it also turns on its axis, an imaginary line that passes between the Poles. This motion, called rotation, occurs once every 24 hours and results in day and night.

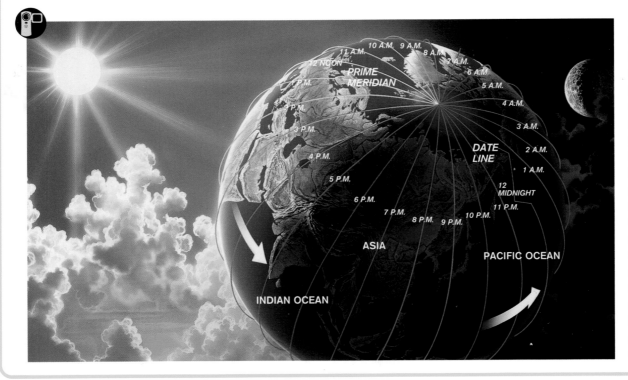

⇦ TIME ZONES. Long ago, when people lived in relative isolation, they measured time by the position of the Sun overhead. That meant that noon in one place was not the same as noon in a place 100 miles (160 km) to the west. Later, with the development of long-distance railroads, people needed to coordinate time. In 1884, a system of 24 standard time zones was adopted. Each time zone reflects the fact that Earth rotates west to east 15 degrees each hour. Time is counted from the prime meridian, which runs through Greenwich, England.

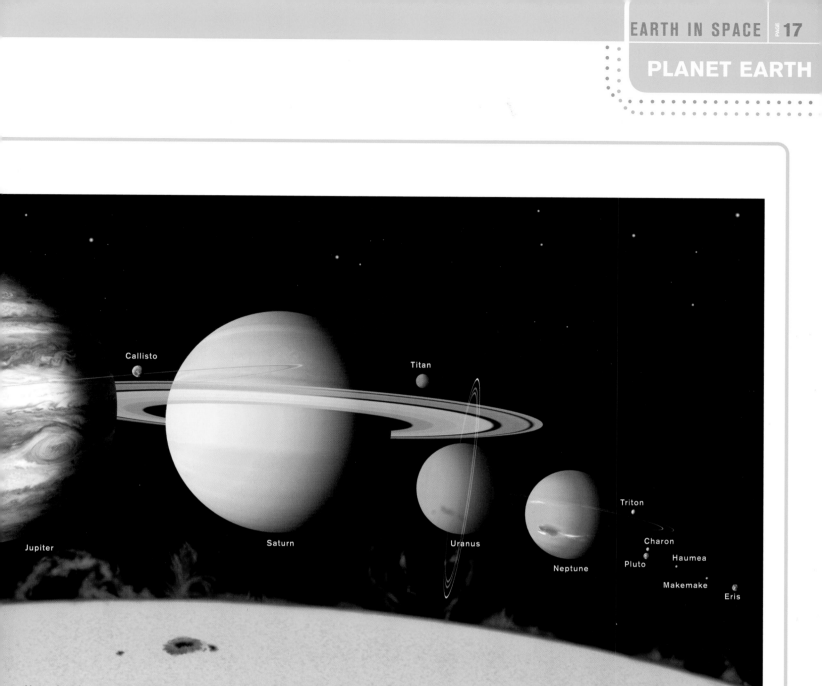

Callisto

Titan

Triton

Jupiter

Saturn

Uranus

Charon

Neptune

Pluto

Haumea

Makemake

Eris

Note: Art shows relative sizes of the Sun and planets, but distances are not to scale.

⇧ SOLAR SYSTEM. The Sun and its family of planets are located near the outer edge of the Milky Way, a giant spiral galaxy. Earth is the third planet from the Sun and one of the four "terrestrial" planets. These planets—Mercury, Venus, Earth, and Mars—are made up of solid rocky material. Beyond these inner planets are the four gas giants—Jupiter, Saturn, Uranus, and Neptune. Recently, astronomers—scientists who study space—have named a new category called "dwarf" planets, including Pluto, Ceres, Eris, Haumea, and Makemake. More of these dwarf planets may soon be identified. Many planets, including Earth, have one or more moons orbiting them. The art above names a few: Io, Callisto, Titan, Triton, and Charon.

⇨ ENVELOPE OF AIR. Earth is enclosed within a thick layer of air called the atmosphere. Made up of a mix of nitrogen, oxygen, and other gases, the atmosphere provides us with the life-giving air that we breathe. It also protects us from dangerous radiation from the Sun. Weather systems move through the atmosphere, redistributing heat and moisture and creating Earth's climates.

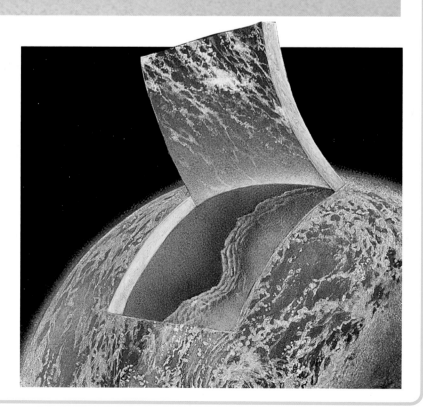

EARTH IN MOTION

If we could step into a time machine and travel 500 million years into the past, we probably would not recognize Earth. Back then, most of the landmasses we call continents were joined together in a single giant landmass called Pangaea. So how did the continents break away from Pangaea and move to their current positions? Where will they be in another 500 million years?

Deep within Earth, pressure and heat cause rocks of the mantle to become partially molten, but near Earth's surface a thin shell of solid rock forms the crust. Currents of heat rise and fall within the mantle, causing the crust to break into large pieces, called plates, which very slowly move about on Earth's surface. These powerful forces are at work today, creating and destroying land features and reshaping Earth's surface.

⇨ CRUST IN MOTION. Earth's major plates are outlined in red on the map at right. Plate edges are the most active parts, with volcanoes and earthquakes (yellow dots on the map) resulting from plates moving together or grinding past each other.

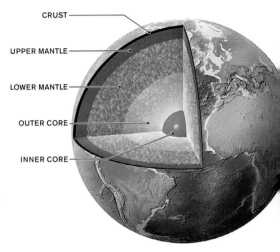

CRUST

UPPER MANTLE

LOWER MANTLE

OUTER CORE

INNER CORE

⇧ A LOOK WITHIN. The distance from Earth's surface to its center is 3,963 miles (6,370 km). There are four layers: a thin, rigid crust; the rocky mantle; the outer core, which is a layer of molten iron; and finally the inner core, which is solid iron.

CONTINENTS ON THE MOVE

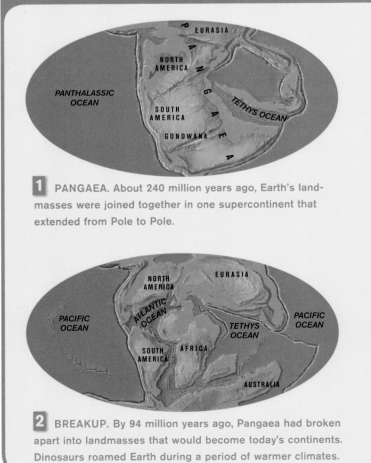

1 PANGAEA. About 240 million years ago, Earth's landmasses were joined together in one supercontinent that extended from Pole to Pole.

2 BREAKUP. By 94 million years ago, Pangaea had broken apart into landmasses that would become today's continents. Dinosaurs roamed Earth during a period of warmer climates.

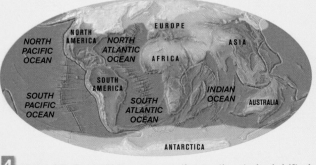

3 EXTINCTION. About 65 million years ago an asteroid smashed into Earth, creating the Gulf of Mexico (∗). This impact may have resulted in the extinction of half the world's species, including the dinosaurs. This was one of several major extinctions.

4 ICE AGE. By 18,000 years ago, the continents had drifted close to their present positions, but most far northern and far southern lands were buried beneath huge glaciers.

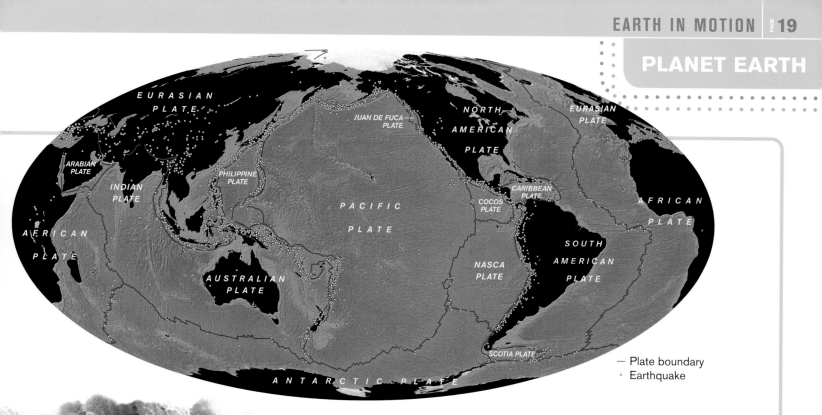

— Plate boundary
° Earthquake

Earth Shapers

Earth's features are constantly undergoing change—being built up, destroyed, or just rearranged. Plates are in constant, very slow motion. Some plates collide, others pull apart, and still others slowly grind past each other. As the plates move, mountains are uplifted, volcanoes erupt, and new land is created.

⇧ VOLCANOES form when molten rock, called magma, rises to Earth's surface. Some volcanoes occur as one plate pushes beneath another plate. Other volcanoes result when a plate passes over a column of magma, called a hot spot, rising from the mantle.

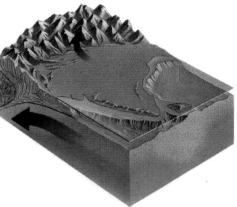

⇧ SPREADING results when oceanic plates move apart. The ocean floor cracks, magma rises, and new crust is created. The Mid-Atlantic Ridge spreads a few centimeters—about an inch—a year, pushing Europe and North America farther apart.

⇩ FAULTING happens when two plates grind past each other, creating large cracks along the edges of the plates. A famous fault is the San Andreas, in California, where the Pacific and North American plates meet, causing damaging earthquakes.

⇧ SUBDUCTION occurs when an oceanic plate dives under a continental plate. This often results in volcanoes and earthquakes, as well as mountain building.

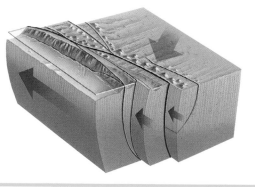

⇧ COLLISION of two continental plates causes plate edges to break and fold, creating mountains, Earth's highest landforms. The Himalaya are the result of the Indian plate colliding with the Eurasian plate, an ongoing process that began 50 million years ago.

THE PHYSICAL WORLD

Earth is dominated by large landmasses called continents—seven in all—and by an interconnected global ocean that is divided into four parts by the continents. More than 70 percent of Earth's surface is covered by oceans, and the remaining 30 percent is made up of land areas.

Different landforms give variety to the surface of the continents. The Rockies and Andes mark the western edge of North and South America, and the Himalaya tower above southern Asia. The Plateau of Tibet forms the rugged core of Asia, while the Northern European Plain extends from the North Sea to the Ural Mountains. Much of Africa is a plateau, and dry plains cover large areas of Australia. Beneath massive ice sheets, mountains rise more than 16,000 feet (4,877 m) in Antarctica.

Mountains and trenches make the ocean floors as varied as any continent (see pages 34–43). A mountain chain called the Mid-Atlantic Ridge runs the length of the Atlantic Ocean. In the western Pacific Ocean, trenches drop to depths greater than 35,000 feet (10,668 m).

⇨ LAND AND WATER. This world physical map shows Earth's seven continents—North America, South America, Europe, Africa, Asia, Australia, and Antarctica—as well as the four oceans: Pacific, Atlantic, Indian, and Arctic. Some people regard the area from Antarctica to 60°S, where the oceans merge, as a fifth ocean called the Southern Ocean.

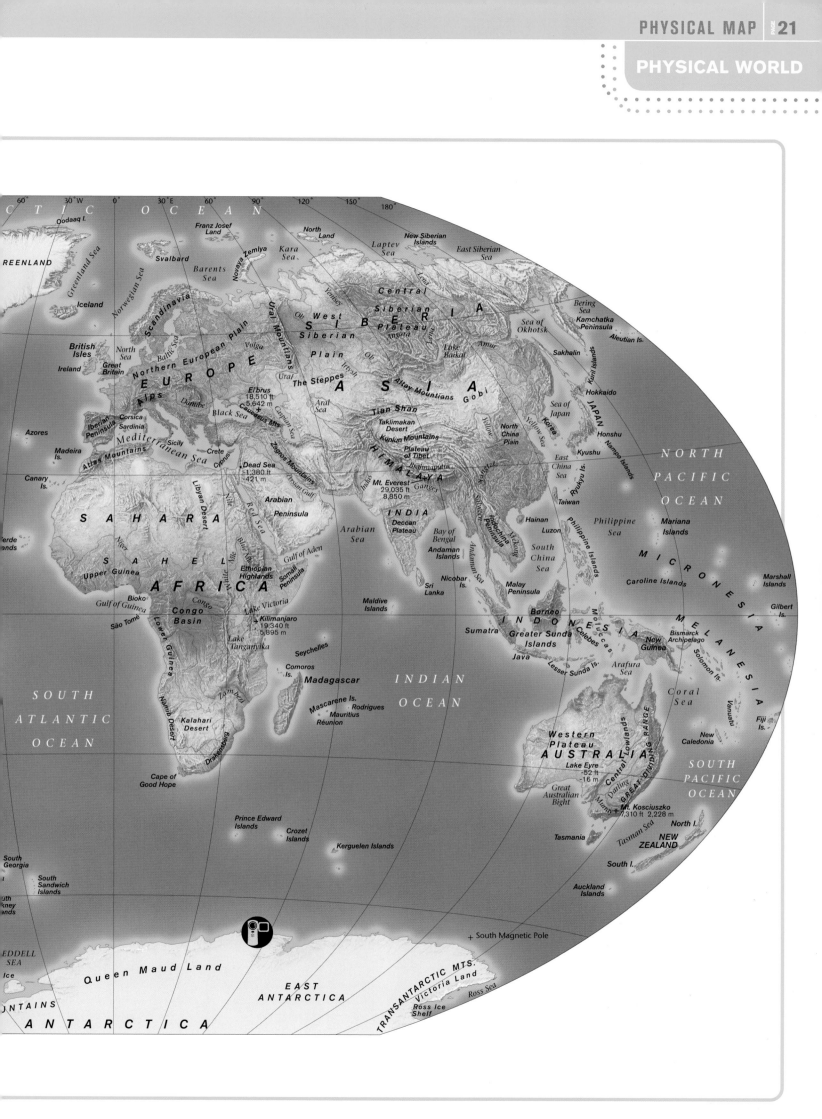

ARCTIC OCEAN

60° 30°W 0° 30°E 60° 90° 120° 150° 180°

GREENLAND

Oodaaq I.

Greenland Sea

Iceland

Franz Josef Land

Svalbard

Novaya Zemlya

North Land

New Siberian Islands

Laptev Sea

East Siberian Sea

Bering Sea

Norwegian Sea

Barents Sea

Kara Sea

Central Siberian Plateau

Kamchatka Peninsula

British Isles

Ireland

North Sea

Great Britain

Baltic Sea

Scandinavia

Northern European Plain

Ural Mountains

Ob

West Siberian Plain

Yenisey

S I B E R I A

Angara

Lena

Sea of Okhotsk

Aleutian Is.

Kuril Islands

Volga

The Steppes

Ob

Irtysh

A S I A

Altay Mountains

Gobi

Lake Baikal

Amur

Sakhalin

Hokkaido

E U R O P E

Alps

Danube

El'brus 18,510 ft 5,642 m

Ural

Caspian Sea

Aral Sea

Tian Shan

Taklimakan Desert

Kunlun Mountains

North China Plain

Sea of Japan

Korea

Yellow Sea

JAPAN

Honshu

Iberian Peninsula

Corsica

Sardinia

Sicily

Crete

Cyprus

Black Sea

Caucasus Mts.

Zagros Mountains

Persian Gulf

Plateau of Tibet

Yellow

East China Sea

Kyushu

Nampo Islands

Ryukyu Is.

Azores

Madeira Is.

Canary Is.

Verde Is.

Atlas Mountains

Mediterranean Sea

Libyan Desert

Nile

Red Sea

Dead Sea -1,380 ft -421 m

Arabian Peninsula

H I M A L A Y A

Mt. Everest 29,035 ft 8,850 m

Indus

Ganges

Brahmaputra

INDIA

Deccan Plateau

Bay of Bengal

Andaman Islands

Salween

Mekong

Yangtze

Hainan

Taiwan

Luzon

Philippine Islands

Philippine Sea

NORTH PACIFIC OCEAN

Mariana Islands

S A H A R A

S A H E L

Upper Guinea

AFRICA

Ethiopian Highlands

Gulf of Aden

Somali Peninsula

Arabian Sea

Maldive Islands

Sri Lanka

Nicobar Is.

Andaman Sea

Malay Peninsula

South China Sea

MICRONESIA

Caroline Islands

Marshall Islands

Gilbert Is.

Bioko

Gulf of Guinea

São Tomé

Blue Nile

White Nile

Congo Basin

Lake Victoria

Kilimanjaro 19,340 ft 5,895 m

Borneo

Sumatra

INDONESIA

Greater Sunda Islands

Java

Celebes

Moluccas

Lesser Sunda Is.

New Guinea

Bismarck Archipelago

Solomon Is.

MELANESIA

Lower Guinea

Lake Tanganyika

Seychelles

Comoros Is.

Madagascar

Arafura Sea

Vanuatu

Fiji Is.

SOUTH ATLANTIC OCEAN

Zambezi

Namib Desert

Kalahari Desert

Drakensberg

Mascarene Is.

Rodrigues

Mauritius

Réunion

INDIAN OCEAN

Coral Sea

New Caledonia

Cape of Good Hope

Western Plateau

AUSTRALIA

Lake Eyre -52 ft -16 m

Great Australian Bight

Central Lowlands

Darling

Murray

GREAT DIVIDING RANGE

Mt. Kosciuszko 7,310 ft 2,228 m

SOUTH PACIFIC OCEAN

South Georgia

South Sandwich Islands

South Orkney Is.

Prince Edward Islands

Crozet Islands

Kerguelen Islands

Tasmania

Tasman Sea

North I.

NEW ZEALAND

South I.

Auckland Islands

WEDDELL SEA

Ice

Mountains

South Magnetic Pole

Queen Maud Land

EAST ANTARCTICA

TRANSANTARCTIC MTS.

Victoria Land

Ross Ice Shelf

Ross Sea

ANTARCTICA

THE LAND

A closer look at Earth's surface reveals many varied forms and features that make each place unique. The drawing (right) captures 42 natural and human-made features in an imaginary landscape that shows how these different land and water features relate to each other. For example, a large moving "river" of ice, called a glacier, descends from a high mountain range. A river passes through a valley and empties into a gulf. And a harbor, built by people, creates safe anchorage for ships.

Features such as these can be found all over the world because the same forces are at work wherever you might go. Internal forces such as volcanoes and the movement of the plates of Earth's crust are constantly creating and building up new landforms, while external forces such as wind, water, and ice continuously wear down surface features.

Earth is dynamic—constantly changing, never the same.

Dormant volcano
Ocean
Island
Archipelago
Strait
Point
Cape
Sound
Peninsula
Bay
Lago
Isthmus
Cliff
G.
Spit
Reef

RIVER

As a river moves through flatlands, it twists and turns. Above, the Rio Los Amigos winds through a rain forest in Peru.

CANYON

Steep-sided valleys called canyons are created mainly by running water. Buckskin Gulch (above) is the deepest slot canyon in the American Southwest.

DESERT

Deserts are a land feature created by climate, specifically by a lack of water. Above, a camel caravan crosses the Sahara, in North Africa.

OASIS

Occasionally, water rises from deep below a desert, creating a refuge that supports trees and sometimes crops, as in this oasis in Africa.

Mountain peak

Mountain range

Glacier

Iceberg

Basin

Desert

Mesa

Oasis

Divide

Plateau

Valley

Waterfall

Escarpment

Lake

Canyon

Canal

Plain

River

Fork

each

Delta

Hills

Harbor

Tributary

Breakwater

A Name for Every Feature

Land has a vocabulary all its own, each name identifying a specific feature of the landscape. A cape, for example, is a broadish chunk of land extending out into the sea. It is not pointed, however, for then it would be a point. Nor does it have a narrow neck. A sizable cape or point with a narrow neck is a peninsula. The narrow neck, of course, is an isthmus.

Such specific identifiers have proven useful over the centuries. In the early days of exploration, even the simplest maps showed peninsulas, bays, and straits. Sailors used these landmarks to reach safe harbor or avoid disastrous encounters.

⇐ EXPLORING THE LANDSCAPE. How many land and water features can you identify in the imaginary landscape at left? Definitions for these terms can be found in the glossary on pages 172–173.

MOUNTAIN

Mountains are Earth's tallest landforms, and Mount Everest (above) rises highest of all at 29,035 feet (8,850 m) above sea level.

GLACIER

Glaciers—"rivers" of ice—such as Alaska's Hubbard (above), move slowly from mountains to the sea. Global warming may be shrinking them.

VALLEY

Valleys, cut by running water or moving ice, may be broad and flat or narrow and steep, such as the Indus River Valley in Ladakh, India (above).

WATERFALL

Waterfalls form when a river reaches an abrupt change in elevation. Above, Kaitur Falls, in Guyana, descends 800 feet (244 m).

WORLD CLIMATE

Weather is the condition of the atmosphere—temperature, precipitation, humidity, wind—at a given place at a given time. Climate, however, is the average weather for a particular place over a long period of time. Different places on Earth have different climates, but climate is not a random occurrence. There is a pattern that is controlled by factors such as latitude, elevation, prevailing winds, temperature of ocean currents, and location on land relative to water. Climate is generally constant, but many are concerned that human activity may be causing a change in the patterns of climate.

THE BASICS

According to the National Oceanic and Atmospheric Administration (NOAA), 2005 ranks first as the hottest year on record, followed by 1998. The global annual temperature for combined land and ocean surfaces was 1°F (.6°C) above the average established between 1880 and 2004.

Ice cores taken from Antarctica and Greenland have enabled scientists to gain detailed information about the history of Earth's climate and its atmosphere—especially the presence of greenhouse gases—dating back thousands of years.

Data collected by satellite imagery suggests that the Sahara, Earth's largest desert, had a wet climate that supported vast forests some 12,000 years ago. Extremely dry conditions did not begin until about 5,000 years ago.

According to climatologists, Earth had what is called the Little Ice Age, which lasted from the 17th century to the late 19th century. During that time, temperatures were cold enough to cause glaciers to advance.

⇩ CLIMATE GRAPHS.
Temperature and precipitation data provide a snapshot of the climate at a particular place. This information can be shown in a special type of graph called a climate graph (see below). Average monthly temperatures (scale on the left side of the graphs) are represented by the lines at the tops of the colored areas, while average monthly precipitation totals (scale on the right side of the graphs) are reflected in the bars. For example, the graph for Belém, Brazil, shows a constant warm temperature with abundant rainfall year-round. In contrast, the graph for Fairbanks, Alaska, shows a cool, variable temperature with only limited precipitation.

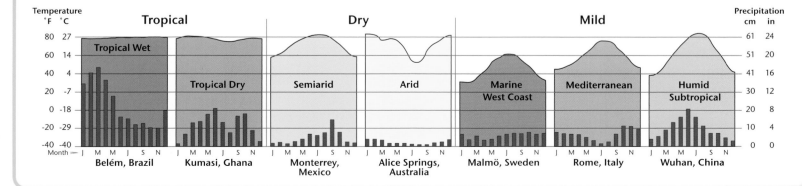

Tropical: Belém, Brazil (Tropical Wet), Kumasi, Ghana (Tropical Dry)

Dry: Monterrey, Mexico (Semiarid), Alice Springs, Australia (Arid)

Mild: Malmö, Sweden (Marine West Coast), Rome, Italy (Mediterranean), Wuhan, China (Humid Subtropical)

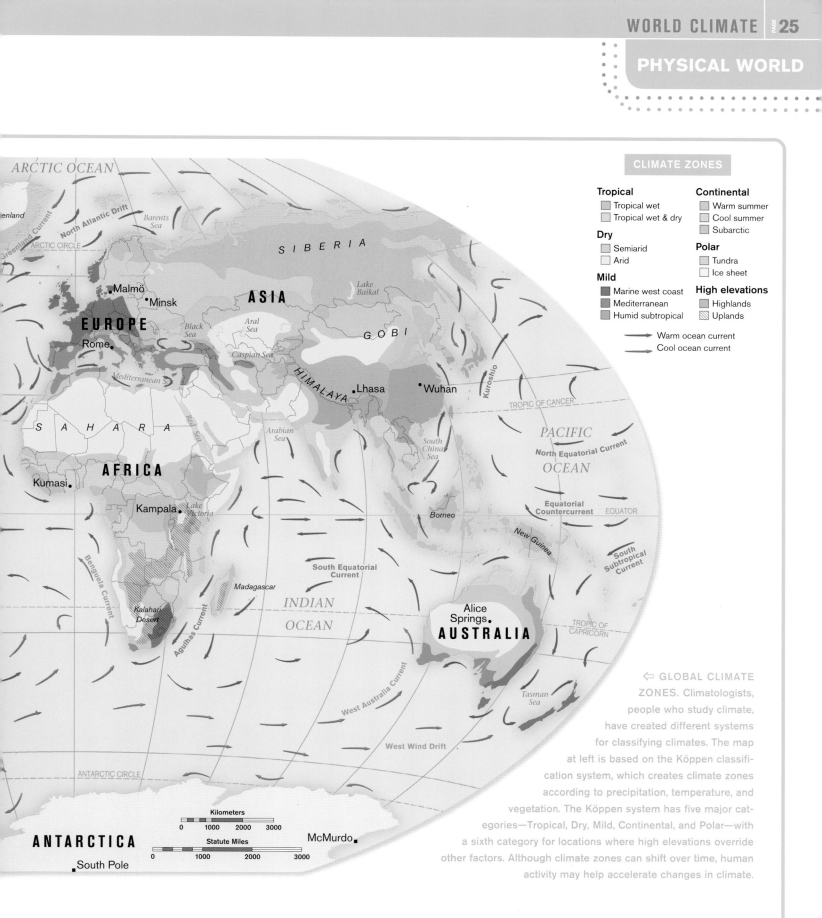

CLIMATE ZONES

Tropical
- Tropical wet
- Tropical wet & dry

Dry
- Semiarid
- Arid

Mild
- Marine west coast
- Mediterranean
- Humid subtropical

Continental
- Warm summer
- Cool summer
- Subarctic

Polar
- Tundra
- Ice sheet

High elevations
- Highlands
- Uplands

→ Warm ocean current
→ Cool ocean current

⇐ GLOBAL CLIMATE ZONES. Climatologists, people who study climate, have created different systems for classifying climates. The map at left is based on the Köppen classification system, which creates climate zones according to precipitation, temperature, and vegetation. The Köppen system has five major categories—Tropical, Dry, Mild, Continental, and Polar—with a sixth category for locations where high elevations override other factors. Although climate zones can shift over time, human activity may help accelerate changes in climate.

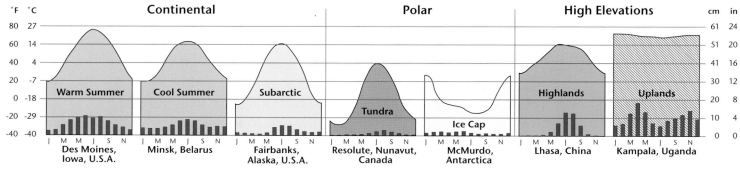

Continental			Polar		High Elevations	
Warm Summer	Cool Summer	Subarctic	Tundra	Ice Cap	Highlands	Uplands
Des Moines, Iowa, U.S.A.	Minsk, Belarus	Fairbanks, Alaska, U.S.A.	Resolute, Nunavut, Canada	McMurdo, Antarctica	Lhasa, China	Kampala, Uganda

FACTORS INFLUENCING CLIMATE

Earth's climate is a bit like a big jigsaw puzzle. In order to understand it, you need to fit all the pieces together because climate is influenced by a number of different, but interrelated factors, including latitude, topography (shape of the land), elevation above sea level, wind systems, ocean currents, and distance from large water bodies. Climate has always affected the way we live, but scientists now believe that the way we live may also be affecting climate. Pollution from industries and motor vehicles may be contributing to global warming. And this could be causing Earth's climates to change.

⇩ TOPOGRAPHY. Mountain ranges are natural barriers to the movement of air. In North America, prevailing westerly winds carry air full of moisture from the Pacific Ocean to the coast. As air rises over the Coast Ranges, light precipitation falls. Farther inland, the much taller Sierra Nevada range triggers heavy precipitation as air rises higher. On the leeward side of the Sierra Nevada, sinking air warms, clouds evaporate, and dry "rain shadow" conditions prevail. As winds continue across the interior plateau, the air remains dry because there is not a significant source of moisture.

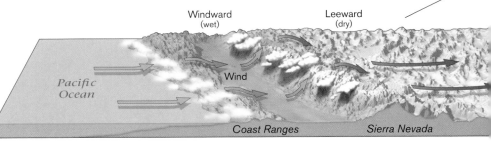

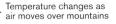

Temperature changes as air moves over mountains

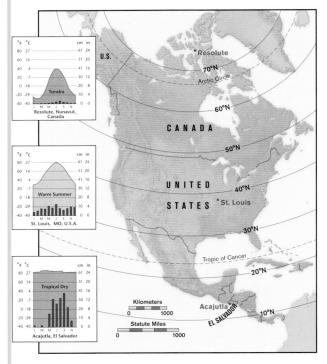

⇧ LATITUDE. Energy from the sun drives global climates. Latitude—distance north or south of the Equator—affects the amount of solar energy received. Places near the Equator (see Acajutla, El Salvador, above) have warm temperatures year-round. As distance from the Equator increases (see St. Louis, U.S.A., and Resolute, Canada, above), average temperatures decline, and cold winters become more pronounced.

⇨ ELEVATION. In general, climate conditions become cooler as elevation increases. Since cooler air holds less moisture, less precipitation falls. As temperature and moisture conditions change, vegetation also changes. In the mountain diagram (right), dense mixed forest grows near the base of the mountain on the windward side. As elevation increases and temperatures decline, the mixed forest changes to all evergreen, followed by alpine meadows, until finally the mountain's rocky peaks are covered by snow and ice. As air moves down the leeward slope of the mountain, it warms and evaporates moisture, causing the leeward side to be drier and have less vegetation.

WINDWARD

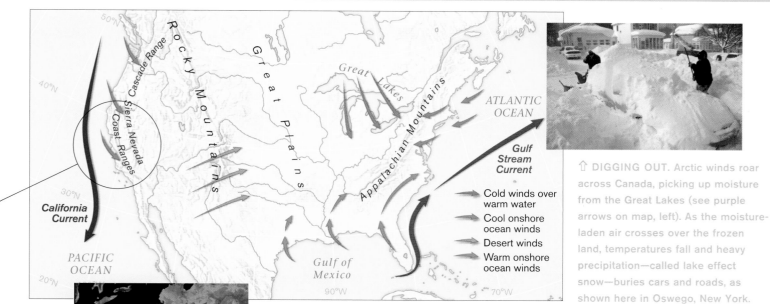

Cold winds over warm water
Cool onshore ocean winds
Desert winds
Warm onshore ocean winds

⇧ DIGGING OUT. Arctic winds roar across Canada, picking up moisture from the Great Lakes (see purple arrows on map, left). As the moisture-laden air crosses over the frozen land, temperatures fall and heavy precipitation—called lake effect snow—buries cars and roads, as shown here in Oswego, New York.

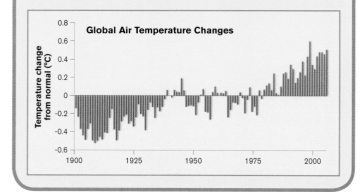

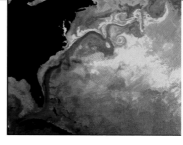

⇦ WARM CURRENT. The Gulf Stream, a warm ocean current averaging 50–93 miles (80–150 km) wide, sweeps up the East Coast of North America (see red arrow on map above). One branch continues across the North Atlantic Ocean and above the Arctic Circle. In this color-enhanced satellite image, the Gulf Stream looks like a dark red river moving up the coast. This "river" of warm water influences climate along its path, bringing moisture and mild temperatures to the East Coast of the United States and causing ice-free ports above the Arctic Circle in Europe.

LEEWARD

GLOBAL WARMING

Earth's climate history has been a story of ups and downs, with warm periods followed by periods of bitter cold. The early part of the 20th century was marked by colder than average temperatures (see graph below), followed by a period of gradual and then steady increase. Scientists are concerned that the current warming trend may be more than a natural cycle. Evidence indicates that human activity is adding to the warming. One sign of change is melting glaciers in Greenland and Antarctica. If glaciers continue to melt, areas of Florida (shown above in red) and other coastal land will be under water.

Global Air Temperature Changes

Temperature change from normal (°C)

0.8
0.6
0.4
0.2
0
-0.2
-0.4
-0.6

1900   1925   1950   1975   2000

WORLD VEGETATION

Natural vegetation—plants that would grow under ideal circumstances at a particular place—depends on several factors. The climate is very important, as is the quality and type of soil that is available. Therefore, vegetation often reflects patterns of climate. (Compare the vegetation map at right with the world climate map on pages 24–25.) Forests thrive in places with ample precipitation; grasses are found in places with less precipitation or with only seasonal rainfall; and xerophytes—plants able to survive lengthy periods with little or no water—are found in arid areas that receive very little precipitation on a yearly basis. Grasses and shrubs cover almost half of Earth's land.

0 miles 2000
0 kilometers 3000

Winkel Tripel Projection

TEMPERATE BROADLEAF FOREST

Broadleaf trees that grow in mid-latitude areas with mild temperatures, such as this one in Shenandoah National Park, are deciduous, meaning they lose their leaves in winter. Many such forests have been cleared for cropland.

DESERT AND DRY SHRUB

Deserts, areas that receive less than 10 inches (25 cm) of rainfall a year, have vegetation that is specially adapted to survive under dry conditions, such as these dry shrubs and cacti growing in the Sonora Desert in Arizona.

TUNDRA

With only two to three months of temperatures above freezing, tundra plants are mostly dwarf shrubs, short grasses, mosses, and lichens. Much of Canada's Yukon has tundra vegetation, which turns red as winter approaches.

CONIFEROUS FOREST

Needleleaf trees with cones to protect their seeds from bitter winters grow in cold climates with short summers, such as British Columbia, Canada. These trees are important in lumber and paper-making industries.

ARCTIC OCEAN

ARCTIC CIRCLE

EUROPE

ASIA

AFRICA

PACIFIC OCEAN

INDIAN
OCEAN

OCEAN

AUSTRALIA

EQUATOR

60°N

60°E

90°E

150°E

30°S

Vegetation Zones

1	Tundra
2	Northern coniferous forest (also called boreal forest or taiga)
3	Temperate coniferous forest
4	Temperate broadleaf forest
5	Temperate grassland
6	Desert and dry shrub
7	Mediterranean shrub
8	Mountain grassland
9	Flooded grassland and savanna
10	Tropical grassland and savanna
11	Tropical dry forest
12	Tropical coniferous forest
13	Tropical moist broadleaf (includes rain forest)
14	Mangrove
15	Permanent ice cover

5

TEMPERATE GRASSLAND

Grasslands, such as this tall-grass prairie in southwestern Missouri, are found in areas where precipitation is too low to support forests. Many temperate grasslands have been converted to cropland for grain production.

10

TROPICAL GRASSLAND

Tall grasses and scattered trees that can survive a hot, dry season dominate low latitude grasslands, also called savannas. Africa's grasslands are home to game animals, such as this male lion crossing the savanna in Botswana.

13

RAIN FOREST

A waterfall tumbles over a cliff in the Costa Rican rain forest. Rain forest trees can grow as much as 200 feet (61 m) above the forest floor. The overlapping branches of the tallest trees keep sunlight from reaching the forest floor.

CROPLAND

People remove natural vegetation in many places to create fields to grow crops to feed both people and animals. Here, a farmer in the Catskill Mountains of New York uses a mechanized harvester to cut corn to feed his dairy cows.

ENVIRONMENTAL HOT SPOTS

Around the world people are putting more and more pressure on the environment by dumping pollutants into the air and water and by removing natural vegetation to extract mineral resources or to turn the land into cropland for farming. In more developed countries, industries create waste and pollution; farmers use fertilizers and pesticides that run off into water supplies; and motor vehicles release exhaust fumes into the air. In less developed countries, forests are cut down for fuel or to clear land for farming; grasslands are turned into deserts as farmers and herders overuse the land; and expanding urban areas face problems of water quality and sanitation.

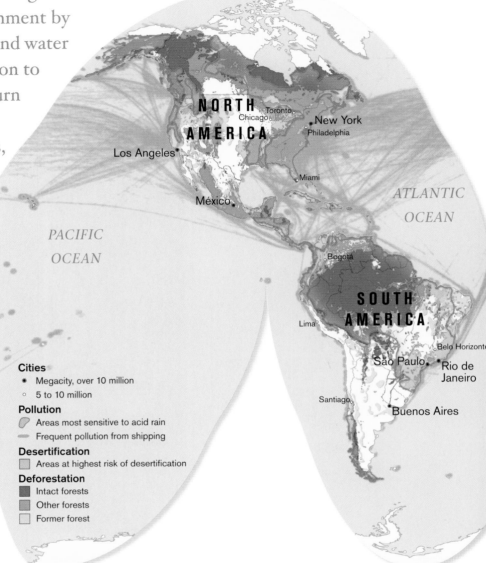

Cities
● Megacity, over 10 million
○ 5 to 10 million

Pollution
Areas most sensitive to acid rain
Frequent pollution from shipping

Desertification
Areas at highest risk of desertification

Deforestation
Intact forests
Other forests
Former forest

ENDANGERED

Human activity poses the greatest threat to Earth's biodiversity—its rich variety of species. Loss of habitat puts many species, including those at right, at great risk. Experts estimate that species are becoming extinct at a rate 100 to 1,000 times higher than natural loss would cause.

Monarch Butterfly

Giant Tree Frog

California Condor

Asian Elephant

Rafflesia Flower

Napoleon Wrasse Fish

POLLUTION

Poor air quality is a serious environmental problem. Industrial plants are a major source of pollution. Smoke containing particles that contribute to acid rain is released from a factory in Poland (above).

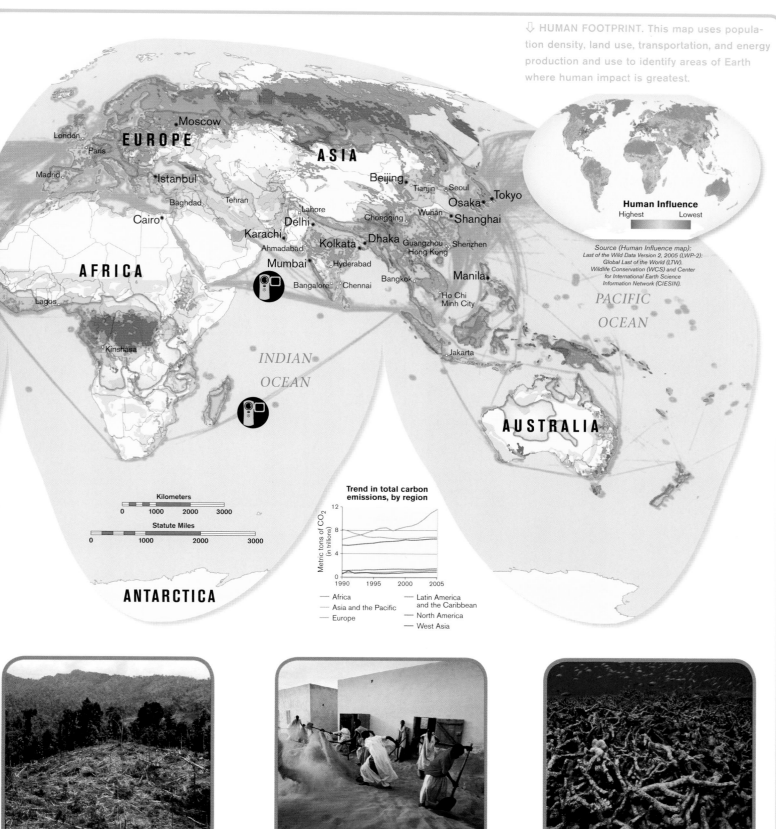

⇩ HUMAN FOOTPRINT. This map uses population density, land use, transportation, and energy production and use to identify areas of Earth where human impact is greatest.

Human Influence
Highest — Lowest

Source (Human Influence map):
Last of the Wild Data Version 2, 2005 (LWP-2):
Global Last of the World (LTW).
Wildlife Conservation (WCS) and Center
for International Earth Science
Information Network (CIESIN).

Trend in total carbon emissions, by region

Metric tons of CO₂ (in trillions)

1990 1995 2000 2005

— Africa
— Asia and the Pacific
— Europe
— Latin America and the Caribbean
— North America
— West Asia

Kilometers
0 1000 2000 3000

Statute Miles
0 1000 2000 3000

DEFORESTATION

Loss of forest cover, such as on this hillside in Malaysia, contributes to a buildup of carbon dioxide in the atmosphere, as well as to a loss of biodiversity. This is a frequent problem in the tropics.

DESERTIFICATION

Villagers in Mauritania, Africa, shovel sand away from their schoolhouse. In semiarid areas, which receive limited and often unreliable rainfall, land that is overgrazed or overcultivated can become desertlike.

DAMAGED REEFS

Coral reefs, such as this one in the Indian Ocean near the Maldives, can be damaged by increases in ocean temperatures. If a reef dies, a habitat for the many marine creatures that live there is lost.

NATURAL DISASTERS

Every world region has its share of natural disasters—the menacing mix just varies from place to place. The Ring of Fire—grinding tectonic plate boundaries that follow the coasts of the Pacific Ocean—shakes with volcanic eruptions and earthquakes. Coastal lives and livelihoods here and along other oceans can be swept away by quake-caused tsunamis. The U.S. heartland endures blizzards in winter and dangerous tornadoes that can strike in spring, summer, or fall. Tropical cyclones batter many coastal areas with ripping winds, torrents of rain, and huge storm surges along their deadly paths.

NORTH AMERICA

ROCKY MOUNTAINS

Tri-State Tornado (1925)

Hawaiian Islands

Galveston Hurricane (1900)

Hurricane Katrina (2005)

ATLANTIC OCEAN

Hurricane Mitch (1998)

PACIFIC OCEAN

ANDES

SOUTH AMERICA

Kilometers
0   1000   2000   3000

Statute Miles
0   1000   2000   3000

Winkel Tripel Projection

KINDS OF DISASTERS

EARTHQUAKE
A shaking of Earth's crust caused by a volcanic eruption or by the release of energy along a fault in the crust

TORNADO
A violently rotating column of air that touches Earth's surface during intense thunderstorm activity

TROPICAL CYCLONE
A huge weather system, fueled by warm water, that can become a rotating storm packing winds of at least 74 miles per hour (119 km/h); called hurricanes in the Atlantic Ocean and eastern Pacific, cyclones in the Bay of Bengal and Indian Ocean, and typhoons in the western Pacific

TSUNAMI
Ocean waves caused by an undersea earthquake or by a volcanic eruption

VOLCANIC ERUPTION
The upward movement and usually forceful release of molten material and gases from Earth's interior onto the surface

⇧ TORNADO. This funnel cloud churns past Union City, Oklahoma. There are more of these storms in "Tornado Alley" (see map) than anywhere else on Earth.

⇨ TSUNAMI. People and pets alike fight to survive the deadly Indian Ocean tsunami of December 2004. The storm, triggered by an undersea earthquake, killed more than 225,000 people.

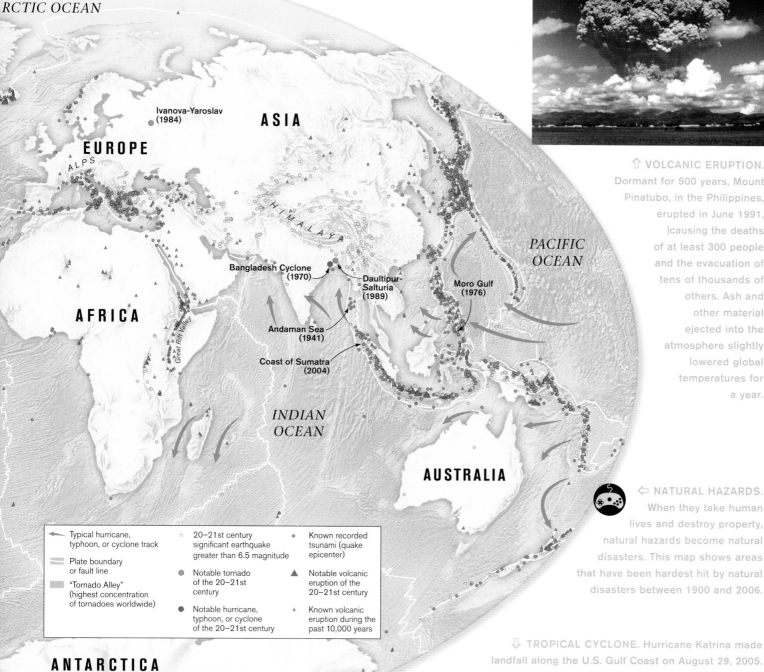

RCTIC OCEAN

ASIA

EUROPE
ALPS

Ivanova-Yaroslav
(1984)

HIMALAYA

AFRICA

Great Rift Valley

Bangladesh Cyclone
(1970)

Daultipur-
Salturia
(1989)

Moro Gulf
(1976)

PACIFIC
OCEAN

Andaman Sea
(1941)

Coast of Sumatra
(2004)

INDIAN
OCEAN

AUSTRALIA

Legend:
- → Typical hurricane, typhoon, or cyclone track
- ▭ Plate boundary or fault line
- ▮ "Tornado Alley" (highest concentration of tornadoes worldwide)
- ◦ 20–21st century significant earthquake greater than 6.5 magnitude
- ● Notable tornado of the 20–21st century
- ● Notable hurricane, typhoon, or cyclone of the 20–21st century
- ● Known recorded tsunami (quake epicenter)
- ▲ Notable volcanic eruption of the 20–21st century
- ▲ Known volcanic eruption during the past 10,000 years

ANTARCTICA

⇧ VOLCANIC ERUPTION. Dormant for 500 years, Mount Pinatubo, in the Philippines, erupted in June 1991, causing the deaths of at least 300 people and the evacuation of tens of thousands of others. Ash and other material ejected into the atmosphere slightly lowered global temperatures for a year.

⇦ NATURAL HAZARDS. When they take human lives and destroy property, natural hazards become natural disasters. This map shows areas that have been hardest hit by natural disasters between 1900 and 2006.

⇩ TROPICAL CYCLONE. Hurricane Katrina made landfall along the U.S. Gulf Coast on August 29, 2005. Four days later, U.S. Army National Guard soldiers assisted stranded victims in New Orleans, Louisiana.

TRACKING QUAKES

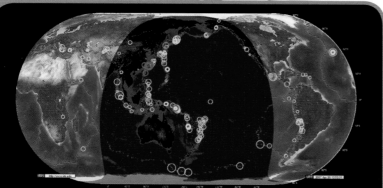

Track seismic events and learn more about them, using the link on page 175.

INVESTIGATING THE OCEANS

The map at right shows that more than 70 percent of Earth's surface is under water, mainly covered by four great oceans. There is growing support for a fifth ocean, called the Southern Ocean, in the area from Antarctica to 60°S latitude. The oceans are really interconnected bodies of water that together form one global ocean.

The ocean floor is as varied as the surface of the continents, but mapping the oceans is challenging. Past explorers cut their way through jungles of the Amazon and conquered icy heights of the Himalaya, but explorers could not march across the floor of the Pacific Ocean, which in places descends to more than 35,000 feet (10,668 m) below the surface of the water.

⇩ UNDERWATER LANDSCAPES. The landscape of the ocean floor is varied and constantly changing. A continental edge that slopes gently beneath the water is called a continental shelf. Mountain ranges, called mid-ocean ridges, rise where ocean plates are spreading and magma flows out to create new land. Other plates plunge into trenches more than 6 miles (10 km) deep. And magma, rising through vents called hot spots, pushes through ocean plates, creating seamounts and volcanoes.

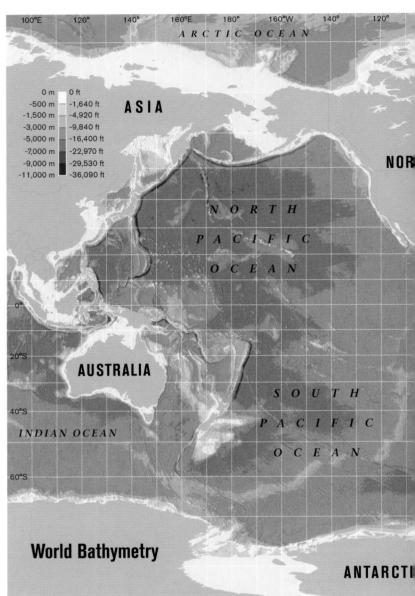

0 m	0 ft
-500 m	-1,640 ft
-1,500 m	-4,920 ft
-3,000 m	-9,840 ft
-5,000 m	-16,400 ft
-7,000 m	-22,970 ft
-9,000 m	-29,530 ft
-11,000 m	-36,090 ft

ARCTIC OCEAN

ASIA

NOR

NORTH PACIFIC OCEAN

AUSTRALIA

INDIAN OCEAN

SOUTH PACIFIC OCEAN

ANTARCTI

World Bathymetry

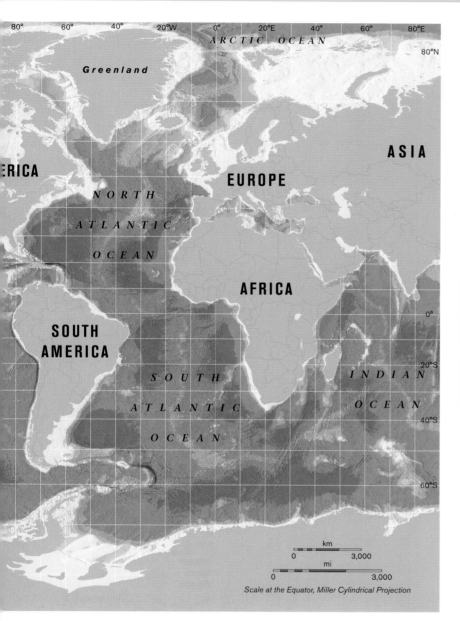

80° 60° 40° 20°W 0° 20°E 40° 60° 80°E

ARCTIC OCEAN

80°N

Greenland

ASIA

EUROPE

ERICA

NORTH

ATLANTIC

OCEAN

AFRICA

0°

SOUTH
AMERICA

20°S

SOUTH

INDIAN

ATLANTIC

OCEAN

40°S

OCEAN

60°S

km
0   3,000
mi
0   3,000

Scale at the Equator, Miller Cylindrical Projection

⇧ FROM OCEAN TO SATELLITE. In the 1990s, scientists developed the Argo Float to collect data from below the ocean surface. Argo Floats sink to a preset depth, often thousands of feet, where they gather data, such as temperature and salt content. At regular intervals, the floats rise to the surface (above) and transmit the data collected to a satellite. Then the cycle starts over again.

⇩ EYE ON THE OCEAN. The Sea-Viewing Wide Field-of-View Sensor (SeaWiFS) satellite records digital images of ocean colors that are used to identify and follow plant and animal activity in the oceans.

⇦ SEEING WITH YOUR EARS. Special instruments, such as this acoustic buoy, use sound waves bounced off the ocean floor to record variations in water temperature. This technique, called Acoustic Thermometry of Ocean Climate (ATOC), may someday help monitor long-term climate changes.

PACIFIC OCEAN

THE BASICS

STATS

Surface area
65,436,200 sq mi
(169,479,000 sq km)

Percent of Earth's water area
47%

Greatest depth
Challenger Deep
(in the Mariana Trench)
-35,827 ft (-10,920 m)

Surface temperatures
Summer high: 90°F (32°C)

Winter low: 28°F (–2°C)

Tides
Highest: 30 ft (9 m)
near Korean peninsula
Lowest: 1 ft (0.3 m)
near Midway Islands

GEO WHIZ

The Pacific Ocean has more islands—tens of thousands of them—than any other ocean.

The ocean's name comes from the Latin *Mare Pacificum,* meaning "peaceful sea," but earthquake and volcanic activity along the Ring of Fire generate powerful waves called tsunamis, which cause death and destruction when they slam ashore.

With the greatest area of tropical waters, the Pacific is also home to the largest number of coral reefs, including Earth's longest: Australia's 1,429-mile-(2,300-km-) long Great Barrier Reef.

The Hawaiian monk seal, the most endangered marine mammal in U.S. waters, lives only on a few islands in the remote northwestern end of the Hawaiian archipelago.

The Pacific Ocean, largest of Earth's oceans, is about 15 times larger than the United States and covers more than 30 percent of Earth's surface. The edges of the Pacific are often called the Ring of Fire because many active volcanoes and earthquakes occur where the ocean plate is moving under the edges of continental plates.

⇧ IN THE MIDST OF DANGER. A false-clown anemonefish swims among the tentacles of a sea anemone off the coast of the Philippines, in the western Pacific. This colorful fish is immune to the anemone's paralyzing sting.

The southwestern Pacific is dotted with many islands. Also in the western Pacific, the Challenger Deep in the Mariana Trench plunges to 35,827 feet (10,920 m) below sea level. Most of the world's fish catch (see page 56) comes from the Pacific, and oil and gas reserves there are an important energy source.

(see page 56)

SCALE AT THE EQUATOR
0   1,000 miles
0   1,000 kilometers
Mercator Projection

⇐ CIRCLE OF LIFE. Atolls, such as this one near Okinawa, Japan, are ocean landforms created by tiny marine animals called corals. These creatures live in warm tropical waters. The circular shape of atolls often marks the coastline of sunken volcanic islands.

3   4   5   6   7   8   9   10

ALASKA

Yukon

A

Continental Shelf

Hudson Bay

Bering Sea

Shirshov Ridge

Aleutian Basin

Bowers Ridge

B

Aleutian Islands

NORTH AMERICA

Emperor Seamounts

Aleutian Trench

Gulf of Alaska

Juan De Fuca Ridge

North

Tufts Plain

Emperor Trough

Columbia

C

Chinook Trough

Hess Rise

Mendocino Fracture Zone

Pioneer Fracture Zone

Colorado

Musicians Seamounts

Escarpment

Parton

NORTH ATLANTIC OCEAN

Midway Islands

Northwest Hawaiian Ridge

Murray Fracture Zone

Pacific

Cedros Trench

D

Mapmaker Seamounts

Hawaiian Islands

Molokai Fracture Zone

TROPIC OF CANCER

Gulf of Mexico

Mexico Basin

Cuba

Greater Antilles

Necker Ridge

Hawai'i

Yucatán Peninsula

Pacific Mountains

Clarion Fracture Zone

Mathematicians Seamounts

Middle America Trench

Caribbean Sea

E

Marshall Islands

Central Pacific

Magellan Rise

Basin

Clipperton Fracture Zone

Line Islands

Guatemala Basin

Galápagos Rift

Cocos Ridge

Panama Basin

EQUATOR

Gilbert Islands

Galápagos Is.

SOUTH AMERICA

Galápagos Fracture Zone

F

Manihiki Plateau

Marquesas Islands

Marquesas Fracture Zone

Galápagos Rise

Peru Basin

Islands

Tuvalu

Tuamotu Archipelago

Vityaz Trench

N. New Vanuatu

North Fiji Basin

Fiji

Fiji Islands

Cook Islands

Society Islands

New Plateau

Hebrides Trench

Lau Basin

Austral Islands

Easter Fracture Zone

Nasca Ridge

G

Lord Howe Rise

Norfolk Ridge

Lau Ridge

Tonga Trench

Sala y Gómez Ridge

Chile Basin

South Fiji Basin

Southwest Pacific

Pacific

man

New Caledonia Basin

Kermadec Trench

Louisville Ridge

Challenger Fracture Zone

Chile Rise

H

NEW ZEALAND

North Island

Agassiz Fracture Zone

Valdivia Fracture Zone

Chatham Rise

Southeast

South Island

Bounty Trough

Basin

arie Ridge

Campbell Plateau

Menard Fracture Zone

Pacific

East

I

Emerald Basin

Eltanin Fracture Zone

Udintsev Fracture Zone

Basin

Humboldt Plain

ATLANTIC OCEAN

THE BASICS

STATS

Surface area
35,338,500 sq mi
(91,526,400 sq km)

Percent of Earth's water area
25%

Greatest depth
Puerto Rico Trench
-28,232 ft (-8,605 m)

Surface temperatures
Summer high: 90°F (32°C)
Winter low: 28°F (-2°C)

Tides
Highest: 52 ft (16 m)
Bay of Fundy, Canada
Lowest: 1.5 ft (0.5 m)
Gulf of Mexico and Mediterranean Sea

GEO WHIZ

In 2005, the Atlantic Ocean produced a record-setting 15 hurricanes. For the first time in a single season, 4 hurricanes—Emily, Katrina, Rita, and Wilma—reached category 5 level, with sustained winds of at least 155 miles per hour (249 km/h).

The Atlantic Ocean is about half the size of the Pacific, but it's growing. Spreading along the Mid-Atlantic Ridge allows molten rock from Earth's interior to escape and form new ocean floor.

Fishermen in the North Atlantic were eyewitnesses to the volcanic eruption that created the island of Surtsey, off the southeastern coast of Iceland, in November 1963.

Each year, the amount of water that flows into the Atlantic Ocean from the Amazon River is equal to 20 percent of Earth's available fresh water.

Among Earth's great oceans, the Atlantic is second only to the Pacific in size. The floor of the Atlantic is split by the Mid-Atlantic Ridge, which is part of the Mid-Ocean Ridge—the longest mountain chain on Earth. The Atlantic poses many hazards to human activity. Tropical storms called hurricanes form in the warm tropical waters off the west coast of Africa and move across the ocean to bombard the islands of the Caribbean and coastal areas of North America with damaging winds, waves, and rain in the late summer and fall. In the cold waters of the North Atlantic, sea ice and icebergs pose a danger to shipping, especially during winter and spring.

The Atlantic has rich deposits of oil and natural gas, but drilling has resulted in pollution problems. In addition, the Atlantic has important marine fisheries, but overfishing has put some species at risk. Sea lanes between Europe and the Americas are among the most heavily trafficked in the world.

⇧ CAMOUFLAGE ON ICE. A young harp seal, called a pup, rests on the ice in Canada's Gulf of St. Lawrence. Pups are cared for by their mothers for only 12 days. Then, they must survive on their own.

⇧ HIDDEN DANGER. Icebergs (above, right) are huge blocks of ice that break away, or calve, from the edges of glaciers. They pose a danger to ships because only about 10 percent of their bulk is visible above the waterline. A tragic disaster associated with an iceberg was the 1912 sinking of the RMS *Titanic*, whose ghostly ruins are shown above, left.

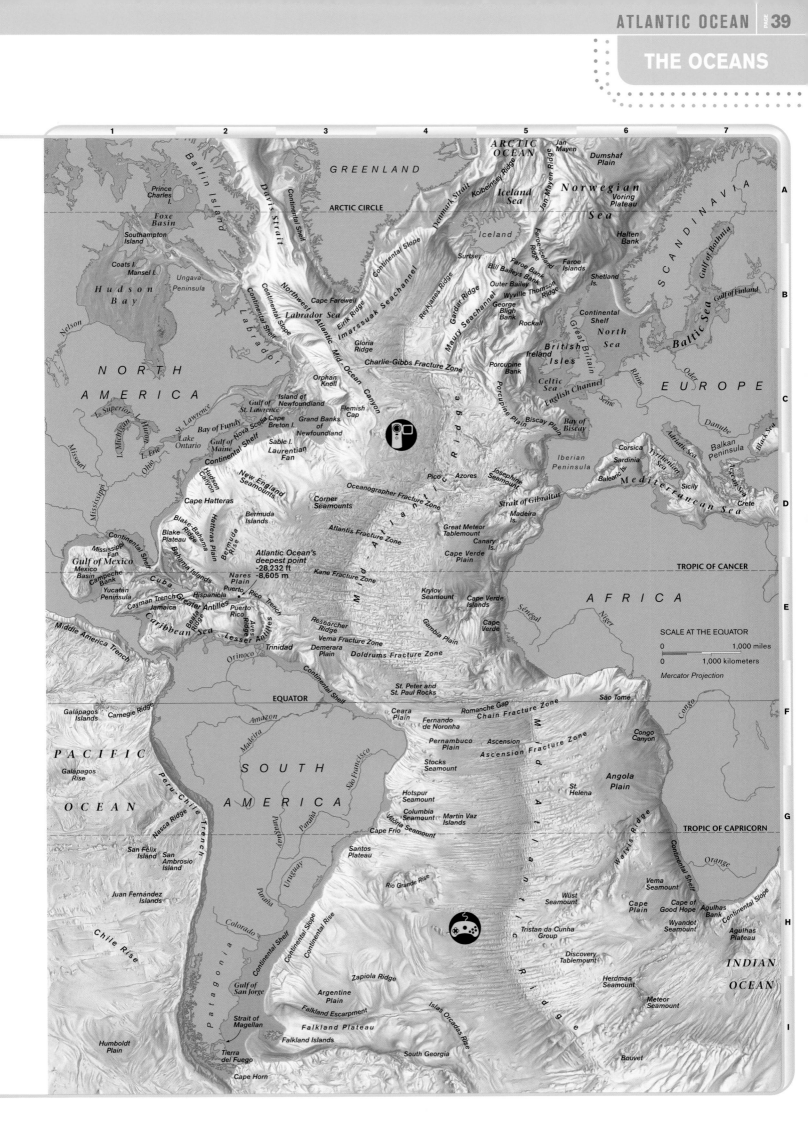

THE BASICS

STATS

Surface area
28,839,800 sq mi
(74,694,800 sq km)

Percent of Earth's water area
21%

Greatest depth
Java Trench
-23,376 ft (-7,125 m)

Surface temperatures
Summer high: 93°F (34°C)
Winter low: 28°F (-2°C)

Tides
Highest: 36 ft (11 m)
Lowest: 2 ft (0.6 m)
Both along Australia's west coast

GEO WHIZ

Each day tankers carrying 17 million barrels of crude oil from the Persian Gulf enter the waters of the Indian Ocean, transporting their cargo for distribution around the world.

Some of the world's largest breeding grounds for humpback whales are in the Indian Ocean, the Arabian Sea, and off the east coast of Africa.

The Bay of Bengal is sometimes called Cyclone Alley because of the large number of tropical storms that occur each year between May and November.

Sailors from what is now Indonesia used seasonal winds called monsoons to reach Africa's east coast. They arrived on the continent long before Europeans did.

The earthquake that caused the tsunami that killed more than 225,000 people in countries bordering the Indian Ocean in December 2004 created waves as high as 49 feet (15 m).

The Indian Ocean has several strategic chokepoints—narrow straits through which shipping must pass. They include Bab el Mandeb, between the Gulf of Aden and the Red Sea; the Strait of Hormuz, between the Persian Gulf and the Arabian Sea; the Gulf of Suez, between the Red Sea and the Suez Canal; and the Strait of Malacca, between Sumatra and the Malay Peninsula.

INDIAN OCEAN

The Indian Ocean stretches from Africa's east coast to the southern coast of Asia and the western coast of Australia. It is the third largest of Earth's great oceans. Changing air pressure systems over the warm waters of the Indian Ocean trigger South Asia's famous monsoon climate— a weather pattern in which winds reverse directions seasonally. The Bay of Bengal, an arm of the Indian Ocean, experiences devastating tropical storms, similar to hurricanes, but called cyclones in this region. Islands along the eastern edge of the Indian Ocean plate experience earthquakes that sometimes cause destructive ocean waves, called tsunamis.

The Arabian Sea, Persian Gulf, and Red Sea, also extensions of the Indian Ocean, are important sources of oil and natural gas reserves and account for an estimated 40 percent of the world's offshore oil production. The sea routes of the Indian Ocean connect the Middle East to the rest of world, carrying much needed energy resources on huge tanker ships.

← LIVING FOSSIL.
A coelacanth swims in the warm waters of the western Indian Ocean off the Comoro Islands. Once thought to have become extinct 65 million years ago along with the dinosaurs, a living coelacanth was discovered in 1938.

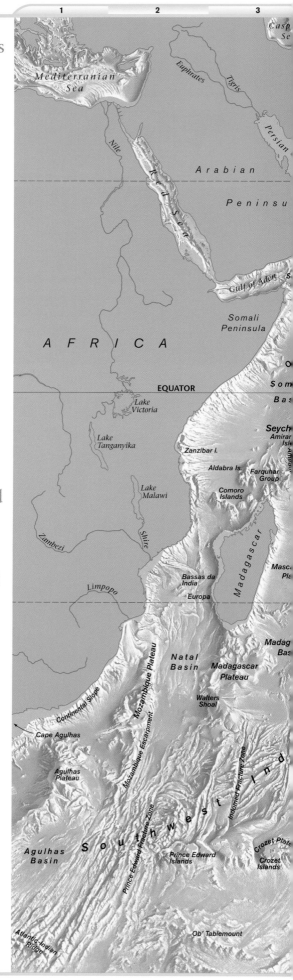

4   5   6   7   8   9   10   11

CALE AT THE EQUATOR

1,000 miles

1,000 kilometers

Mercator Projection

A S I A

Indus

Brahmaputra

Ganges

Yellow

Yangtze

Yellow
Sea

Honshu

Japan Trench

JAPAN

Shikoku

Kyushu

Izu Trench

East
China
Sea

PACIFIC

Bonin Trench

Bonin Is.

TROPIC OF CANCER

Mekong

Salween

Taiwan

Ryukyu Islands

Ryukyu Trench

Kyushu-Palau Ridge

OCEAN

Mariana Trough

Mariana Islands

Gulf of Oman

Ra's al Hadd

Continental Shelf

I N D I A

Irrawaddy

Bay of
Bengal

Ganges Fan

Indochina
Peninsula

Hainan

South

Paracel
Islands

Macclesfield
Bank

Luzon

Philippine Sea

Philippine

Philippine Islands

Benham
Seamount

Philippine
Basin

West
Mariana
Basin

Continental Shelf

Guam

Arabian
Sea

Arabian
Basin

Andaman
Islands

Andaman
Basin

China

Gulf of Thailand

Sea

Sulu
Basin

Philippine Trench

World's greatest
ocean depth
-35,827 ft
-10,920 m

Mariana
Trench
Challenger
Deep

Carlsberg
Ridge

Laccadive Plateau

Chagos Trench

Sri Lanka
(Ceylon)

Nicobar
Islands

Continental Shelf

Palawan Trough

Celebes
Basin

Mindanao

Palau

Palau Trench

Yap Trench

Caroline Islands

West
Caroline
Basin

Eauripik Rise

East
Caroline
Basin

o-De-Mer
amounts

Maldive
Islands

Chagos
Archipelago

Diego
Garcia

Vema Fracture Zone

Nikitin
Seamount

Mid-Indian

Basin

Celebes

I N D O N E S I A

Greater
Java Sea

Sunda Islands

New
Guinea

ascarene
Bank

azareth
Bank

ados
agos
ank

Saya de
Malha Bank

Mid-Indian Ridge

Osborn
Plateau

Investigator Ridge

Java

Christmas I.

Indian Ocean's
deepest point
-23,376 ft
-7,125 m

Bali

Java Ridge

Java Trench

Lesser Sunda Islands

Flores Sea

Banda Sea

Timor

Weber Basin

Arafura Sea

Continental Shelf

Coral
Sea

Ninetyeast Ridge

North
Australian
Basin

Gulf
of
Carpentaria

Rodrigues

Rodrigues
Fracture Zone

Egeria Fracture Zone

Wharton Basin

Exmouth
Plateau

TROPIC OF CAPRICORN

Mid Indian Ridge

Wallaby
Plateau

Cuvier
Plateau

East Indiamen Ridge

A U S T R A L I A

Perth

Basin

Darling

Broken   Ridge

Diamantina Fracture Zone

Naturaliste
Plateau

Continental Slope

Continental Shelf

Great
Australian
Bight

Murray

rozet

asin

Amsterdam
St. Paul

South Australian Basin

Bass Strait

South Tasman Rise

Tasmania

Ridge

Kerguelen
Islands

S o u t h e a s t   I n d i a n   R i d g e

Kerguelen
Plateau

THE BASICS

STATS

Surface area
5,390,000 sq mi (13,960,100 sq km)

Percent of Earth's water area
4%

Greatest depth
Molloy Deep: -18,599 ft (-5,669 m)

Surface temperatures
Summer high: 41°F (5°C)
Winter low: 28°F (-2°C)

Tides
Less than a 1-ft (0.3-m) variation
throughout the ocean

GEO WHIZ

Satellite monitoring of Arctic sea
ice, which began in the late 1970s,
shows that the extent of the sea ice is
shrinking by approximately 8 percent
every 10 years. Scientists think this may
be caused by global warming.

The geographic North Pole lies roughly
in the middle of the Arctic Ocean under
13,000 feet (3,962 m) of water.

Many of the features on the Arctic
Ocean floor are named for early Arctic
explorers and bordering landmasses.

Mapping of the Arctic Ocean floor did
not begin until 2001. The initial research
was by a joint U.S.-German operation
called AMORE (Arctic Mid-Ocean Ridge
Expedition). Surprise findings included
12 volcanoes, hydrothermal vents, and a
vast continental shelf off Siberia.

ARCTIC OCEAN

The Arctic Ocean lies mostly north of the Arctic Circle, bounded by North America, Europe, and Asia. Unlike the other oceans, the Arctic is subject to persistent cold throughout the year. Also, because of its very high latitude, the Arctic experiences winters of perpetual night and summers of continual daylight. Except for coastal margins, the Arctic Ocean is covered by permanent drifting pack ice that averages almost 10 feet (3 m) in thickness. Some scientists are concerned that the polar ice may be melting due to global warming, putting at risk the habitat of polar bears and other arctic animals.

← ARCTIC RESEARCH.
Scientists wearing cold weather survival suits prepare to measure salt content, nutrients, and plant and animal life in ice and meltwater. They also monitor changes related to global warming, such as the shrinking of the polar ice cap.

⇨ FREE RIDE.
A baby polar bear catches a ride as its mother crosses Canada's Arctic. Polar bear populations are showing signs of stress as sea ice shrinks.

Azimuthal Equidistant Projection

200 miles
200 kilometers

4 5 6 7 8 9 10 11

EUROPE

Northern Dvina

Khatanga

Upper Taymyr

Taymyr Peninsula

Yenisey Gulf

Gulf of Ob

Yamal Peninsula

Baydarata Bay

Pechora Bay

Chesha Bay

White Sea

Continental Shelf

Kara Sea

East Novaya Zemlya Trough

Novaya Zemlya

Gusinaya Bank

Continental Shelf

Kola Peninsula

ARCTIC CIRCLE

Gulf of Bothnia

Continental Shelf

ntinental Shelf

aptev Sea

Cape Chelyuskin

Bol'shevik I.

October Revolution I.

North Land

Komsomolets I.

Voronin Trough

Svyataya Anna Trough

Franz Josef Land

Graham Bell I.

George Land

Alexandra Land

Olga Basin

Barents Sea

Murmansk Rise

North Cape

SCANDINAVIA

Nansen Basin

Nansen Ridge

Pole Plain

Svyataya Anna Fan

Soyataya Anna

North East Land

Svalbard

Continental Shelf

Spitsbergen Bank

Bjørnya

Røst Bank

Halten Bank

Continental Shelf

Wrangel Plain

Lomonosov Ridge

Fram Basin Ridge

Fletcher Plain

Spitzbergen

Arctic Ocean's deepest point -18,599 ft -5,669 m

Yermak Plateau

Molloy Deep

Voring Plateau

Continental Slope

Norwegian

Norwegian Basin

akarov Basin

eyev Ridge

North Pole

Basin

Barents Plain

Spitsbergen Fracture Zone

Boreas Plain

Greenland Fracture Zone

Greenland Plain

Mohns Ridge

Dumshaf Plain

Aegir Ridge

deleyev Plain

Alpha Cordillera

Marvin Spur

Morris Jesup Rise

Oodaaq Island

Wandel Sea

Ob' Bank

Continental Shelf

Belgica Bank

Greenland Sea

Jan Mayen Fracture Zone

Jan Mayen

Jan Mayen Ridge

Iceland Plateau

Iceland Sea

Basin

Lincoln Sea

Continental Slope

Continental Shelf

Axel Heiberg Island

Ellesmere Island

GREENLAND

Kolbeinsey Ridge

Iceland

Surtsey

Sverdrup Islands

Prince Patrick Island

Mackenzie King I.

Ellef Ringnes I.

Queen Elizabeth Islands

M'Clure Strait

Melville Island

Parry Islands

Bathurst Island

Cornwallis I.

Devon Island

Baffin Bay

Reykjanes Ridge

nks Island

Parry Channel

Viscount Melville Sound

Barrow Str.

Lancaster Sound

Bylot I.

Qeqertarsuaq (Disko)

ARCTIC CIRCLE

ATLANTIC OCEAN

Victoria Island

M'Clintock Channel

Somerset Island

Prince of Wales Island

Prince Regent Inlet

Brodeur Pen.

Baffin Island

Continental Slope

AMERICA

King William Island

Gulf of Boothia

Boothia Peninsula

Melville Pen.

Davis Strait

Cape Farewell

THE POLITICAL WORLD

Earth's land area is mainly made up of seven giant continents, but people have divided much of the land into smaller political units called countries. Australia is a continent with a single country, and Antarctica is set aside for scientific research. But the other five continents include almost 200 independent countries. The political map (right) shows boundaries—imaginary lines agreed by treaties—that separate countries. Some boundaries, such as the one between the United States and Canada, are very stable and have been recognized for many years. Other boundaries, such as the one between Ethiopia and Eritrea in northeast Africa, are relatively new and still disputed.

Countries come in all shapes and sizes. Russia and Canada are giants. Other countries, such as Luxembourg in western Europe, are small. Some countries are long and skinny—look at Chile in South America! Still other countries—like Indonesia and Japan in Asia—are made up of groups of islands. The political map is a clue to the diversity that makes Earth so fascinating.

⇨ **COUNTRIES AND CAPITALS.** The world political map looks a bit like a patchwork quilt. Each country's boundary is outlined in one color. Some countries also include territory beyond the main land area. For example, the United States is outlined in bright green, but so are Alaska and Hawai'i, which are also U.S. states. Most countries have one city—called the capital—that is the center of political decision-making. For example, Beijing is the capital of China. But a few countries have more than one capital, such as La Paz and Sucre in Bolivia. The capital of each country is marked with a star inside a circle.

SCALE AT THE EQUATOR
0 — 2,000 miles
0 — 2,000 kilometers
Winkel Tripel Projection, Central Meridian 0°

WORLD POPULATION

How big is a billion? It's hard to imagine. But Earth's population is 6.8 billion and rising, with more than a billion living in both China and India. And more than 80 million people are added to the world each year. Most growth occurs in the less-developed countries of Asia, Africa, and Latin America, while some countries in Europe are hardly increasing at all. Population changes can create challenges for countries. Fast-growing countries with young populations need food, housing, and schools. Countries with low growth rates and older populations need workers to sustain their economies.

MOST POPULOUS COUNTRIES

	(mid-2009 data)
1.	China 1,362,069,000
2.	India 1,171,000,000
3.	United States 306,805,000
4.	Indonesia 243,306,000
5.	Brazil 191,481,000
6.	Pakistan 180,808,000
7.	Bangladesh 162,221,000
8.	Nigeria 152,616,000

MOST CROWDED COUNTRIES

	Population Density (People per sq mi/sq km; mid-2006 data)
1.	Monaco 45,455/17,500
2.	Singapore 19,000/7,335
3.	Bahrain 4,255/1,642
4.	Malta 3,393/1,310
5.	Bangladesh 2,918/1,127
6.	Maldives 2,739/1,057
7.	Mauritus 1,619/625
8.	Nauru 1,233/476

⇨ DENSITY. Demographers, people who study population, use density to measure how concentrated population is. For example, the population density of Egypt is almost 200 people per square mile (77 per sq km). This assumes that the population is evenly spread throughout the country, but this is not the case in Egypt. Almost all of the people live along the banks of the Nile River. Likewise, Earth's population is not evenly spread across the land. Some places, like central Australia, are almost empty, but others, such as Europe or India, are very crowded.

⇨ CITY DWELLERS. Almost half the world's people have shifted from rural areas to urban centers, with some countries adding more than 100 million to their urban populations between 1955 and 2005 (see map, right). In more-developed countries, about 74 percent of the population is urban, compared with just 43 percent in less-developed countries. But the fastest growing urban areas are in less-developed countries, where thousands flock to cities, such as Dhaka, Bangladesh (photo, far right), in search of a better life. By 2015 there could be as many as 22 cities with populations of 10 million or more.

Los Angeles

México

PACIFIC OCEAN

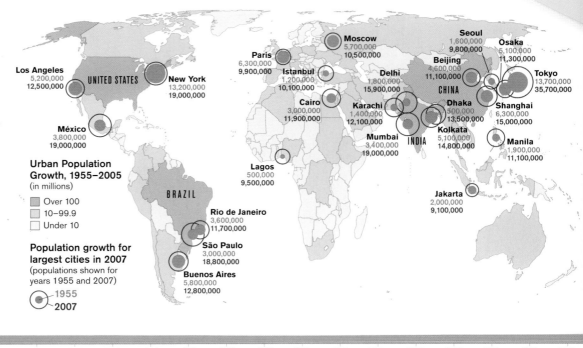

Urban Population Growth, 1955–2005 (in millions)
- ☐ Over 100
- ☐ 10–99.9
- ☐ Under 10

Population growth for largest cities in 2007 (populations shown for years 1955 and 2007)
- 1955
- **2007**

Los Angeles 5,200,000 12,500,000

UNITED STATES

New York 13,200,000 19,000,000

México 3,800,000 19,000,000

BRAZIL

Rio de Janeiro 3,600,000 11,700,000

São Paulo 3,000,000 18,800,000

Buenos Aires 5,800,000 12,800,000

Lagos 500,000 9,500,000

Paris 6,300,000 9,900,000

Istanbul 1,200,000 10,100,000

Cairo 3,000,000 11,900,000

Moscow 5,700,000 10,500,000

Delhi 1,800,000 15,900,000

Karachi 1,400,000 12,100,000

Mumbai 3,400,000 19,000,000

INDIA

Seoul 1,600,000 9,800,000

Beijing 4,600,000 11,100,000

CHINA

Dhaka 500,000 13,500,000

Kolkata 5,100,000 14,800,000

Osaka 5,100,000 11,300,000

Tokyo 13,700,000 35,700,000

Shanghai 6,300,000 15,000,000

Manila 1,900,000 11,100,000

Jakarta 2,000,000 9,100,000

50	100	150	200	250	300	350	400	450	500	550	600	650	700	750	800	850	900	950

Year

ARCTIC OCEAN

NORTH
AMERICA

EUROPE
Moscow
London
Paris
Madrid
Istanbul
Tehran
Baghdad
Cairo

ASIA
Beijing
Tianjin
Seoul
Tokyo
Osaka
Wuhan
Chongqing
Shanghai
Lahore
Delhi
Guangzhou
Karachi
Kolkata
Dhaka
Shenzhen
Ahmadabad
Hong Kong
Mumbai
Hyderabad
Bangalore
Chennai
Bangkok
Manila
Ho Chi Minh City

Toronto
New York
Philadelphia
cago

Miami

ATLANTIC
OCEAN

AFRICA

Lagos

Kinshasa

PACIFIC
OCEAN

Bogotá

SOUTH
AMERICA

INDIAN
OCEAN

Jakarta

AUSTRALIA

Belo Horizonte
Rio de Janeiro
São Paulo

ntiago

Buenos Aires

Kilometers
0   1000   2000   3000

Statute Miles
0   1000   2000   3000

**People per
Square Mile**
More than 500
150–500
25–149
1–24
0–1
No data

**People per
Square Km**
More than 195
60–195
10–59
1–9
Less than 1
No data

**Urban Area
Population**
(in millions)
■ More than 20
▲ 15–20
● 10–14.9
○ 5–9.9

ANTARCTICA

⇨ **MEASURING GROWTH.**
This graph traces the
growth of Earth's popula-
tion for more than 2,000
years. Asia, including
population giants China
and India, dominates,
followed by Africa and
Latin America. The United
Nations projects that
the world population will
increase to 9.2 *billion*
people by 2050.

Asia
Africa
Latin America
Europe
North America
Australia/Oceania

9
8
7
6
5
4
3
2
1
0

Billions of people

1100 1150 1200 1250 1300 1350 1400 1450 1500 1550 1600 1650 1700 1750 1800 1850 1900 1950 2000 2050
Year

WORLD LANGUAGES & LITERACY

Earth's 6.8 billion people live in 194 independent countries, but they speak more than 5,000 languages. Some countries, such as Japan, have one official language. Others speak many languages, such as India, where 23 are official. Experts believe that humans may once have spoken as many as 10,000 languages, but that number has dropped by one-half and is still declining.

Literacy is the ability to read and write in one's native language. High literacy rates are associated with more-developed countries. But literacy is also a gender issue, since women in less-developed countries often lack access to education (see pages 52–53).

NORTH AMERICA

Toronto
New York
Los Angeles
México

PACIFIC OCEAN

ATLANTIC OCEAN

SOUTH AMERICA

São Paulo
Buenos Aires

Major Language Families Today
- Afro-Asiatic
- Altaic
- Austro-Asiatic
- Austronesian
- Dravidian
- Indo-European
- Japanese/Korean
- Kam-Tai
- Niger-Congo
- Nilo-Saharan
- Sino-Tibetan
- Uralic
- Other

LEADING LANGUAGES

Some languages have only a few hundred speakers, but 23 languages stand out with more than 50 million speakers each. Earth's population giant, China, has 845 million speakers of Mandarin, more than double the next largest group of language speakers. Colonial expansion, trade, and migration account for the spread of the other most widely spoken languages. With growing use of the Internet, English is becoming the language of the technology age.

Population of first language speakers (in millions)

Language	
Chinese (Mandarin)	845
Spanish	329
English	328
Arabic	221
Hindi	182
Bengali	181
Portuguese	178
Russian	144
Japanese	122
German	90

Languages

⇧ EDUCATION AND LITERACY. These Nenet boys in Siberia spend hours learning the national language—Russian—but this may result in the loss of their native language. Literacy means good jobs in the future for these boys and economic success for their country.

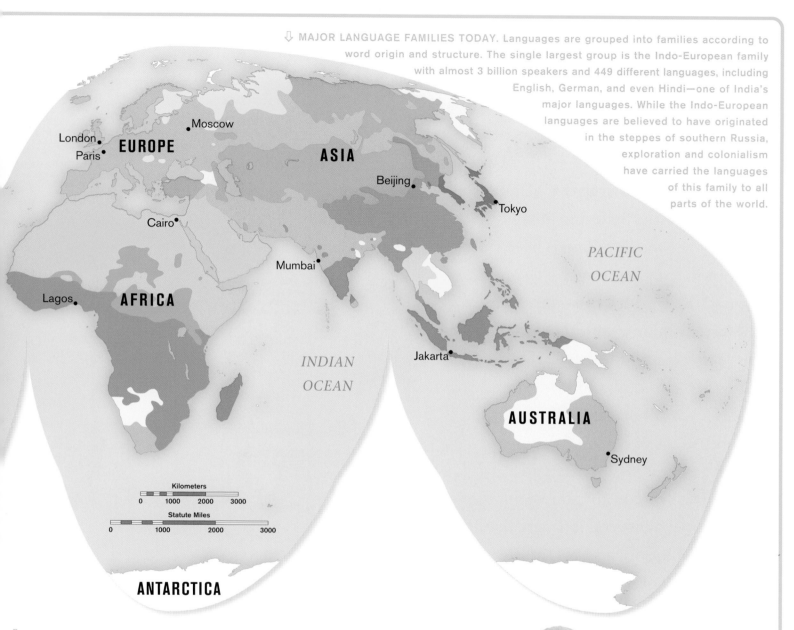

⇩ MAJOR LANGUAGE FAMILIES TODAY. Languages are grouped into families according to word origin and structure. The single largest group is the Indo-European family with almost 3 billion speakers and 449 different languages, including English, German, and even Hindi—one of India's major languages. While the Indo-European languages are believed to have originated in the steppes of southern Russia, exploration and colonialism have carried the languages of this family to all parts of the world.

⇩ ONE LANGUAGE, TWO FORMS. Some languages, including Chinese, use characters instead of letters. The Golden Arches provide a clue to the meaning of the characters on the restaurant sign. Many signs, such as the one in the foreground, also show words in pinyin, a spelling system that uses the Western alphabet.

⇧ UNIVERSAL LANGUAGE. The widespread use of technology—for example, the electronic games that hold the attention of these children in France—has crossed over the language barrier. Computers, the Internet, and electronic communications devices use a universal language that knows no national borders.

WORLD RELIGIONS

Rooted in people's attempts to explain the unknown, religion takes many forms. Some belief systems, such as Christianity, Islam, and Judaism, are monotheistic, meaning that followers believe in just one supreme being. Others, like Hinduism, Shintoism, and most native belief systems, are polytheistic, believing in many gods.

All of the major religions have their origins in Asia, but they have spread around the world. Christianity, with the largest number of followers, has three divisions—Roman Catholic, Eastern Orthodox, and Protestant. Islam, with about one-fifth of all believers, has two main divisions—Sunni and Shia. Hinduism and Buddhism account for almost another one-fifth of believers. Judaism, dating back some 4,000 years, is the oldest of all the major monotheistic religions.

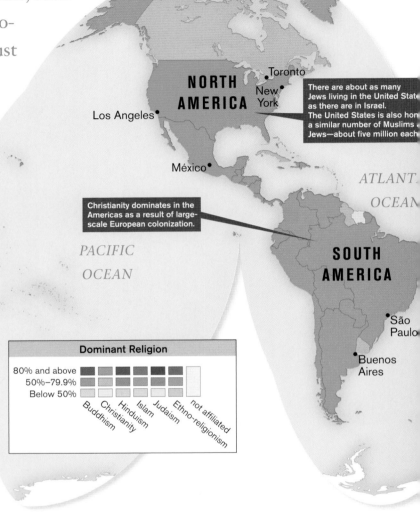

NORTH AMERICA

Toronto
New York
Los Angeles
México

There are about as many Jews living in the United States as there are in Israel. The United States is also home a similar number of Muslims Jews—about five million each

ATLANTIC OCEAN

PACIFIC OCEAN

Christianity dominates in the Americas as a result of large-scale European colonization.

SOUTH AMERICA

São Paulo

Buenos Aires

Dominant Religion

	Buddhism	Christianity	Hinduism	Islam	Judaism	Ethno-religionism	not affiliated
80% and above							
50%–79.9%							
Below 50%							

BUDDHISM

Founded about 2,500 years ago in northern India by a Hindu prince, Gautama Buddha, Buddhism spread throughout East and Southeast Asia. Buddhist temples have statues, such as the Mihintale Buddha (above) in Sri Lanka.

CHRISTIANITY

Based on the teachings of Jesus Christ, a Jew born some 2,000 years ago in the area of modern-day Israel, Christianity has spread worldwide and actively seeks converts. Followers in Switzerland (above) participate in a procession with lanterns and crosses.

HINDUISM

Dating back more than 4,000 years, Hinduism is practiced mainly in India. Hindus follow sacred texts known as the Vedas and believe in reincarnation. During the festival of Diwali, Hindus light candles (above) to symbolize the victory of good over evil.

The Caucasus are deeply divided, with Azerbaijan 88% Muslim and Georgia and Armenia 83% Christian.

In China and in North and South Korea, people with no religious affiliation form the largest group. China, however, is still home to more than 100 million Buddhists, 100 million Christians, and 100 million atheists.

Moscow

ASIA

London
Paris EUROPE

Beijing

Tokyo

Cairo

AFRICA

Mumbai

Lagos

Sandwiched between vast Christian and Muslim strongholds, Nigeria is 45% Muslim and 45% Christian.

Home to 94% of the world's one billion Hindus, India is also home to more than 168 million Muslims.

INDIAN OCEAN

PACIFIC OCEAN

Jakarta

AUSTRALIA

Sydney

Kilometers
0   1000   2000   3000

Statute Miles
0   1000   2000   3000

This map is intended to be a general indication of the geography of religions worldwide.

ANTARCTICA

ISLAM

Muslims believe that the Koran, Islam's sacred book, records the words of Allah (God) as revealed to the Prophet Muhammad around A.D. 610. Believers (above) circle the Kabah in the Haram Mosque in Mecca, the spiritual center of the faith.

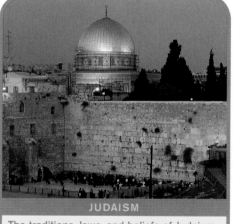

JUDAISM

The traditions, laws, and beliefs of Judaism date back to Abraham, the founder, and the Torah, the first five books of the Old Testament. Followers (above) pray before the Western Wall, which stands below Islam's Dome of the Rock in Jerusalem.

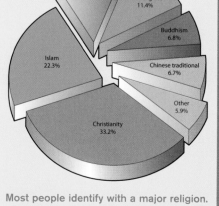

RELIGIOUS FOLLOWERS

Hinduism 13.7%

Non-religious 11.4%

Buddhism 6.8%

Chinese traditional 6.7%

Islam 22.3%

Other 5.9%

Christianity 33.2%

Most people identify with a major religion. Some are non-religious.

WORLD ECONOMIES

People use resources together with human energy and ingenuity to produce goods and services that meet their needs and generate income. This map shows patterns of economic activity around the world.

A country's economy can be divided into three parts, or sectors—agriculture, industry, and services. The economies of the United States and Western Europe are dominated by the service sector. These economies enjoy a high GDP (Gross Domestic Product) per capita—the value of goods and services produced each year, averaged per person in each country. In contrast, some economies in Africa and Asia still depend mostly on agriculture. Many farmers produce only enough crops to support their own families—a practice called subsistence farming—and therefore have a low standard of living. Other economies, such as those of oil-producing countries of the Middle East, have a very high GDP per capita, but wealth is unevenly divided among the population, and many people remain poor.

No country produces everything its people need or want. Therefore, trade is a critical part of the world economy.

HIGHEST GDP PER CAPITA*	
1. Liechtenstein	$122,100
2. Qatar	$121,400
3. Luxembourg	$77,600
4. Norway	$59,300
5. Kuwait	$55,800
6. Singapore	$50,300
7. Brunei	$50,100
8. United States	$46,400
9. Andorra	$42,500
10. Ireland	$42,200

LOWEST GDP PER CAPITA*	
1. Zimbabwe	$200
2. Democratic Republic of the Congo	$300
3. Burundi	$300
4. Liberia	$500
5. Somalia	$600
6. Guinea-Bissau	$600
7. Eritrea	$700
8. Niger	$700
9. Central African Republic	$700

*All data as of 2009.

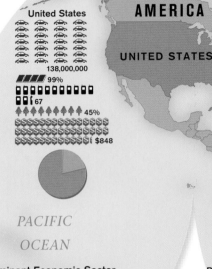

NORTH AMERICA

UNITED STATES

United States
138,000,000
99%
67
45%
$848

ATLANTIC OCEAN

SOUTH AMERICA
BRAZIL

PACIFIC OCEAN

Dominant Economic Sector (as a percentage of GDP)

	Agriculture	Industry*	Services
70%–100%			
50%–69.9%			
0%–49.9%			
No data			

*Includes the mining industry

Brazil
25,700,000
89%
46
43%
$167

⬆ INDUSTRY. A man assembles a hybrid Prius car on an automated assembly line in a Toyota factory in Japan. Manufacture of cars is an important industrial activity and a key part of the global economy.

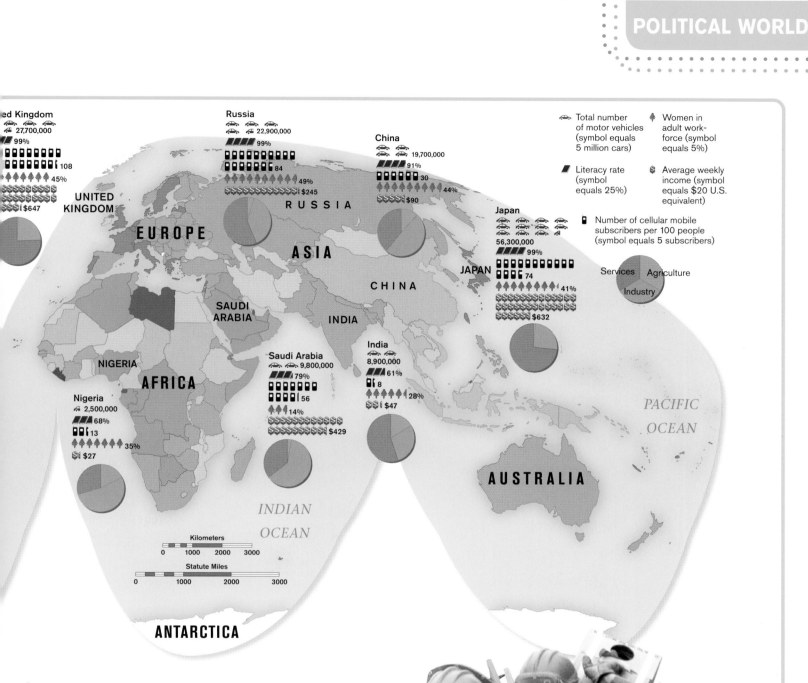

ed Kingdom
🚗🚗🚗 27,700,000
▰▰ 99%
🔲🔲🔲🔲🔲🔲🔲🔲🔲🔲 108
🌲🌲🌲🌲🌲🌲🌲🌲🌲 45%
$$$$$$$$
$$$ $647

UNITED
KINGDOM

EUROPE

Russia
🚗🚗 22,900,000
▰▰▰▰ 99%
🔲🔲🔲🔲🔲🔲🔲🔲 84
🌲🌲🌲🌲🌲🌲🌲🌲🌲🌲 49%
$$$$$$$$$$ $245

RUSSIA

ASIA

China
🚗🚗🚗🚗 19,700,000
▰▰▰▰ 91%
🌲🌲🌲🌲🌲🌲 30
🌲🌲🌲🌲🌲🌲🌲🌲 44%
$$$$ $90

CHINA

Total number
of motor vehicles
(symbol equals
5 million cars)

Literacy rate
(symbol
equals 25%)

Women in
adult work-
force (symbol
equals 5%)

Average weekly
income (symbol
equals $20 U.S.
equivalent)

Number of cellular mobile
subscribers per 100 people
(symbol equals 5 subscribers)

Japan
🚗🚗🚗🚗🚗🚗🚗🚗🚗🚗🚗 56,300,000
▰▰▰▰ 99%
🔲🔲🔲🔲🔲🔲🔲🔲🔲🔲🔲 74
🌲🌲🌲🌲🌲🌲🌲🌲🌲 41%
$$$$$$$$$$
$$$$$$ $632

JAPAN

Services   Agriculture

Industry

SAUDI
ARABIA

INDIA

NIGERIA

AFRICA

Nigeria
🚗 2,500,000
▰▰ 68%
🔲🔲🔲 13
🌲🌲🌲🌲🌲🌲🌲 35%
$ $27

Saudi Arabia
🚗🚗 9,800,000
▰▰▰ 79%
🔲🔲🔲🔲🔲🔲🔲🔲 56
🌲🌲🌲 14%
$$$$$$$$$$$ $429

India
🚗🚗🚗 8,900,000
▰▰ 61%
🔲 8
🌲🌲🌲🌲🌲🌲 28%
$$ $47

PACIFIC

OCEAN

AUSTRALIA

INDIAN

OCEAN

Kilometers
0 1000 2000 3000

Statute Miles
0 1000 2000 3000

ANTARCTICA

⇩ AGRICULTURE. Farms in more-developed countries, such as this one in Saskatchewan, Canada, use machinery to make agriculture more efficient and productive. Farmers in less-developed countries often use less-efficient traditional farming tools and methods.

⇧ SERVICES. People employed in the service sector, such as these national forest firefighters in Washington State, use their skills and training to provide services rather than products. Teachers, lawyers, and store clerks, among others, are also part of the service sector.

WORLD WATER

Water is Earth's most precious resource. Although more than two-thirds of Earth is covered by water, fresh water, which is needed by plants and animals—including humans—is only about 2.5 percent of all the water on Earth. Much of this is trapped deep underground or frozen in ice sheets and glaciers. Of the small amount of water that is fresh, less than 1 percent is available for human use.

The map at right shows Earth's major watersheds—large areas in which all surface and groundwater drains into a large river. Unfortunately, human activity often puts great stress on vital watersheds. For example, in Brazil, plans are being made to build large dams on the Amazon. This will alter the natural flow of water in this giant watershed. And heavy use of chemical fertilizers and pesticides has created toxic runoff that threatens the health of the Mississippi watershed in the United States.

Access to clean fresh water is critical for human health. But in many places, safe water is scarce due to population pressure and pollution.

WATER FACTS

Rivers that have been dammed to generate electricity are the source of almost 90 percent of Earth's renewable energy resources.

North America's Great Lakes hold about 20 percent of Earth's available fresh water.

If all the glaciers and ice sheets on Earth's surface melted, they would raise the level of Earth's oceans by about 230 feet (70 m). It is estimated that during the last ice age, when glaciers covered about one-third of the land, sea level was 400 feet (122 m) lower than it is today.

Desalination is the process of removing salt from ocean water so that it can be used for irrigation, water for livestock, and for drinking. Most of the world's desalination plants are in the arid countries of the Arabian Peninsula.

Because of the water cycle, Earth has roughly the same amount of water now as it has had for two billion years.

If all the world's water were placed in a gallon jug, the fresh water available for humans to use would equal only about one tablespoon.

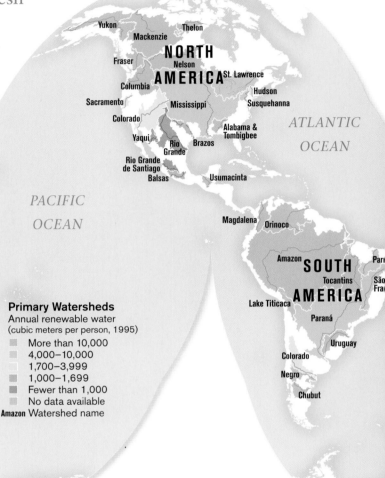

Yukon
Mackenzie
Thelon
Fraser
NORTH AMERICA
Nelson
St. Lawrence
Columbia
Hudson
Sacramento
Mississippi
Susquehanna
Colorado
Alabama & Tombigbee
ATLANTIC OCEAN
Yaqui
Rio Grande
Brazos
Rio Grande de Santiago
Balsas
Usumacinta

PACIFIC OCEAN

Magdalena
Orinoco
Amazon
SOUTH AMERICA
Parr
Tocantins
São Fra
Lake Titicaca
Paraná
Uruguay
Colorado
Negro
Chubut

Primary Watersheds
Annual renewable water
(cubic meters per person, 1995)

More than 10,000
4,000–10,000
1,700–3,999
1,000–1,699
Fewer than 1,000
No data available
Amazon Watershed name

⇨ BIG SPLASH! Water sports are a favorite recreational activity, especially in hot places such as Albuquerque, New Mexico, where these young people cool down in a giant wave pool.

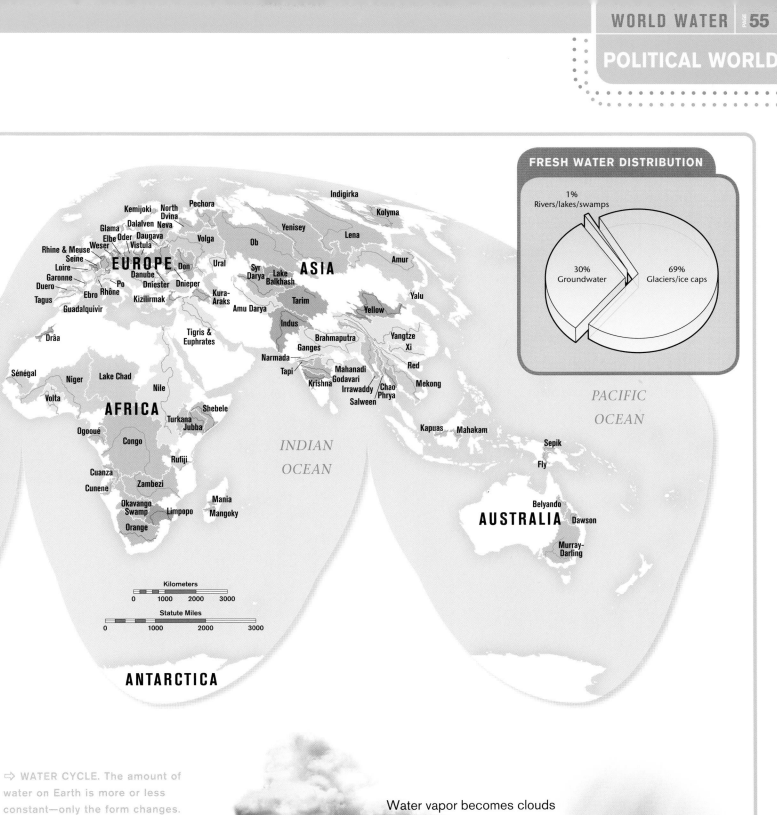

FRESH WATER DISTRIBUTION

1%
Rivers/lakes/swamps

30%
Groundwater

69%
Glaciers/ice caps

EUROPE

ASIA

AFRICA

AUSTRALIA

ANTARCTICA

INDIAN OCEAN

PACIFIC OCEAN

Kemijoki · North Dvina · Pechora · Indigirka · Kolyma · Glama · Dalalven · Neva · Yenisey · Lena · Elbe · Oder · Daugava · Volga · Ob · Amur · Weser · Vistula · Rhine & Meuse · Seine · Ural · Syr Darya · Loire · Danube · Don · Lake Balkhash · Yalu · Garonne · Dniester · Dnieper · Kura-Araks · Duero · Po · Rhône · Tarim · Yellow · Tagus · Ebro · Kizilirmak · Amu Darya · Guadalquivir · Indus · Brahmaputra · Yangtze · Xi · Drâa · Tigris & Euphrates · Ganges · Narmada · Red · Sénégal · Niger · Lake Chad · Nile · Tapi · Mahanadi · Mekong · Volta · Krishna · Godavari · Chao Phrya · Ogooué · Shebele · Irrawaddy · Salween · Kapuas · Mahakam · Congo · Turkana · Jubba · Sepik · Rufiji · Fly · Cuanza · Cunene · Zambezi · Belyando · Dawson · Okavango Swamp · Limpopo · Mania · Mangoky · Murray-Darling · Orange

Kilometers
0 1000 2000 3000

Statute Miles
0 1000 2000 3000

⇨ **WATER CYCLE.** The amount of water on Earth is more or less constant—only the form changes. As the sun warms Earth's surface, liquid water is changed to water vapor in a process called evaporation. Plants lose water from the surface of leaves in a process called transpiration. As water vapor rises into the air, it cools and changes form again. This time it becomes clouds in a process called condensation. Water droplets fall from the clouds as precipitation, which then travels as groundwater or runoff back to the lakes, rivers, and oceans, where the cycle starts all over again.

Water vapor becomes clouds

Precipitation falls and runs off into the ground

Lake

River

Water evaporates

Groundwater

Ocean

WORLD FOOD

Earth produces enough food for all its inhabitants— all 6.8 billion and growing—but not everyone gets enough to eat. It's a matter of distribution. Agricultural regions, shown in the map at right, are unevenly spread around the world, and it is sometimes difficult to move food supplies from areas of surplus to areas of great need. Africa, in particular, has regions where hunger and malnourishment rob people of healthy, productive lives.

In recent decades, food production has increased, especially production of meat and cereals, such as corn, wheat, and rice. Cereal grains play an important role in world trade. They also dominate the calorie supply of people, especially in Africa and Asia. But increased yields of grain require intensive use of fertilizers and irrigation, which are not only expensive but also possibly a threat to the environment. Most advances in food production have occurred in Asia and Latin America, but new research now focuses on Africa.

⇨ FISHING AND AQUACULTURE. The world's yearly catch of ocean fish is more than four times what it was in 1950. The most heavily harvested areas are in the North Atlantic and western Pacific Oceans. Overfishing is becoming a serious problem. At least seven of the most-fished species are considered to be at their limit.

Aquaculture—raising fish and seaweed in controlled ponds—accounts for 40 percent of the fish people eat. This practice began some 4,000 years ago in China, where it continues today, accounting for about two-thirds of total output. Fish are among the most widely traded food products, with 75 percent of the total catch sold on the international market each year.

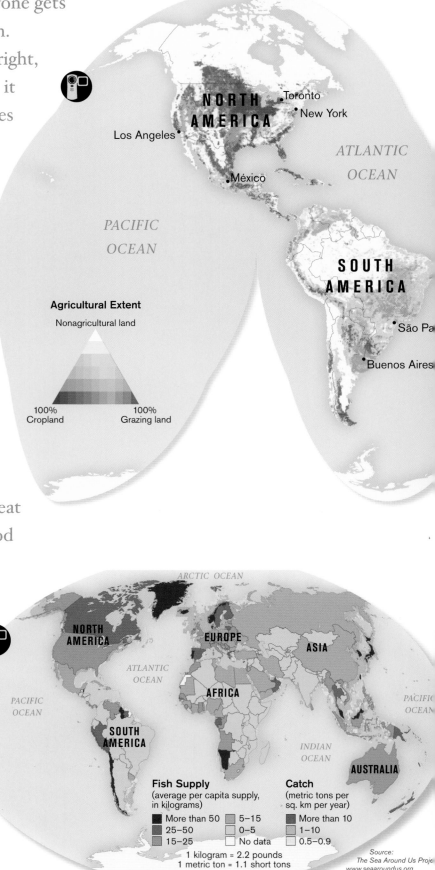

Agricultural Extent

Nonagricultural land

100% Cropland   100% Grazing land

Fish Supply
(average per capita supply, in kilograms)

More than 50	5–15
25–50	0–5
15–25	No data

Catch
(metric tons per sq. km per year)

More than 10
1–10
0.5–0.9

1 kilogram = 2.2 pounds
1 metric ton = 1.1 short tons

Source: The Sea Around Us Project www.seaaroundus.org

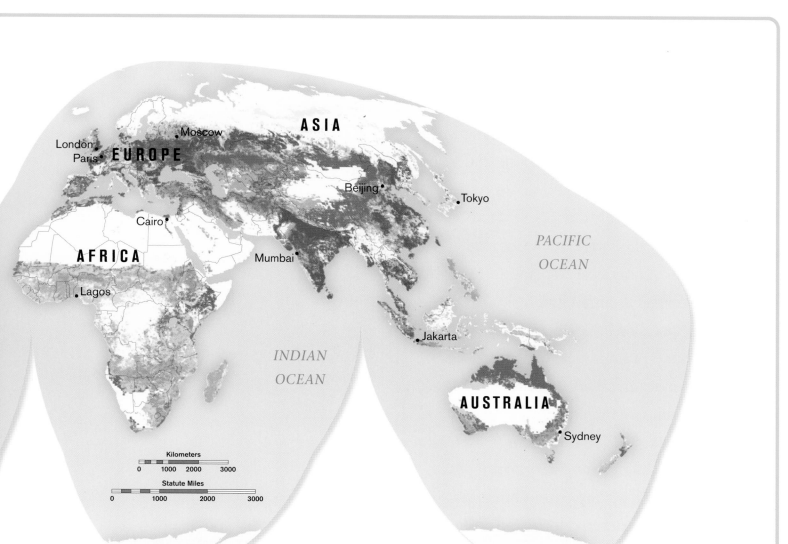

ASIA

Moscow

London
Paris EUROPE

Beijing

Tokyo

Cairo

PACIFIC
OCEAN

AFRICA

Mumbai

Lagos

INDIAN
OCEAN

Jakarta

AUSTRALIA

Sydney

Kilometers
0 1000 2000 3000

Statute Miles
0 1000 2000 3000

ANTARCTICA

⇧ CASTING NETS. Fishermen in Orissa, India, cast their nets on the Birupa River. Fish is an important source of protein in their diets. Any surplus catch can be sold in the local market.

STAPLE GRAINS

CORN. A staple in prehistoric México and Peru, corn (or maize) is native to the New World. By the time Columbus's crew first tasted it, corn was already a hardy crop in much of North and South America.

WHEAT. Among the two oldest grains (barley is the other), wheat was important in ancient Mediterranean civilizations. Today, it is the most widely cultivated grain. Wheat grows best in temperate climates.

RICE. Originating in Asia many millennia ago, rice is the staple grain for about half the world's people. It is a labor-intensive plant that grows primarily in paddies (flooded fields) and thrives in the hot, humid tropics.

WORLD ENERGY & MINERALS

Almost everything people do—from cooking to powering a space shuttle—requires energy. But energy comes in different forms. Traditional energy sources, still used by many people in the developing world, include burning dried animal dung and wood. Industrialized countries and urban centers around the world rely on coal, oil, and natural gas—called fossil fuels because they formed from decayed plant and animal material accumulated from long ago. Fossil fuel deposits, either in the ground or under the ocean floor, are unevenly distributed on Earth (see map, right), and only some countries can afford to buy them.

Carbon dioxide from the burning of fossil fuels as well as other emissions may be contributing to global warming. Concerned scientists are looking at new ways to harness renewable sources of energy, such as water, wind, and sun.

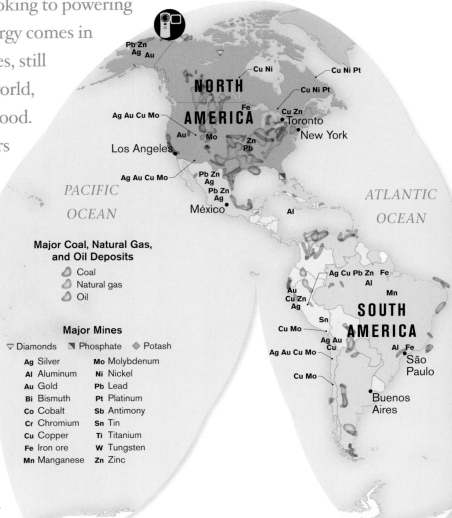

Major Coal, Natural Gas, and Oil Deposits

- Coal
- Natural gas
- Oil

Major Mines

▽ Diamonds   ◩ Phosphate   ◆ Potash

Ag	Silver	**Mo**	Molybdenum
Al	Aluminum	**Ni**	Nickel
Au	Gold	**Pb**	Lead
Bi	Bismuth	**Pt**	Platinum
Co	Cobalt	**Sb**	Antimony
Cr	Chromium	**Sn**	Tin
Cu	Copper	**Ti**	Titanium
Fe	Iron ore	**W**	Tungsten
Mn	Manganese	**Zn**	Zinc

OIL, GAS, AND COAL

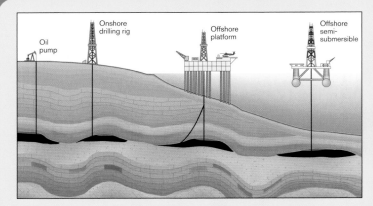

⇧ DRILLING FOR OIL AND GAS. The type of equipment depends on whether oil or natural gas is in the ground or under the ocean. This illustration shows some of the different kinds of onshore and offshore drilling equipment.

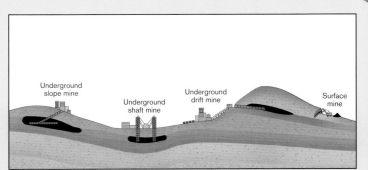

⇧ COAL MINING. The mining of coal made the industrial revolution possible, and coal still provides a major energy source. Work that was once done by people using picks and shovels now relies heavily on mechanized equipment. This diagram shows some of the various kinds currently in use.

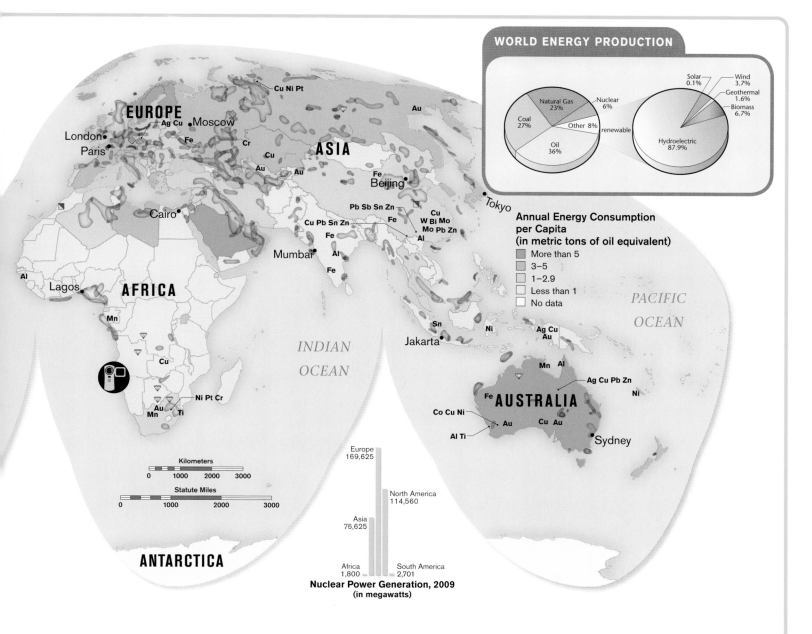

WORLD ENERGY PRODUCTION

Natural Gas 23%
Coal 27%
Oil 36%
Nuclear 6%
Other 8% renewable

Solar 0.1%
Wind 3.7%
Geothermal 1.6%
Biomass 6.7%
Hydroelectric 87.9%

Annual Energy Consumption per Capita (in metric tons of oil equivalent)

- More than 5
- 3–5
- 1–2.9
- Less than 1
- No data

EUROPE — London, Paris, Moscow
Cu Ni Pt
Ag Cu
Fe
Cr
Cu
Au
Au
Au
Fe — Beijing
ASIA
Au
Pb Sb Sn Zn
Cu Pb Sn Zn
Fe
Cu W Bi Mo
Mo Pb Zn
Al
Tokyo
Cairo
Fe
Mumbai
Al
Fe
Al
AFRICA
Lagos
Mn
Cu
Ni Pt Cr
Au
Mn
Ti
Sn
Ni
Ag Cu Au
Jakarta
INDIAN OCEAN
PACIFIC OCEAN
Mn
Al
Ag Cu Pb Zn
Ni
Fe AUSTRALIA
Co Cu Ni
Au
Cu Au
Al Ti
Sydney

ANTARCTICA

Nuclear Power Generation, 2009 (in megawatts)

- Europe 169,625
- North America 114,560
- Asia 76,625
- Africa 1,800
- South America 2,701

Kilometers
0 1000 2000 3000

Statute Miles
0 1000 2000 3000

HYDROELECTRIC POWER

Hydroelectric plants, such as Santiago del Estero in Argentina (above), use dams to harness running water to generate clean, renewable energy.

GEOTHERMAL POWER

Geothermal power, originating from groundwater heated by magma, provides energy for this power plant in Iceland. Swimmers enjoy the warm, mineral-rich waters of a lake created by the power plant.

SOLAR POWER

Solar panels on Samso Island in Denmark capture and store energy from the sun, an environmentally friendly alternative to the use of fossil fuels.

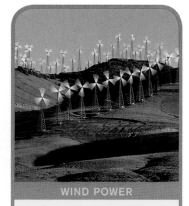

WIND POWER

Strong winds blowing through California's mountain passes spin the blades of windmills on an energy farm, powering giant turbines that generate electricity for the state.

THE CONTINENT:
NORTH AMERICA

Mount McKinley (Denali), Alaska

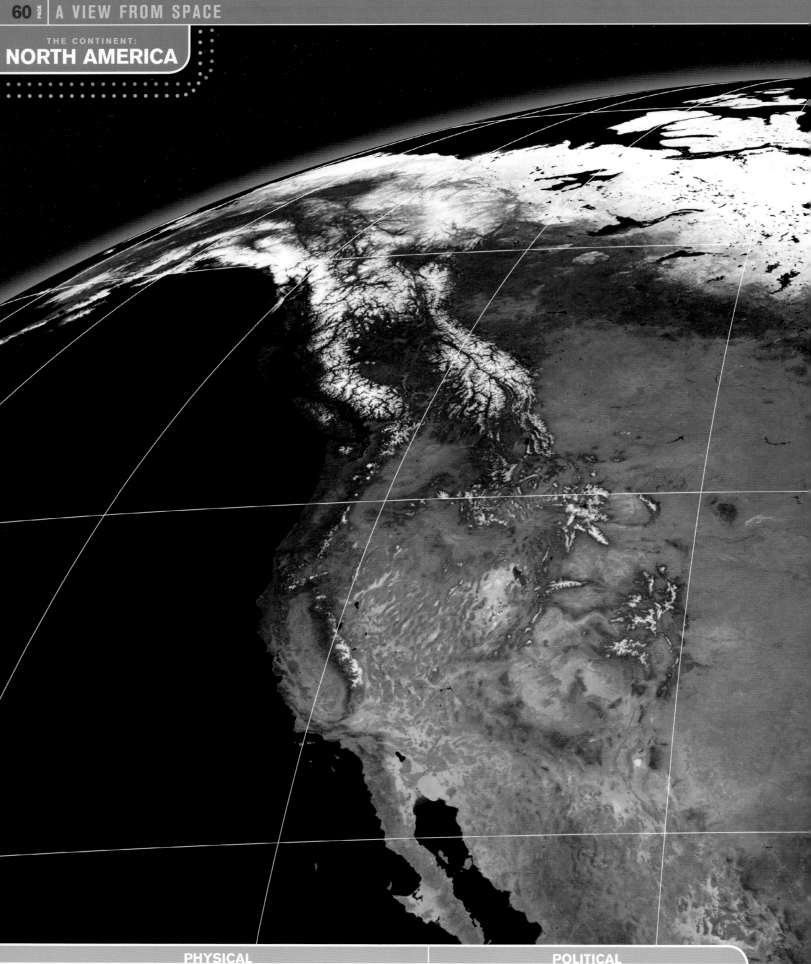

PHYSICAL

Land area
9,449,000 sq mi (24,474,000 sq km)

Highest point
Mount McKinley (Denali), Alaska
20,320 ft (6,194 m)

Lowest point
Death Valley, California
-282 ft (-86 m)

Longest river
Mississippi-Missouri,
United States
3,710 mi (5,971 km)

Largest lake
Lake Superior, U.S.-Canada
31,700 sq mi (82,100 sq km)

POLITICAL

Population
534,232,000

Largest metropolitan area
México City, México
Pop. 19,485,000

Largest country
Canada
3,855,101 sq mi (9,984,670 sq km)

Most densely populated country
Barbados
1,693 people per sq mi (653 per sq km)

Economy
Farming: cattle, grains, cotton, sugar
Industry: machinery, metals, mining
Services

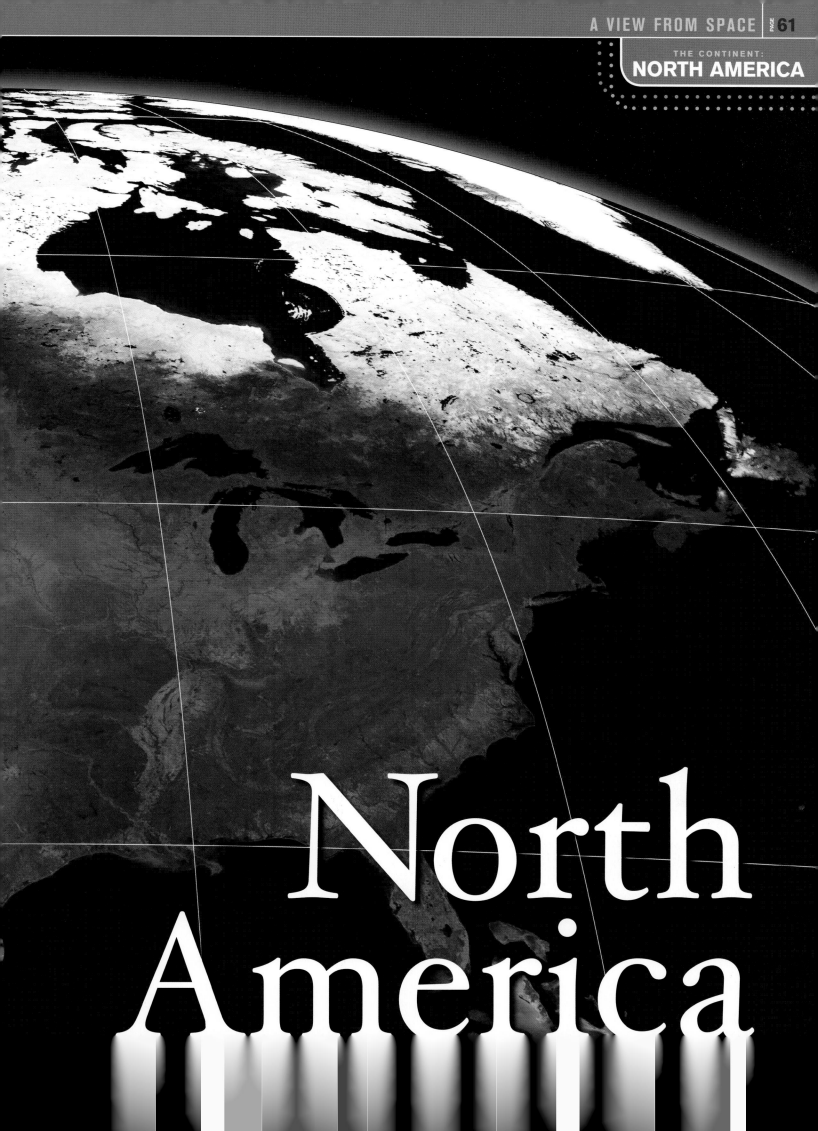

North America

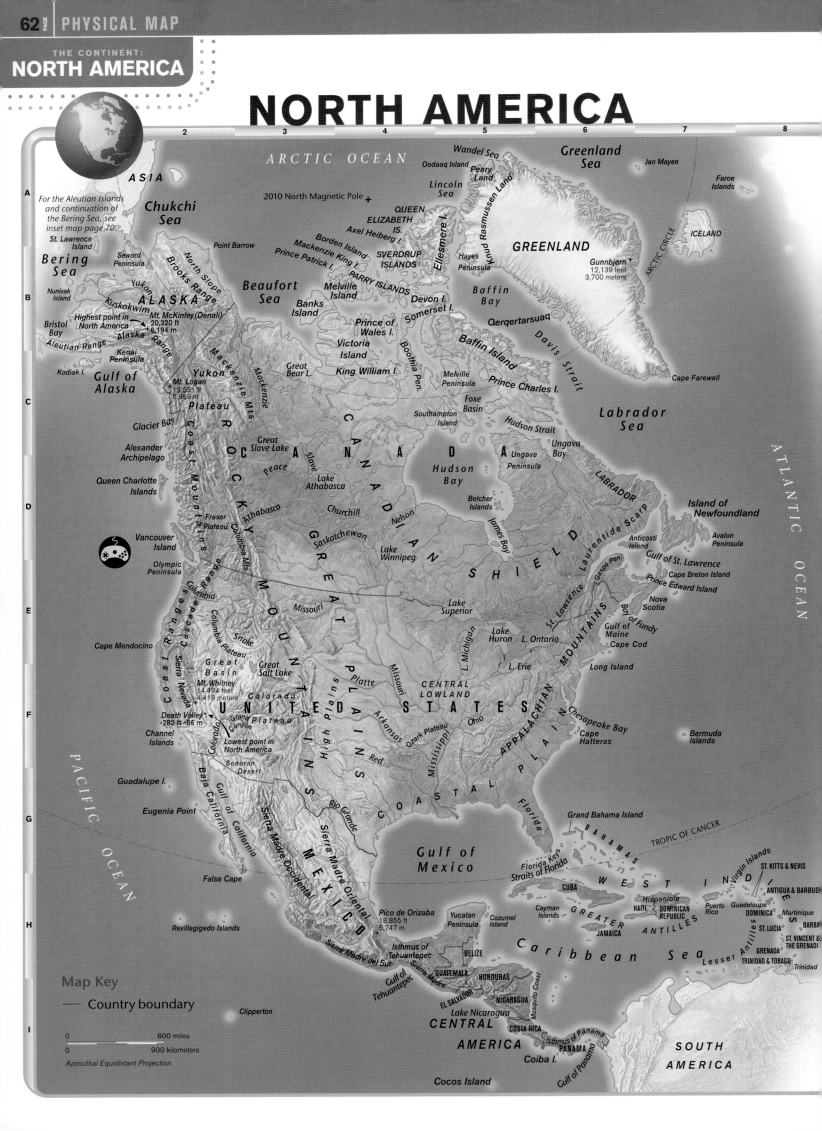

NORTH AMERICA

ARCTIC OCEAN

For the Aleutian Islands and continuation of the Bering Sea, see inset map page 70.

ASIA

Chukchi Sea

St. Lawrence Island

Bering Sea

Nunivak Island

Bristol Bay

Aleutian Range

Kodiak I.

Gulf of Alaska

Seward Peninsula

ALASKA

Kuskokwim

Yukon

Brooks Range

North Slope

Point Barrow

Highest point in North America
Mt. McKinley (Denali)
20,320 ft
6,194 m

Alaska Range

Kenai Peninsula

Mt. Logan
19,551 ft
5,959 m

Yukon Plateau

Mackenzie Mts.

Coast Mountains

Glacier Bay

Alexander Archipelago

Queen Charlotte Islands

Fraser Plateau

Columbia Mts.

Vancouver Island

Olympic Peninsula

Cape Mendocino

Coast Ranges

Cascade Range

Columbia

Snake

Columbia Plateau

Great Basin

Sierra Nevada

Mt. Whitney
14,494 feet
4,418 meters

Death Valley
-282 ft -86 m

Lowest point in North America

Channel Islands

Guadalupe I.

Eugenia Point

False Cape

ROCKY MOUNTAINS

Great Salt Lake

Colorado Plateau

Grand Canyon

Colorado

Sonoran Desert

Baja California

Gulf of California

Sierra Madre Occidental

MEXICO

Revillagigedo Islands

Sierra Madre del Sur

Isthmus of Tehuantepec

Gulf of Tehuantepec

Pico de Orizaba
18,855 ft
5,747 m

Sierra Madre

GUATEMALA

EL SALVADOR

BELIZE

HONDURAS

NICARAGUA

Lake Nicaragua

Mosquito Coast

COSTA RICA

CENTRAL AMERICA

PANAMA

Isthmus of Panama

Gulf of Panama

Coiba I.

Cocos Island

Clipperton

Mackenzie

Great Bear L.

Great Slave Lake

Peace

Slave

Athabasca

Lake Athabasca

Saskatchewan

Churchill

Nelson

Lake Winnipeg

CANADA

CANADIAN GREAT SHIELD

Missouri

Lake Superior

L. Michigan

Lake Huron

L. Ontario

L. Erie

GREAT PLAINS

High Plains

Platte

Missouri

Arkansas

Red

Mississippi

Ozark Plateau

Ohio

UNITED STATES

CENTRAL LOWLAND

APPALACHIAN MOUNTAINS

COASTAL PLAIN

Florida

Rio Grande

Gulf of Mexico

Yucatan Peninsula

Cozumel Island

2010 North Magnetic Pole +

QUEEN ELIZABETH IS.

Axel Heiberg I.

Borden Island

Mackenzie King I.

Prince Patrick I.

PARRY ISLANDS

Melville Island

Banks Island

Beaufort Sea

Victoria Island

Prince of Wales I.

King William I.

Boothia Pen.

Melville Peninsula

Southampton Island

SVERDRUP ISLANDS

Devon I.

Somerset I.

Ellesmere I.

Hayes Peninsula

Knud Rasmussen Land

Baffin Bay

Qeqertarsuaq

Davis Strait

GREENLAND

Gunnbjørn +
12,139 feet
3,700 meters

Wandel Sea

Oodaaq Island

Peary Land

Lincoln Sea

Greenland Sea

Jan Mayen

ICELAND

Faroe Islands

ARCTIC CIRCLE

Cape Farewell

Labrador Sea

Baffin Island

Foxe Basin

Hudson Strait

Ungava Bay

Ungava Peninsula

Belcher Islands

Hudson Bay

James Bay

Prince Charles I.

LABRADOR

Laurentide Scarp

St. Lawrence

Gaspé Pen.

Island of Newfoundland

Avalon Peninsula

Anticosti Island

Gulf of St. Lawrence

Cape Breton Island

Prince Edward Island

Nova Scotia

Gulf of Maine

Bay of Fundy

Cape Cod

Long Island

Chesapeake Bay

Cape Hatteras

ATLANTIC OCEAN

Bermuda Islands

Grand Bahama Island

BAHAMAS

TROPIC OF CANCER

Florida Keys

Straits of Florida

CUBA

Cayman Islands

GREATER ANTILLES

Hispaniola

HAITI

DOMINICAN REPUBLIC

JAMAICA

Puerto Rico

Virgin Islands

WEST INDIES

ST. KITTS & NEVIS

ANTIGUA & BARBUDA

Guadeloupe

DOMINICA

Martinique

ST. LUCIA

BARBA

ST. VINCENT & THE GRENADI

GRENADA

TRINIDAD & TOBAGO

Trinidad

Lesser Antilles

Caribbean Sea

SOUTH AMERICA

PACIFIC OCEAN

Map Key

— Country boundary

| 0 | 600 miles |
| 0 | 900 kilometers |

Azimuthal Equidistant Projection

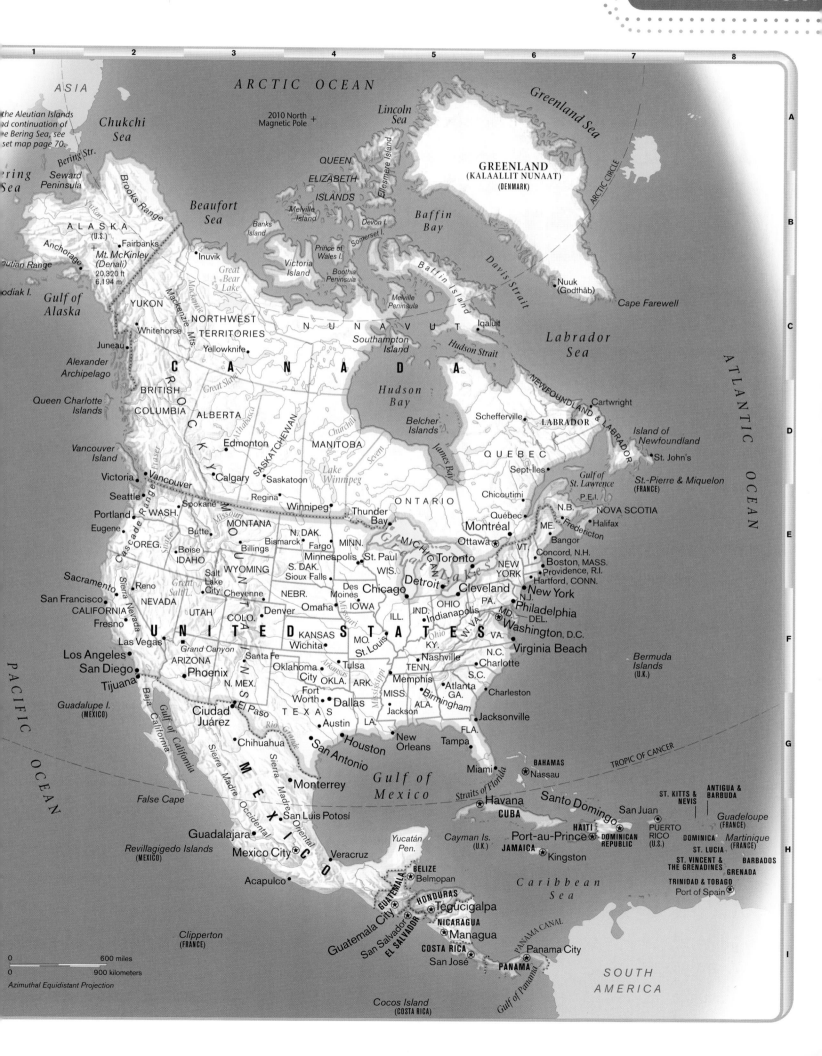

Azimuthal Equidistant Projection

North America

LAND OF CONTRASTS

From the windswept tundra of Alaska to the rain forest of Panama, the third-largest continent stretches 5,500 miles (8,850 km), spanning natural environments that support wildlife from polar bears to jaguars. Over thousands of years, Native American groups spread across these varied landscapes. But this rich mosaic of cultures largely disappeared before the onslaught of European fortune hunters and land seekers. While abundant resources and fast-changing technology have brought prosperity to Canada and the United States, other countries wrestle with the most basic needs. Promise and problems abound across this contrasting realm of 23 countries and 534 million people.

⇧ STORY IN THE ROCKS. Slanting sun rays reveal layers in the rocks of the Grand Canyon. Each rock layer—oldest on the canyon floor, youngest at the canyon's rim—tells us about Earth's changing history.

⇦ DRESSED TO CELEBRATE. This boy in México's southern state of Chiapas wears traditional clothing, including a brightly colored string tie and a broad-brimmed sombrero with elaborate stitching around the edge.

⬇ HOLD TIGHT. These daring rafters are running the roaring rapids of the Kicking Horse River in British Columbia, Canada's westernmost province. Rivers tumbling down the steep slopes of the Rocky Mountains provide many recreational opportunities.

⬅ STREET MUSIC. People from around the world visit New Orleans, Louisiana, to hear jazz musicians fill the air with their music.

➡ NIGHT SONG. This coyote sends his mournful howl into the dark Montana night. Members of the dog family, coyotes originated in the southwestern United States but are now found throughout North America—even in urban areas.

more about
NORTH AMERICA

⇧ DWELLINGS FROM THE PAST. Between A.D. 1000 and A.D. 1300 native people known as Ancestral Puebloans built cliff dwellings called pueblos, such as this one in Mesa Verde, Colorado.

⇧ MAYA TREASURE. Pyramid of the Magician marks the ruins of Uxmal on the Yucatán Peninsula. Nearly four million people of Maya descent still live in southern México and Central America.

⇦ FROZEN SUMMER. Because it lies so far north, even summers are cold in Greenland. Here local people navigate their boat among icebergs in waters off the village of Augpilagtoq.

⇓ HIGH FLYER. A young Kutchin boy sails off a snow bank on snowshoes in Canada's Yukon. The Kutchin, an Athabascan tribe, live in the forested lands of eastern Alaska and western Canada. The name Kutchin means "people."

⇑ FISH BAIT. Palometa fish investigate the toes of a vacationer wading in the warm waters of the Caribbean near St. John in the U.S. Virgin Islands. Tropical waters are habitat for many species of fish.

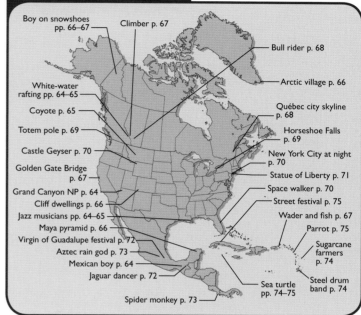

WHERE THE PICTURES ARE

Boy on snowshoes pp. 66–67
Climber p. 67
Bull rider p. 68
White-water rafting pp. 64–65
Arctic village p. 66
Coyote p. 65
Québec city skyline p. 68
Totem pole p. 69
Horseshoe Falls p. 69
Castle Geyser p. 70
New York City at night p. 70
Golden Gate Bridge p. 67
Statue of Liberty p. 71
Grand Canyon NP p. 64
Space walker p. 70
Cliff dwellings p. 66
Street festival p. 75
Jazz musicians pp. 64–65
Wader and fish p. 67
Maya pyramid p. 66
Parrot p. 75
Virgin of Guadalupe festival p. 72
Sugarcane farmers p. 74
Aztec rain god p. 73
Mexican boy p. 64
Steel drum band p. 74
Jaguar dancer p. 72
Sea turtle pp. 74–75
Spider monkey p. 73

⇑ WESTERN GATEWAY. The Golden Gate Bridge marks the entrance to San Francisco Bay. Beyond the bridge, captured above in the warm glow of twilight, is the California port city named after the bay.

⇓ DON'T LOOK DOWN. Clinging to a sheer rock face, this young woman demonstrates great skill as she climbs a cliff in Banff National Park in Canada. Covering more than 2,500 square miles (6,475 sq km) in the Canadian Rockies, Banff is a major tourist attraction.

THE CONTINENT:
NORTH AMERICA

CANADA

1 2

Topped only by Russia in area, Canada has just 33 million people—fewer than live in the U.S. state of California. Ancient rocks yield abundant minerals. Lakes and rivers in Québec are tapped for hydropower, and wheat farming and cattle ranching thrive across the western Prairie Provinces. Vast forests attract loggers, and mountain slopes provide a playground for nature lovers. Enormous deposits of oil sands lie waiting for technology to find a cheap way to convert them to hundreds of billions of barrels of oil. Most Canadians live within a hundred miles (160 km) of the U.S. border. Here, too, are its leading cities: Asia-focused Vancouver, ethnically diverse Toronto, capital Ottawa, and French-speaking Montréal.

THE BASICS

STATS

Area
3,855,101 sq mi (9,984,670 sq km)

Population
33,707,000

Predominant languages
English, French (both official)

Predominant religion
Christianity (Roman Catholic, Protestant)

GDP per capita
$38,400

Life expectancy
81 years

Literacy rate
99%

GEO WHIZ

Canada ranks second behind Saudi Arabia in largest oil reserves thanks to oil contained in the Athabasca tar sands in northern Alberta.

The Inuit territory of Nunavut has issued license plates for cars, motorcycles, and snowmobiles in the shape of a polar bear.

Canada is a constitutional monarchy with Britain's Queen Elizabeth II as its head of state.

Montréal is the second most populous French-speaking city in the world after Paris, France.

Canada's many bays, inlets, and islands give it the longest coastline of any country: 151,023 miles (243,042 km).

Geologists believe Réservoir Manicouagan in Québec may have been created by the impact of a meteorite more than 200 million years ago.

⇒ COWBOY TRADITION. Across the continent's western regions, rodeos showcase cowboy skills of riding, roping, and racing. This bull rider at the Calgary Stampede in Alberta fights for balance atop 1,300 pounds (590 kg) of bucking bull.

URANIUM PRODUCTION FROM MINES

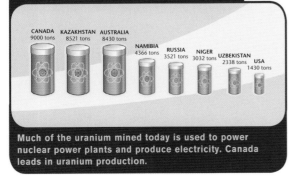

CANADA
9000 tons

KAZAKHSTAN
8521 tons

AUSTRALIA
8430 tons

NAMIBIA
4366 tons

RUSSIA
3521 tons

NIGER
3032 tons

UZBEKISTAN
2338 tons

USA
1430 tons

Much of the uranium mined today is used to power nuclear power plants and produce electricity. Canada leads in uranium production.

⇒ FRENCH ENCLAVE. Chateau Frontenac sparkles in Québec City's nighttime skyline. Settled by the French in the early 1600s, the province of Québec has maintained close ties to Europe and to its French heritage.

Map labels

ARCTIC CIRCLE

ALASKA (U.S.)

Inuvik

Tukto

MACKENZIE MTS

YUKON

Yukon

SELWYN MTS

Mt. Logan
19,551 ft
5,959 m

St. Elias Mts.

Haines Junction

Whitehorse

ROCKY

PACIFIC OCEAN

QUEEN CHARLOTTE IS.

Prince Rupert

Dawson Creek

BRITISH

Prince George

Gr.
P.

COLUMBIA

MOUNTAIN

Campbell River

Fraser

Vancouver Island

Kamloops

Nanaimo

Kelowna

Victoria

Vancouver

Columbia

← KNOWING WHO WE ARE. Native people of the Pacific Northwest preserve their family stories and legends in massive carved poles called totems, such as this one in Stanley Park in Vancouver, British Columbia.

Map Key

⊛ Country capital
◉ Province capital
• • • City or town
· · · · · · Boundary

0 ————————— 500 miles
0 ————————— 500 kilometers

Azimuthal Equidistant Projection

ARCTIC OCEAN

QUEEN ELIZABETH

SVERDRUP ISLANDS

Ellesmere Island

GREENLAND
(KALAALLIT NUNAAT)
(DENMARK)

Prince Patrick Island

ISLANDS

PARRY ISLANDS

Melville I.

Bathurst Island

BAFFIN BAY

BEAUFORT SEA

Banks Island

Resolute.

Devon Island

Parry Channel

Pond Inlet

Prince of Wales Island

Somerset Island

BAFFIN ISLAND

DAVIS STRAIT

Amundsen Gulf

NORTHWEST

Victoria Island

Boothia Peninsula

Melville Peninsula

Igloolik

Cambridge Bay

King William I.

Prince Charles Island

Kugluktuk

FOXE BASIN

Iqaluit

ATLANTIC OCEAN

eat Bear Lake

N U N A V U T

Cape Dorset

Great Slave Lake

RRITORIES

Yellowknife

Southampton Island

Ivujivik

Hudson Strait

River

Whale Cove

Chesterfield Inlet

Coats I.

A

LABRADOR SEA

Fort Smith

N

A

Mansel Island

Ungava Peninsula

Ungava Bay

NEWFOUNDLAND & LABRADOR

Uranium City

Arviat

D

A

Kuujjuaq

LABRADOR

L'Anse aux Meadows

Fort Murray

HUDSON BAY

Churchill

Belcher Islands

Schefferville

Happy Valley-Goose Bay

Reindeer Lake

Churchill

Fort Severn

Labrador City

St. John's

Thompson

Nelson

James Bay

Réservoir Manicouagan

ISLAND OF NEWFOUNDLAND

BERTA

SASKATCHEWAN

MANITOBA

Chisasibi

Sept-Îles

Cape Race

Edmonton

Prince Albert

The Pas

Akimiski Island

Île d'Anticosti

ed Deer

Lake Winnipeg

Fort Albany

QUÉBEC

Gaspé Peninsula

Gulf of St. Lawrence

Cabot Strait

ST.-PIERRE & MIQUELON (FRANCE)

lgary

Saskatoon

ONTARIO

Chicoutimi

Rimouski

PRINCE EDWARD ISLAND

Cape Breton Island

Moose Jaw

Lake Manitoba

Winnipeg

Lake Nipigon

Québec

NEW BRUNSWICK

Charlottetown

bridge

Medicine Hat

Regina

Brandon

Thunder Bay

Timmins

North Bay

Montréal

St. Lawrence

Fredericton

NOVA SCOTIA

Halifax

Sable Island

UNITED STATES

Lake Superior

Sudbury

Sault Ste. Marie

Lake Huron

Lake Michigan

Kingston

Oshawa

Ottawa

Toronto

L. Ontario

Bay of Fundy

Cape Sable

Hamilton

London

Niagara Falls

Windsor

Lake Erie

← ICE-AGE REMNANT. The Niagara River, which formed as glaciers of the last ice age began to melt, cascades over Canada's Horseshoe Falls. The falls, which stretch across the border between Canada and the United States, are a major tourist attraction.

THE CONTINENT:
NORTH AMERICA

UNITED STATES

From "sea to shining sea" the United States is blessed with a rich bounty of natural resources. Mineral treasures abound—oil, coal, iron, and gold—and croplands are among the most productive in the world. Americans have used—and too often overused—this storehouse of raw materials to build an economic base unmatched by any other country. An array of high-tech businesses populate the Sunbelt of the South and West. By combining its natural riches and the creative ideas of its ethnically diverse population, this land of opportunity has become the leading global power.

⇧ CALLING HOME.
A U.S. astronaut takes an extravehicular space walk high above planet Earth, during a mission of the space shuttle *Atlantis*.

⇐ WORLD CITY. The lights of Manhattan glitter around New York City's Chrysler Building. The city's influence as a financial and cultural center extends across the United States and around the world.

⇨ LETTING OFF STEAM. Castle Geyser is just one of many active geological features in Yellowstone National Park in Wyoming. The park is part of a region that sits on top of a major tectonic hot spot.

← LADY LIBERTY. The Statue of Liberty, a gift from France, stands in New York City's harbor. The statue has become a symbol of hope for millions of immigrants coming to the United States in search of a better life.

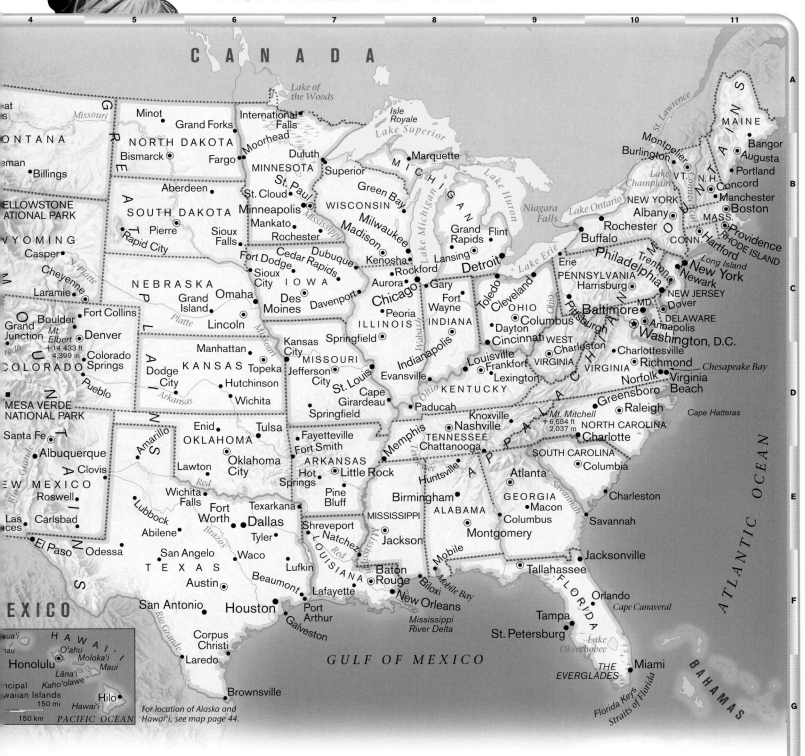

CANADA

Lake of the Woods

Isle Royale

Lake Superior

St. Lawrence

MAINE

Minot
Grand Forks
International Falls
Montpelier
Burlington
VT.
N.H.
Bangor
Augusta
Portland
Concord
Manchester

NORTH DAKOTA
Moorhead
Duluth
Marquette
Bismarck
Fargo
MINNESOTA
Superior
Lake Champlain
NEW YORK
Albany
Boston
MASS.

Aberdeen
St. Cloud
St. Paul
Green Bay
MICHIGAN
Lake Huron
Lake Ontario
Niagara Falls
Rochester
Providence
RHODE ISLAND

SOUTH DAKOTA
Minneapolis
WISCONSIN
Milwaukee
Buffalo
CONN.
Hartford

Pierre
Mankato
Madison
Grand Rapids
Flint
Lake Erie
Erie
Philadelphia
Trenton
New York
Long Island
Newark

Sioux Falls
Rochester
Kenosha
Lansing
Detroit
Cleveland
PENNSYLVANIA
Harrisburg
NEW JERSEY

Rapid City
Fort Dodge
Cedar Rapids
Dubuque
Rockford
Chicago
Gary
Toledo
OHIO
Pittsburgh
Baltimore
MD.
Dover
DELAWARE

NEBRASKA
Sioux City
IOWA
Aurora
Fort Wayne
Columbus
Dayton
WEST
Charleston
Annapolis
Washington, D.C.

Grand Island
Omaha
Des Moines
Davenport
Peoria
ILLINOIS
INDIANA
Indianapolis
Cincinnati
VIRGINIA
Charlottesville

Boulder
Fort Collins
Lincoln
Springfield
Louisville
Frankfort
VIRGINIA
Richmond
Chesapeake Bay

Grand Junction
Denver
Manhattan
Kansas City
MISSOURI
St. Louis
Evansville
Lexington
Norfolk
Virginia Beach

Mt. Elbert
+14,433 ft
4,399 m
Colorado Springs
Topeka
Jefferson City
Cape Girardeau
KENTUCKY
Greensboro
Raleigh

COLORADO
Dodge City
KANSAS
Hutchinson
Springfield
Paducah
Mt. Mitchell
+6,684 ft
2,037 m
Cape Hatteras

Pueblo
Wichita
Knoxville
Nashville
NORTH CAROLINA
Charlotte

MESA VERDE NATIONAL PARK
Enid
Tulsa
Fayetteville
Memphis
TENNESSEE
Chattanooga
SOUTH CAROLINA
Columbia

Santa Fe
OKLAHOMA
Fort Smith
Huntsville
Charleston

Albuquerque
Lawton
Oklahoma City
ARKANSAS
Hot Springs
Little Rock
Birmingham
Atlanta
GEORGIA
Macon

Clovis
Wichita Falls
Pine Bluff
ALABAMA
Columbus
Savannah

NEW MEXICO
Roswell
Lubbock
Fort Worth
Texarkana
MISSISSIPPI
Montgomery

Carlsbad
Abilene
Dallas
Tyler
Shreveport
Natchez
Jackson
Mobile
Jacksonville

El Paso
Odessa
San Angelo
Waco
LOUISIANA
FLORIDA

TEXAS
Austin
Beaumont
Lafayette
Baton Rouge
Biloxi
Mobile Bay
Tallahassee
Orlando
Cape Canaveral

San Antonio
Houston
Port Arthur
New Orleans
Mississippi River Delta
Tampa
St. Petersburg
Lake Okeechobee

Corpus Christi
Galveston
GULF OF MEXICO
THE EVERGLADES
Miami

Laredo
Florida Keys
Straits of Florida
BAHAMAS

Brownsville

ATLANTIC OCEAN

For location of Alaska and Hawai'i, see map page 44.

HAWAI'I
Honolulu
O'ahu
Moloka'i
Maui
Lāna'i
Kaho'olawe
Hilo
Hawai'i
150 mi
150 km
PACIFIC OCEAN

MONTANA
Billings
WYOMING
Casper
Cheyenne
Laramie
Missouri
N. Platte
Platte
Arkansas
Red
Rio Grande
Brazos
Mississippi
Ohio
Wabash
Tennessee

Map Key

⊛ Country capital
◉ State capital
••• City or town
••••• Boundary

0 ———— 200 miles
0 ———— 200 kilometers

Albers Conic Equal-Area Projection

NATION OF IMMIGRANTS

Mexico 189,989

Figures represent the number of immigrants obtaining legal permanent resident status in 2008

China 80,271
India 63,352
Philippines 54,030
Cuba 49,500

From its founding, the United States has attracted people from other lands. Today, most immigrants come from Latin America and Asia.

THE CONTINENT:
NORTH AMERICA

MÉXICO & CENTRAL AMERICA

⇧ PAST MEETS PRESENT.
A boy prepares to become a jaguar dancer in Tabasco State, México. This dance to bring rain dates back to the Olmec culture.

THE BASICS

STATS

Largest country
México
758,449 sq mi (1,964,375 sq km)

Smallest country
El Salvador
8,124 sq mi (21,041 sq km)

Most populous country
México
109,610,000

Least populous country
Belize
329,000

Predominant languages
English, Spanish, Mayan, various Amerindian languages

Predominant religion
Christianity (Roman Catholic, Protestant)

Highest GDP per capita
México
$13,200

Lowest GDP per capita
Nicaragua
$2,800

Highest life expectancy
Costa Rica
78 years

Highest literacy rate
Costa Rica
95%

GEO WHIZ

México takes its name from the word "Mexica," another name for the Aztec, the last of the indigenous cultures to rule México before it fell to Spanish conquerors in 1521.

Scientists believe that the crater of the comet that struck Earth 65 million years ago, causing the dramatic climate changes that led to the extinction of the dinosaurs, is at Chicxulub, on the Yucatán Peninsula.

Coral colonies growing along much of the coast of Belize form the longest barrier reef in the Western Hemisphere and the second longest in the world, after Australia's Great Barrier Reef.

Vampire bats, which are only about the size of an adult person's thumb, drink the blood of other animals to survive. They are found throughout Central America.

A new set of locks on the Panama Canal will allow ships with 2.5 times the cargo capacity of ships now traveling the canal to take this shortcut between the Atlantic and Pacific Oceans.

⇨ CELEBRATION.
Traditional costumes and musical instruments combine with Christian beliefs during the annual Virgin of Guadalupe festival, observed throughout México. The festival marks the appearance of the Virgin Mary to a peasant in 1531.

México and most Central American countries share a backbone of mountains, a legacy of powerful Native American empires, and a largely Spanish colonial history. Once-abundant rain forests now are largely gone. México dwarfs its seven Central American neighbors in area, population, and natural resources. Its economy boasts a rich diversity of agricultural crops, highly productive oil fields, a growing manufacturing base, and strong trade with the U.S. and Canada. Overall, Central American countries rely on agricultural products such as bananas and coffee, though tourism is increasing. Modern-day México and Central America struggle to fulfill the hopes of growing populations, some of whom search for better lives by migrating—both legally and illegally—north to the United States.

1

Tijuana
Ensenada
Mexicali
Nogales
Hermosi
BAJA CALIFORNIA
Gulf of California
Guaymas
Ciudad Obregón
Los Moch
La Paz
False Cape

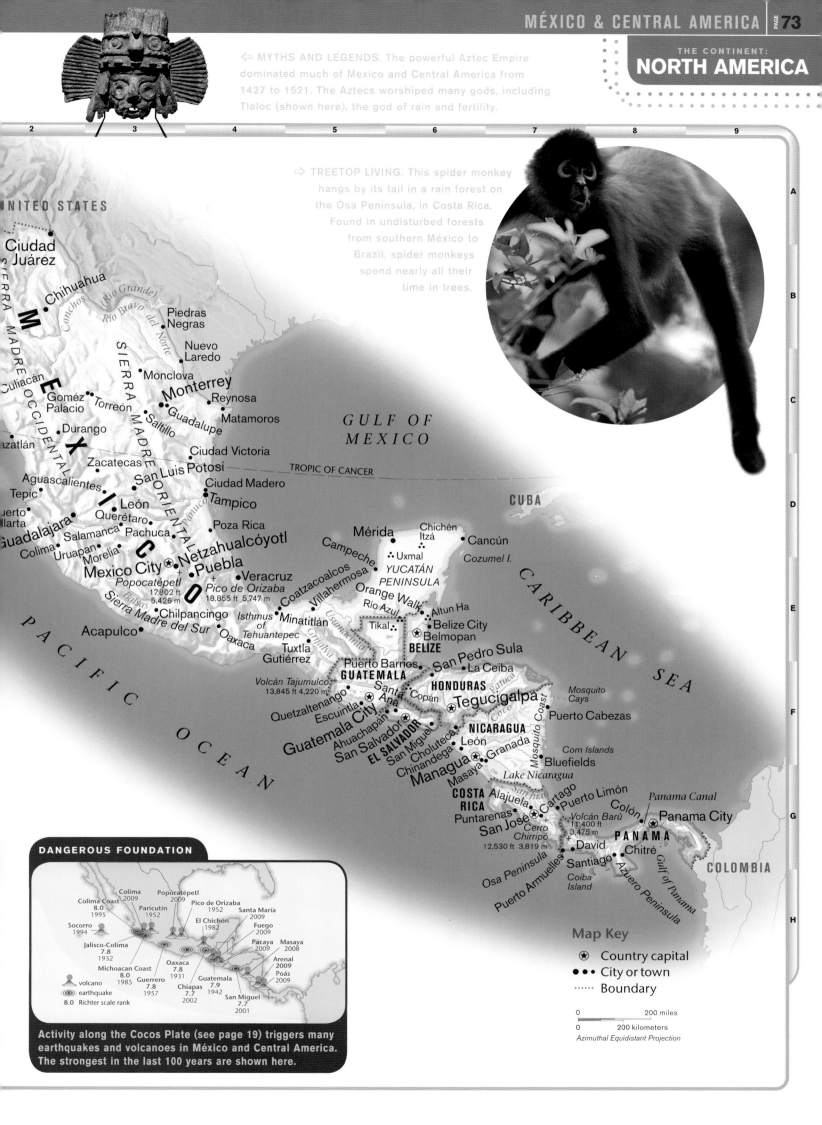

← MYTHS AND LEGENDS. The powerful Aztec Empire dominated much of Mexico and Central America from 1427 to 1521. The Aztecs worshiped many gods, including Tlaloc (shown here), the god of rain and fertility.

⇨ TREETOP LIVING. This spider monkey hangs by its tail in a rain forest on the Osa Peninsula, in Costa Rica. Found in undisturbed forests from southern México to Brazil, spider monkeys spend nearly all their time in trees.

UNITED STATES

Ciudad Juárez

Chihuahua

Rio Grande
(Río Bravo del Norte)
Conchos

Piedras Negras

Nuevo Laredo

Monclova

Monterrey
Reynosa

SIERRA MADRE OCCIDENTAL

Culiacán

Gomez Palacio
Torreón
Saltillo
Guadalupe
Matamoros

Durango

azatlán

SIERRA MADRE ORIENTAL

Ciudad Victoria

Zacatecas
San Luis Potosí

TROPIC OF CANCER

GULF OF MEXICO

CUBA

Aguascalientes

Ciudad Madero

Tepic

Puerto
llarta

León
Querétaro
Pachuca

Guadalajara
Salamanca

Pánuco

Tampico

Poza Rica

M É X I C O

Mérida

Chichén Itzá

Cancún

Colima
Uruapan
Morelia

Netzahualcóyotl

Campeche

Cozumel I.

Uxmal

YUCATÁN PENINSULA

Mexico City
Popocatépetl
17,802 ft
5,426 m

Puebla
Veracruz

Pico de Orizaba
18,855 ft 5,747 m

Coatzacoalcos

Villahermosa

Orange Walk

Río Azul

Altun Ha

Chilpancingo
Sierra Madre del Sur

Isthmus
of
Tehuantepec

Minatitlán

Tikal

Belize City

Belmopan

Acapulco

Oaxaca

Tuxtla Gutiérrez

Usumacinta

Grijalva

BELIZE

Volcán Tajumulco
13,845 ft 4,220 m

Puerto Barrios

San Pedro Sula

La Ceiba

Mosquito Cays

GUATEMALA

Santa
Ana

HONDURAS

Copán

Tegucigalpa

Patuca

Quetzaltenango

Escuintla

Guatemala City
Ahuachapán
San Salvador

NICARAGUA

Puerto Cabezas

Coco

León
San Miguel

Choluteca

Chinandega

EL SALVADOR

Masaya
Managua

Granada

Corn Islands

Bluefields

Masaya

Lake Nicaragua

Mosquito Coast

PACIFIC OCEAN

COSTA
RICA

Alajuela

San Juan

Cartago

Puerto Limón

Panama Canal

Colón

Puntarenas

San José

Volcán Barú
11,400 ft
3,475 m

David

Panama City

Cerro Chirripó
12,530 ft 3,819 m

PANAMA

Chitré

Osa Peninsula

Santiago

Puerto Armuelles

Coiba Island

Azuero Peninsula

Gulf of Panama

COLOMBIA

CARIBBEAN SEA

DANGEROUS FOUNDATION

Colima Coast
8.0
1995

Colima
2009

Popocatépetl
2009

Pico de Orizaba
1952

Santa María
2009

Paricutín
1952

El Chichón
1982

Fuego
2009

Socorro
1994

Jalisco-Colima
7.8
1932

Michoacan Coast
8.0
1985

Oaxaca
7.8
1931

Pacaya
2009

Masaya
2008

Arenal
2009

Guerrero
7.8
1957

Guatemala
7.9
1942

Poás
2009

▲ volcano

◎ earthquake

8.0 Richter scale rank

Chiapas
7.7
2002

San Miguel
7.7
2001

Activity along the Cocos Plate (see page 19) triggers many earthquakes and volcanoes in México and Central America. The strongest in the last 100 years are shown here.

Map Key

⊛ Country capital

••• City or town

······ Boundary

0   200 miles

0   200 kilometers

Azimuthal Equidistant Projection

THE CONTINENT:
NORTH AMERICA

WEST INDIES & THE BAHAMAS

THE BASICS

STATS

Largest country
Cuba
42,803 sq mi (110,860 sq km)

Smallest country
St. Kitts and Nevis
104 sq mi (269 sq km)

Most populous country
Cuba
11,225,000

Least populous country
St. Kitts and Nevis
50,000

Predominant languages
Spanish, English, French, French patois

Predominant religion
Christian (Roman Catholic, Protestant, and others)

Highest GDP per capita
Bahamas
$29,800

Lowest GDP per capita
Haiti
$1,300

Highest life expectancy
Cuba
77 years

Highest literacy rate
Cuba, Barbados
100%

GEO WHIZ

Voodoo, a religion that combines elements of West African spiritualism and Roman Catholic saints, is common in Haiti, the Dominican Republic, Cuba, Jamaica, and the Bahamas.

On the seafloor just off San Salvador, in the Bahamas, there is a bronze monument marking the site where Christopher Columbus is believed to have anchored his ship in 1492.

Pico Duarte (10,417 ft/3,175 m), on the island of Hispaniola, is the highest peak in the Caribbean.

Boiling Lake, in Morne Trois Pitons National Park on Dominica, is one of the world's largest thermal lakes.

Grenada, which is nicknamed the Spice Island, is one of the world's chief sources of nutmeg, mace, and other spices.

⇧ RHYTHM OF THE TROPICS.
When traditional drums were banned in Trinidad in 1884, plantation workers looked for new instruments, including 55-gallon (208-L) oil drums, which were the origin of today's steel drums or "pans."

This region of tropical islands stretches from the Bahamas, off the eastern coast of Florida, to Trinidad and Tobago, off the northern coast of South America. The Greater Antilles—Cuba, Jamaica, Hispaniola, and U.S. territory Puerto Rico—account for nearly 90 percent of the region's land area and most of its 40 million people. A necklace of smaller islands called the Lesser Antilles plus the Bahamas make up most of the rest of this region. Lush vegetation, warm waters, and scenic beaches attract vacationers from across the globe. While these visitors bring much needed income, most people in this region remain poor.

⇦ WHITE GOLD. Sugarcane is an important economic resource throughout the Caribbean. This woman carries freshly cut cane on her head in a field in Barbados.

FUN IN THE SUN

*Figures represent tourist arrivals, 2004

3,450,000*	2,017,000	1,561,000	1,415,000	552,000	443,000	296,000	245,384	118,000	98,244
Dominican Republic	Cuba	Bahamas	Jamaica	Barbados	Trinidad and Tobago	St. Lucia	Antigua and Barbuda	St. Kitts and Nevis	Grenada

These island countries are the region's most popular destinations for tourists seeking sandy beaches, blue waters, and warm breezes.

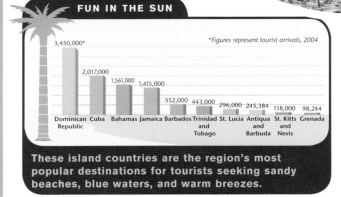

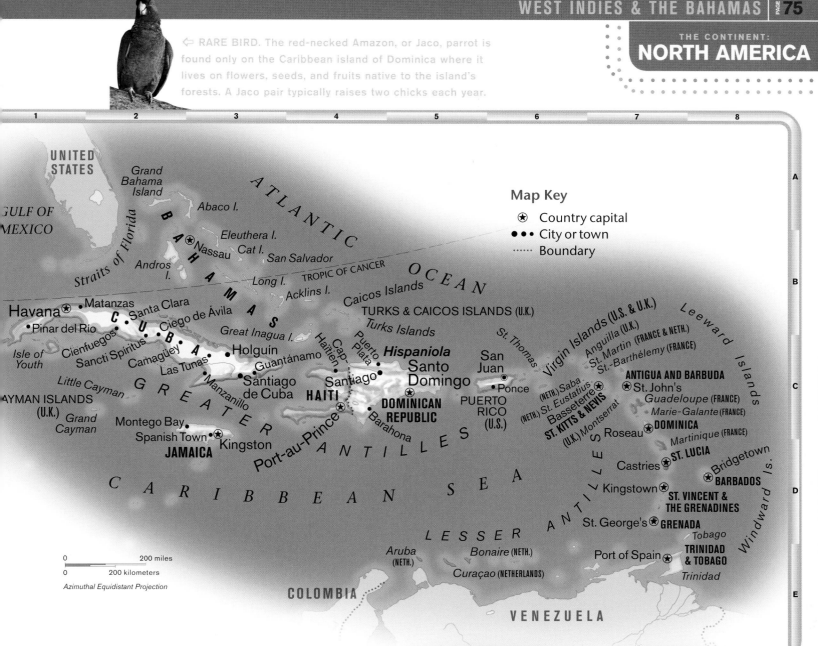

← RARE BIRD. The red-necked Amazon, or Jaco, parrot is found only on the Caribbean island of Dominica where it lives on flowers, seeds, and fruits native to the island's forests. A Jaco pair typically raises two chicks each year.

Map Key

⊛ Country capital
••• City or town
······ Boundary

UNITED STATES

Grand Bahama Island

Abaco I.

ATLANTIC

GULF OF MEXICO

Straits of Florida

BAHAMAS

Nassau ⊛

Eleuthera I.

Cat I.

San Salvador

Andros I.

Long I.   TROPIC OF CANCER

OCEAN

Acklins I.

Caicos Islands

TURKS & CAICOS ISLANDS (U.K.)

Turks Islands

St. Thomas

Virgin Islands (U.S. & U.K.)

Anguilla (U.K.)

Leeward Islands

Havana ⊛   • Matanzas

• Pinar del Rio

C   • Santa Clara

U   Ciego de Ávila

B   Great Inagua I.

Isle of Youth

• Cienfuegos

Sancti Spíritus

Camagüey

A

Holguín

Las Tunas

Manzanillo

Little Cayman

CAYMAN ISLANDS (U.K.)

Grand Cayman

Montego Bay

Spanish Town ⊛

JAMAICA   Kingston

GREATER

Santiago de Cuba

Guantánamo

Cap-Haïtien

Puerto Plata

Hispaniola

Santiago

Santo Domingo

HAITI

Port-au-Prince

Barahona

DOMINICAN REPUBLIC

ANTILLES

San Juan

• Ponce

PUERTO RICO (U.S.)

(NETH.) Saba

(NETH.) St. Eustatius ⊛

St. Martin (FRANCE & NETH.)

St.-Barthélemy (FRANCE)

Basseterre ⊛

ST. KITTS & NEVIS

(U.K.) Montserrat

Roseau •

LESSER   ANTILLES

ANTIGUA AND BARBUDA

⊛ St. John's

Guadeloupe (FRANCE)

• Marie-Galante (FRANCE)

DOMINICA

Martinique (FRANCE)

Castries ⊛ ST. LUCIA

Kingstown ⊛

ST. VINCENT & THE GRENADINES

St. George's ⊛ GRENADA

Bridgetown

BARBADOS

Windward Is.

CARIBBEAN   SEA

LESSER

Aruba (NETH.)

Bonaire (NETH.)

Curaçao (NETHERLANDS)

Port of Spain ⊛

Tobago

TRINIDAD & TOBAGO

Trinidad

COLOMBIA

VENEZUELA

0 ——— 200 miles
0 ——— 200 kilometers
Azimuthal Equidistant Projection

⬇ WATER WORLD. The clear waters of the Caribbean allow face-to-face interaction with sea life, such as this green sea turtle. Adult sea turtles can remain under water for two hours without breathing.

⬆ CELEBRATION. Stilt walkers in brightly colored costumes tower above this street in Old Havana, Cuba, during the annual celebration of Carnival. Introduced by Catholic colonizers from Spain, this festival occurs prior to the beginning of the religious season of Lent.

THE CONTINENT:
SOUTH AMERICA

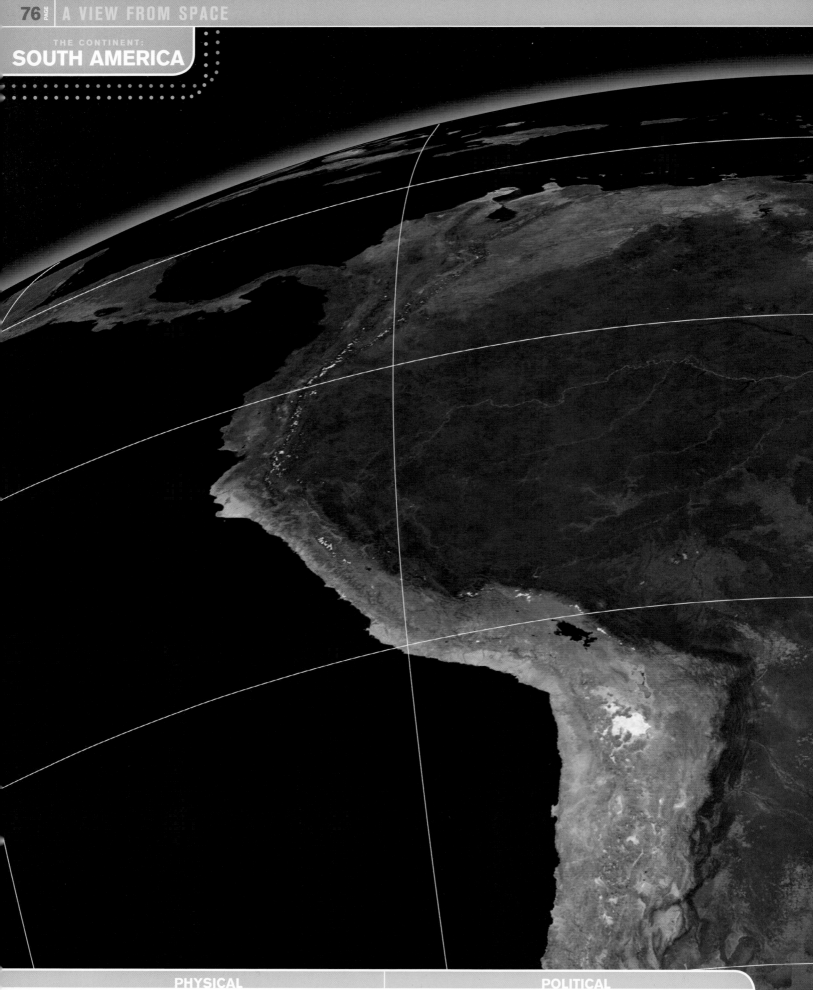

PHYSICAL

Land area	Lowest point	Largest lake
6,880,000 sq mi (17,819,000 sq km)	Laguna del Carbón, Argentina -344 ft (-105 m)	Lake Titicaca, Bolivia-Peru 3,200 sq mi (8,290 sq km)
Highest point	Longest river	
Cerro Aconcagua, Argentina 22,831 ft (6,959 m)	Amazon 4,000 mi (6,437 km)	

POLITICAL

Population	Largest country	Economy
386,030,000	Brazil 3,300,169 sq mi (8,547,403 sq km)	Farming: cattle, coffee, fruit
Largest metropolitan area	Most densely populated country	Industry: mining, oil, manufacturing
São Paulo, Brazil: Pop. 19,582,000	Ecuador 124 people per sq mi (48 per sq km)	Services

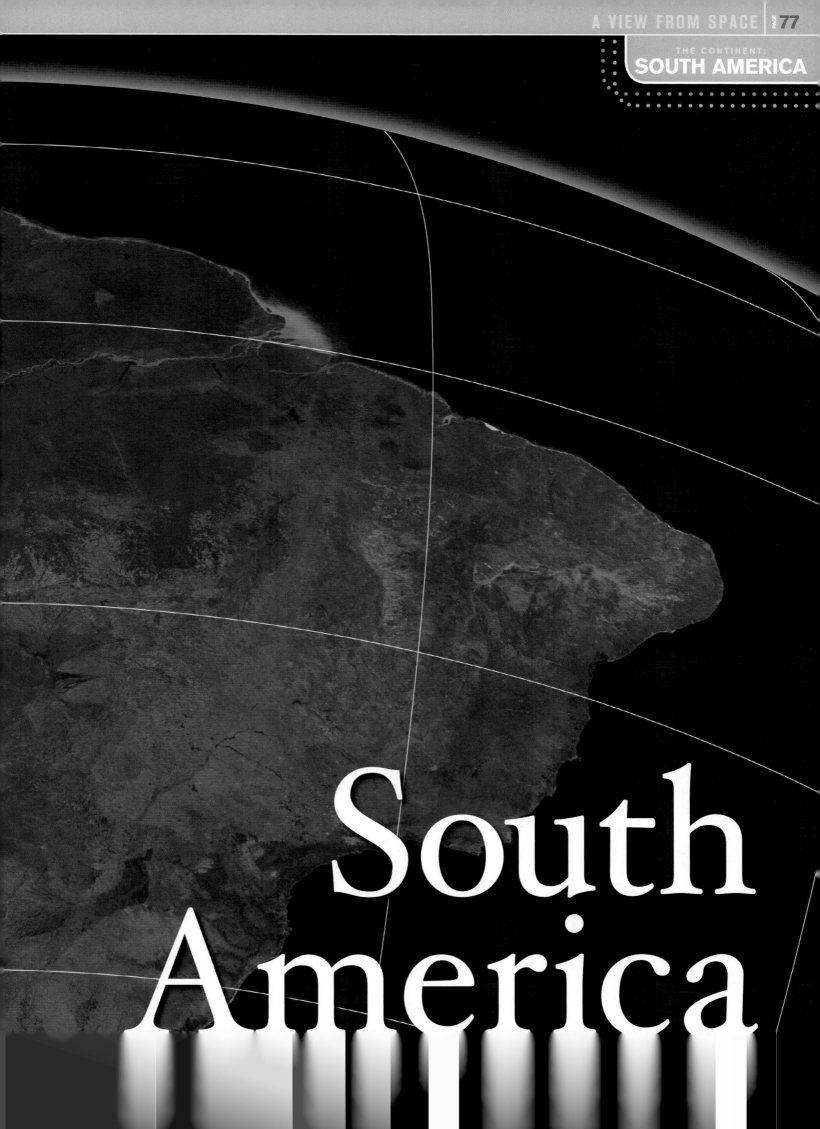

South America

SOUTH AMERICA

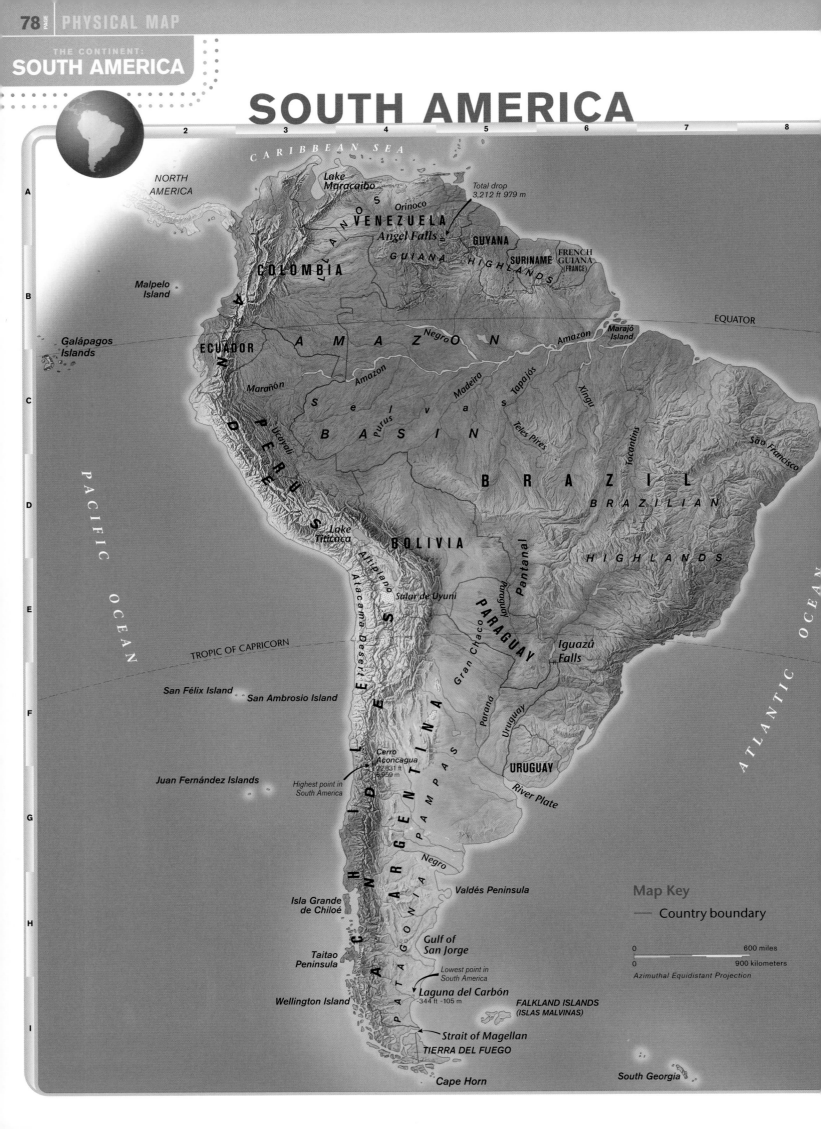

CARIBBEAN SEA

NORTH AMERICA

Lake Maracaibo

Orinoco

Total drop 3,212 ft 979 m

VENEZUELA

GUYANA

Angel Falls

GUIANA HIGHLANDS

SURINAME

FRENCH GUIANA (FRANCE)

COLOMBIA

Malpelo Island

EQUATOR

Galápagos Islands

Negro

Amazon

Marajó Island

ECUADOR

A M A Z O N

Marañón

Amazon

Madeira

Tapajós

Xingu

São Francisco

Selva

Purus

Teles Pires

Tocantins

Ucayali

B A S I N

BRAZIL

PERU

BRAZILIAN

PACIFIC OCEAN

Lake Titicaca

BOLIVIA

Pantanal

HIGHLANDS

Altiplano

Salar de Uyuni

Paraguay

Atacama Desert

PARAGUAY

Iguazú Falls

TROPIC OF CAPRICORN

Gran Chaco

ATLANTIC OCEAN

San Félix Island

San Ambrosio Island

Paraná

Uruguay

Cerro Aconcagua *22,831 ft 6,959 m*

URUGUAY

Juan Fernández Islands

Highest point in South America

PAMPAS

River Plate

A R G E N T I N A

C H I L E

A N D E S

Negro

Valdés Peninsula

Isla Grande de Chiloé

P A T A G O N I A

Gulf of San Jorge

Taitao Peninsula

Lowest point in South America

Wellington Island

Laguna del Carbón *-344 ft -105 m*

FALKLAND ISLANDS (ISLAS MALVINAS)

Strait of Magellan

TIERRA DEL FUEGO

Cape Horn

South Georgia

Map Key

— Country boundary

0		600 miles

0		900 kilometers

Azimuthal Equidistant Projection

2 3 4 5 6 7 8

1 2 3 4 5 6 7 8

CARIBBEAN SEA

NORTH
AMERICA

Santa Marta
Barranquilla
Cartagena
Maracaibo
Lake
Maracaibo
Barquisimeto
Caracas
Valencia
Maracay
Ciudad Guayana
Orinoco
Cúcuta
Bucaramanga
San Cristóbal
VENEZUELA
Georgetown
Paramaribo
GUYANA
Cayenne
Medellín
Angel Falls
GUIANA HIGHLANDS
SURINAME
FRENCH GUIANA
(FRANCE)
Manizales
Ibagué
Bogotá
COLOMBIA
Boa Vista
Amapá
Cali
Boundary claimed
by Suriname
Malpelo Island
(COLOMBIA)
Esmeraldas
Pasto
EQUATOR
Quito
ECUADOR
A M A Z O N
Negro
Amazon
Marajó
Island
Belém
Galápagos
Islands
(ECUADOR)
Guayaquil
Cuenca
Iquitos
Manaus
Santarém
São Luís
Parnaíba
Marañón
Amazon (Solimões)
Madeira
Tapajós
Marabá
Teresina
Fortaleza
Piura
S
Selva
B A S I N
Xingu
Natal
João Pessoa
Campina Grande
Chiclayo
Purus
Porto Velho
Teles Pires
Recife
Trujillo
Rio
Branco
Tocantins
Maceió
Chimbote
B R A Z I L
Aracaju
Feira de Santana
Callao
Lima
Machu Picchu
Cusco
B R A Z I L I A N
Salvador
(Bahia)
Ayacucho
L. Titicaca
Trinidad
São Francisco
Ilhéus
P E R U
La Paz
Brasília
Governador Valadares
Arequipa
BOLIVIA
Goiânia
HIGHLANDS
Arica
Oruro
Cochabamba
Santa Cruz
Uberlândia
Uberaba
Belo Horizonte
Altiplano
Sucre
Campo
Grande
São José do
Rio Preto
Ribeirão Preto
Iquique
Salar
de Uyuni
Pantanal
Nova Iguaçu
Tarija
Londrina
Campinas
TROPIC OF CAPRICORN
Antofagasta
PARAGUAY
Paraguay
São Paulo
Santos
Rio de Janeiro
San Félix Island
(CHILE)
San Ambrosio Island
Salta
Gran Chaco
Asunción
Iguazú Falls
Curitiba
San Miguel
de Tucumán
Resistencia
Corrientes
Passo
Fundo
Florianópolis
La Serena
Paraná
Uruguaiana
Santa
Maria
Porto Alegre
Cerro
Aconcagua
22,831 ft
6,959 m
Córdoba
Uruguay
URUGUAY
Valparaíso
Mendoza
ARGENTINA
Santa Fe
Rosario
Montevideo
Santiago
P A M P A S
Buenos
Aires
River Plate
Talca
La Plata
Juan Fernández Islands
(CHILE)
Concepción
Mar del Plata
Temuco
Negro
Bahia Blanca
Puerto Montt
Viedma
Isla Grande
de Chiloé
Valdés Peninsula
C O R D I L L E R A N
Taitao
Peninsula
Comodoro Rivadavia
Gulf of San Jorge
600 miles
900 kilometers
Azimuthal Equidistant Projection
Wellington I.
Laguna del Carbón
-344 ft -105 m
Stanley
FALKLAND ISLANDS (ISLAS MALVINAS)
(UNITED KINGDOM)
Rio Gallegos
Strait of Magellan
Punta Arenas
TIERRA DEL FUEGO
Ushuaia
Cape Horn
South Georgia
(U.K.)

PACIFIC
OCEAN

ATLANTIC OCEAN

PATAGONIA

South America
A MIX OF OLD AND NEW

South America stretches from the warm waters of the Caribbean to the frigid ocean around Antarctica. Draining a third of the continent, the mighty Amazon carries more water than the world's next ten biggest rivers combined. Its basin contains the planet's largest rain forest. The Andes tower along the continent's western edge from Colombia to southern Chile. The Amerindian peoples who lived in the Andes were no match for the gold-seeking Spanish who arrived in 1532. They, along with the Portuguese, ruled most of the continent for almost 300 years. Centuries of ethnic blending have woven Amerindian, European, African, and Asian heritage into South America's rich cultural fabric.

⇧ SILENT STALKER. The jaguar is the largest member of the cat family native to the Americas. The largest populations of this at-risk species are found in the southern Amazon basin.

⇐ ROYAL CITY. Built by an Inca ruler between 1460 and 1470, Machu Picchu reveals the Inca's skill as stone masons. Massive blocks of granite were carved so carefully that all seams fit tightly without the use of mortar.

⇩ SOUTHERN METROPOLIS. A 1,300-foot (396-m)-high block of granite called Sugar Loaf dominates the harbor of Brazil's second largest city, Rio de Janeiro. Rio was Brazil's capital until 1960 and remains the country's most popular tourist destination.

⇐ NATURAL HERITAGE. Extending 2.5 miles (4 km) along the border between Brazil and Argentina, Iguazú Falls, which means "great water" in the local Guaraní language, is clouded in mist as the water drops 269 feet (90 m) into the Iguazú River.

⇒ MOUNTAIN BUDDIES. An Aymara woman, with her llama, follows a traditional mountain lifestyle in the Andes of Peru.

THE CONTINENT:
SOUTH AMERICA

more about
SOUTH AMERICA

⬆ STAPLE CROP. Corn, a food plant native to the Americas, is an important part of the diet of people throughout South America. Against a backdrop of Bolivia's Lake Titicaca, these men spread newly harvested corn to dry on a blanket. The dried corn will be stored for use throughout the year.

⬆ ICY COLD. Rising to an elevation of almost 11,000 feet (3,353 m), Fitzroy Massif in southern Argentina's Patagonia region presents major challenges to adventurous climbers who must contend with strong winds and bitter cold.

⬅ QUIET VIGIL. A young Pinare Indian sits beside a rushing stream in Venezuela, holding his traditional spear ready to catch a fish. Many groups of native people live in relative isolation from the modern world.

⇧ JUICY HARVEST. Grapes hang in heavy clusters ready for picking in a vineyard near Santiago, Chile. Second only to Italy, Chile produces almost one-quarter of the world's supply of fresh grapes. Grapes are Chile's leading fresh-fruit export.

WHERE THE PICTURES ARE

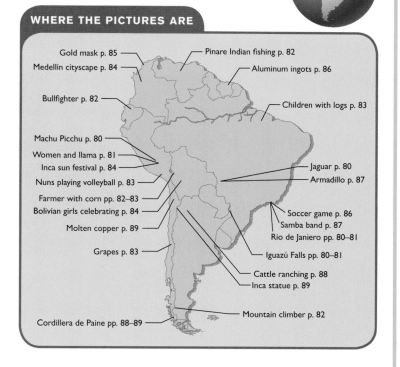

Gold mask p. 85

Medellín cityscape p. 84

Bullfighter p. 82

Machu Picchu p. 80

Women and llama p. 81

Inca sun festival p. 84

Nuns playing volleyball p. 83

Farmer with corn pp. 82–83

Bolivian girls celebrating p. 84

Molten copper p. 89

Grapes p. 83

Cordillera de Paine pp. 88–89

Pinare Indian fishing p. 82

Aluminum ingots p. 86

Children with logs p. 83

Jaguar p. 80

Armadillo p. 87

Soccer game p. 86

Samba band p. 87

Rio de Janiero pp. 80–81

Iguazú Falls pp. 80–81

Cattle ranching p. 88

Inca statue p. 89

Mountain climber p. 82

⇧ ENVIRONMENTAL TRAGEDY. These giants of the rain forest dwarf two children in the Amazon village of Paragominas in Brazil. Harvesting such trees provides income for villagers but poses a serious long-term threat to the environment.

⇐ *EL TORRO!* Introduced to South America during the Spanish colonization, bullfighting is a popular sport and the focus of many festivals. Here, in Cayambe, Ecuador, a matador flashes his red cape before the bull.

⇩ BREAK TIME. Colonization of South America by Spain and Portugal in the 16th century brought a new religion—Roman Catholicism—to the region. Here, Catholic nuns in Arequipa, Peru, take a break from prayers to engage in a game of volleyball.

NORTHWESTERN SOUTH AMERICA

THE BASICS

STATS

Largest country
Peru
496,224 sq mi (1,285,216 sq km)

Smallest country
Ecuador
109,483 sq mi (283,560 sq km)

Most populous country
Colombia
46,065,000

Least populous country
Bolivia
9,863,000

Predominant languages
Spanish, Amerindian languages and dialects, English

Predominant religion
Christianity (Roman Catholic)

Highest GDP per capita
Venezuela
$13,200

Lowest GDP per capita
Bolivia
$4,600

Highest life expectancy
Ecuador
75 years

Highest literacy rate
Colombia, Venezuela
93%

GEO WHIZ

 On the llanos of Venezuela, capybaras, the world's largest rodents, are stalked and killed by anacondas, snakes weighing as much as 550 pounds (250 kg).

Some of the world's finest emeralds come from Colombia. Emeralds were sacred stones to the Inca, and some of the mines these ancient people worked are still a source of quality gemstones.

 The world's only marine iguanas are among the unique animal species that live on the Galápagos, a volcanic chain of islands in the Pacific that belongs to Ecuador.

Bolivia's Madidi National Park is home to more plant and animal species than any other preserve in South America.

⇧ HAIL THE SUN. The ancient Inca celebrated the new year on June 24 in the festival of Inti Raymi. The tradition continues today in Cuzco, Peru, with the Festival of the Sun, when the celestial body is honored through music and dance.

Like a huge letter "C," five countries crest the continent's northwest—Venezuela, Colombia, Ecuador, Peru, and Bolivia. Each has a seacoast except land-locked Bolivia. Dominated by the volcano-studded Andes range, the region contains huge rain forests in the upper Amazon and Orinoco River basins. Colombia and Venezuela share an extensive tropical grassland called Los Llanos. Though Spanish conquistador Pizarro defeated the Inca in the 16th century, Quechua, the Inca language, is still spoken by millions of Amerindians living in the altiplanos—high plateaus of the Andes. Rich oil resources are centered around Lake Maracaibo, in Venezuela. Many people in the region are poor, and drug wars have caused political instability, but recent democratic successes offer some hope for the future.

⇩ FOLKLORE CENTER. Founded as a mining town, Oruro, Bolivia, is a UNESCO cultural heritage site. Each November a week-long festival celebrates traditional Andean culture with ancient dances, music, and rituals.

⇩ OLD MEETS NEW. Against a backdrop of skyscrapers, a modern urban train speeds past the old government palace in Medellín, Colombia. Known as a center of illegal drug trafficking, the city has worked hard to change its image, introducing economic and social changes that have improved safety.

⟵ ANCIENT ARTISANS. Early cultures of Colombia left no great stone monuments, but they distinguished themselves with their fine gold work, which may have encouraged Europeans to search for El Dorado, the legendary City of Gold.

Map Key

⊛ Country capital
••• City or town
······ Boundary

0 ___ 200 miles
0 ___ 300 kilometers
Azimuthal Equidistant Projection

CARIBBEAN SEA

Aruba (Neth.)
Bonaire (Netherlands)
Curaçao (Neth.)
GRENADA

Santa Marta
Barranquilla
Cartagena
Valledupar
Sincelejo
Montería

PANAMA

Cauca

Barrancabermeja

Medellín
Manizales
Pereira
Armenia
Tuluá
Ibagué
Buenaventura
Cali
Palmira
Neiva
Popayán
Pasto

Cúcuta
San Cristóbal
Bucaramanga

Sogamoso
Tunja

⊛ Bogotá
Villavicencio

COLOMBIA

San José del Guaviare

Florencia

Cabimas
Ojeda
Mérida

Maracaibo
Ciudad Ojeda
Lake Maracaibo
Pico Bolívar
16,427 ft 5,007 m

Puerto Cabello
Maracay
⊛ Caracas
Los Teques
Valencia
Barquisimeto
Barcelona

Cumaná
Puerto La Cruz
Maturín

TRINIDAD & TOBAGO

ATLANTIC OCEAN

Barinas

VENEZUELA

Meta

Ciudad Bolívar

Orinoco

Ciudad Guayana

GUIANA HIGHLANDS

Angel Falls
Total drop
3,212 ft 979 m

Mt. Roraima
9,094 ft 2,772 m

GUYANA

Orinoco

EQUATOR

A N D E S

Ibarra
Cayambe
Portoviejo
⊛ Quito
Manta
Chimborazo
20,702 ft 6,310 m
Riobamba
Guayaquil
Milagro
Machala
Cuenca
Loja

ECUADOR

Putumayo

A M A Z O N

Iquitos

Amazon

Negro

Amazon (Solimões)

B A S I N

Talara
Sullana
Piura

Marañón
Ucayali

B R A Z I L

Chiclayo
Cajamarca

Trujillo
Chimbote
Nevado Huascarán
22,205 ft
6,768 m

Pucallpa

PERU

Huánuco

Purus

Madeira

Callao
⊛ Lima

Huancayo

Machu Picchu
Cusco
Ica

Apurímac

Madre de Dios

Guaporé

Mamoré

Trinidad

Arequipa
Puno

Lake Titicaca

⊛ La Paz
(administrative capital)

BOLIVIA

Tacna

Nevado Sajama
21,463 ft 6,542 m

Altiplano

Oruro

Cochabamba

Santa Cruz

⊛ Sucre
(constitutional capital)

Potosí

Salar de Uyuni

Tarija

A N D E S

PACIFIC OCEAN

CHILE

PARAGUAY

ARGENTINA

Pantanal

INDIGENOUS PEOPLE

Bolivia	55%
Peru	45%
Ecuador	25%
Guyana	9%
Chile	5%
Argentina	3%
Suriname	2%
Colombia	1%
Brazil	0%
Paraguay	0%
Uruguay	0%
Venezuela	0%

Amerindians are concentrated largely in Andean countries. More than half of Bolivia's population is made up of these indigenous people.

NORTHEASTERN SOUTH AMERICA

THE BASICS

STATS

Largest country
Brazil
3,300,169 sq mi (8,547,403 sq km)

Smallest country
Suriname
63,037 sq mi (163,265 sq km)

Most populous country
Brazil
191,481,000

Least populous country
Suriname
502,000

Predominant languages
Portuguese, English, Dutch, Hindi

Predominant religions
Christianity (Roman Catholic, Protestant), Hindu, Islam

Highest GDP per capita
Brazil
$10,200

Lowest GDP per capita
Guyana
$3,900

Highest life expectancy
Brazil
72 years

Highest literacy rate
Guyana
99%

GEO WHIZ

Guyana has as many as 300 species of catfish, roughly a quarter of the total number living in South America. Locals hunt them and other fish for the international aquarium trade by probing hollow tree trunks submerged on river bottoms.

Paramaribo, Suriname's capital, is a melting pot of Dutch, Chinese, Hindu, East Indian, and Javanese cultures. Dutch is the only official language.

Brazil covers almost half of South America's land area. It is the world's largest Portuguese-speaking country and the largest Catholic country.

The Pantanal, the world's largest freshwater wetland, is almost ten times the size of the Florida Everglades. It is formed by the seasonal flooding of several rivers in southwestern Brazil.

⇧ GOAL! Maracana Stadium in Rio de Janeiro is packed with enthusiastic soccer fans. Brazil has a long history of producing world-class soccer players and strong teams—winning the coveted World Cup five times.

Brazil dominates the region as well as the continent in size (it is the world's fifth largest country in area) and population (half of South America's 386 million people live here). Leading cities São Paulo and Rio de Janeiro are among the world's largest, and the country's vast agricultural lands make it a top global exporter of coffee, soybeans, beef, orange juice, and sugar. The vast Amazon rain forest, once a dense wilderness of unmatched biodiversity, is now threatened by farmers, loggers, and miners. To Brazil's north are lands colonized by the British, Dutch, and French—now sparsely settled Guyana, Suriname, and a French overseas department where the European Space Agency maintains its Spaceport, a launch site for explorations beyond Earth. Formerly known as the Guianas, these lands are populated by a mix of people with African, South Asian, and European heritage.

⇩ BAUXITE TO ALUMINUM. By exploiting rich deposits of bauxite, the ore from which aluminum is made, and inexpensive hydropower, the small country of Suriname produces aluminum ingots for export, such as these headed for global markets.

VAST WATERSHED

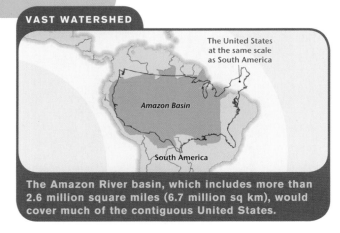

The United States at the same scale as South America

Amazon Basin

South America

The Amazon River basin, which includes more than 2.6 million square miles (6.7 million sq km), would cover much of the contiguous United States.

⇦ SIX-BANDED ARMADILLO, found throughout dry grass-land areas of northeastern South America, lives on plants and insects. Also known as the yellow armadillo, it is unlike others of its species in that it remains active during the day.

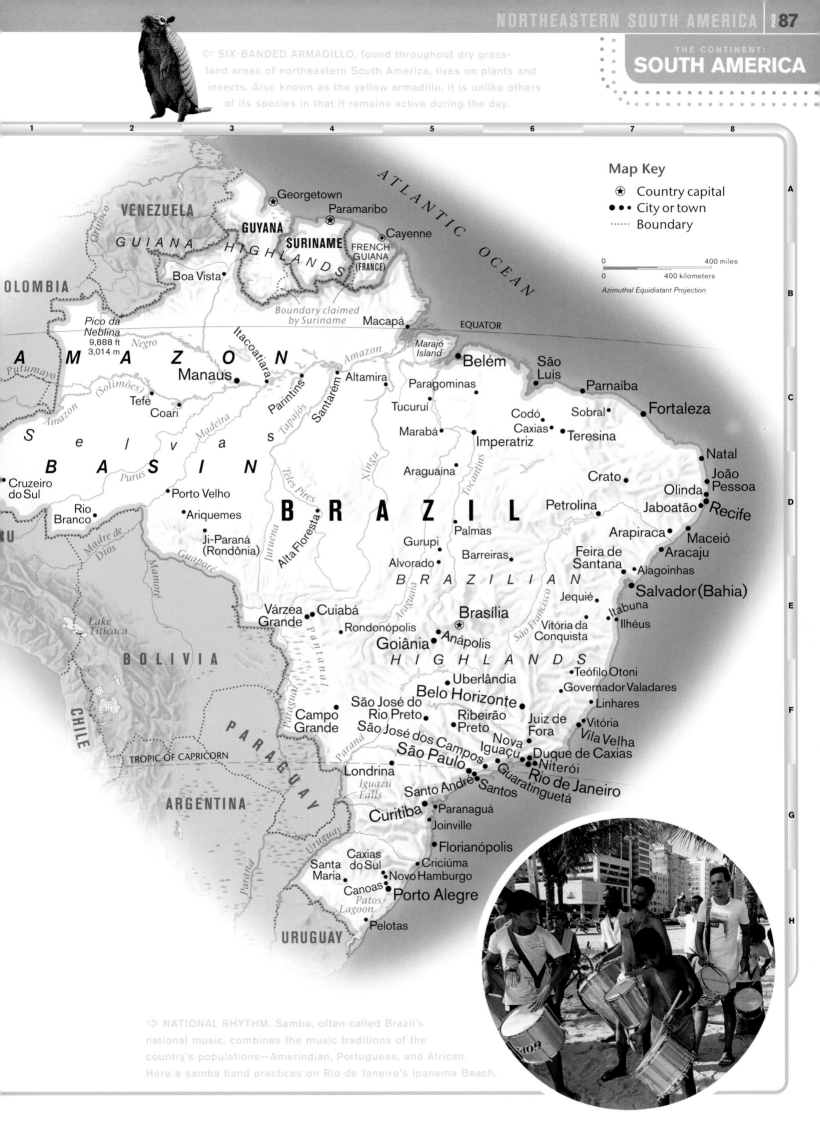

Map Key
- ⊛ Country capital
- ●●● City or town
- ······ Boundary

0 ————— 400 miles
0 ————— 400 kilometers
Azimuthal Equidistant Projection

VENEZUELA

ATLANTIC OCEAN

Orinoco

GUIANA HIGHLANDS

Georgetown
Paramaribo
GUYANA
SURINAME
Cayenne
FRENCH GUIANA (FRANCE)

Boa Vista

Boundary claimed by Suriname

COLOMBIA

Pico da Neblina
9,888 ft
3,014 m
Negro

Macapá
EQUATOR

Marajó Island

Belém
São Luís

Parnaíba

Itacoatiara

Amazon

A M A Z O N

Manaus
Altamira

Paragominas

Tucuruí

Codó
Caxias

Sobral
Teresina

Fortaleza

Putumayo

(Solimões)

Tefé
Coari

Parintins
Santarém
Tapajós

Marabá
Imperatriz

Natal

Amazon

Selva

Madeira

B A S I N

Araguaína

Crato

João Pessoa
Olinda
Recife

Cruzeiro do Sul

Purus

Porto Velho

B R A Z I L

Petrolina

Jaboatão

Rio Branco

Ariquemes

Palmas

Arapiraca

Maceió

Madre de Dios

Ji-Paraná (Rondônia)

Gurupi

Barreiras

Feira de Santana

Aracaju
Alagoinhas

Teles Pires

Alvorado

B R A Z I L I A N

Jeciué

Salvador (Bahia)

Guaporé

Alta Floresta

Juruena

Xingu

Tocantins

São Francisco

Itabuna
Ilhéus

Mamoré

Várzea Grande
Cuiabá

Araguaia

Brasília

Vitória da Conquista

Lake Titicaca

BOLIVIA

Rondonópolis

Anápolis

H I G H L A N D S

Goiânia

Teófilo Otoni
Governador Valadares

CHILE

Pantanal

Uberlândia

Belo Horizonte

Linhares

São José do Rio Preto

Ribeirão Preto

Juiz de Fora

Vitória
Vila Velha

P A R A G U A Y

Campo Grande

São José dos Campos

Nova Iguaçu

Duque de Caxias

TROPIC OF CAPRICORN

Paraná

São Paulo
Santo André
Santos

Niterói
Rio de Janeiro
Guaratinguetá

Londrina

Iguazú Falls

ARGENTINA

P A R A G U A Y

Paranaguá

Curitiba

Joinville

Uruguay

Florianópolis

Caxias do Sul

Criciúma

Santa Maria

Novo Hamburgo

Canoas

Porto Alegre

Patos Lagoon

Paraná

Pelotas

URUGUAY

⇨ NATIONAL RHYTHM. Samba, often called Brazil's national music, combines the music traditions of the country's populations—Amerindian, Portuguese, and African. Here a samba band practices on Rio de Janeiro's Ipanema Beach.

THE BASICS

STATS

Largest country
Argentina
1,073,518 sq mi (2,780,400 sq km)

Smallest country
Uruguay
68,037 sq mi (176,215 sq km)

Most populous country
Argentina
40,267,000

Least populous country
Uruguay
3,364,000

Predominant languages
Spanish, Guarani, English, Italian, German, French

Predominant religion
Christianity (Roman Catholic, Protestant)

Highest GDP per capita
Chile
$14,700

Lowest GDP per capita
Paraguay
$4,100

Highest life expectancy
Argentina, Chile
77 years

Highest literacy rate
Uruguay
98%

GEO WHIZ

Guanacos, a member of the camel family that is most numerous in the Patagonia region of Chile and Argentina, keeps enemies at bay by spitting at them.

The Itaipú Dam, which spans the Paraná River between Brazil and Paraguay, is currently the world's largest operating hydroelectric power plant.

Guarani is the name of a people native to Paraguay, the country's basic unit of money, and one of its two official languages. Spanish is the other.

Argentinians eat 150 pounds (68 kg) of beef per person each year, making the country the world's largest per capita consumer of this meat.

Chile's Chuquicamata mine is among the largest open-pit copper mines.

SOUTHERN SOUTH AMERICA

Four countries make up this region, which is sometimes called the Southern Cone because of its shape. Long north-south distances in Chile and Argentina result in varied environments. Chile's Atacama Desert in the north contrasts with much cooler, moister lands in the country's south where there are fjords and glaciers. Nine of ten Chileans live in Middle Chile, in and around booming Santiago. Similarly, most neighboring Argentinians live in the central Pampas region, where wheat and cattle flourish on the fertile plains. Farther south lie the arid, windswept plateaus of Patagonia. Landlocked Paraguay is small in comparison, less urbanized, and one of South America's poorest countries. Compact Uruguay is smaller still, but possesses a strong agricultural economy, including cattle- and sheep-raising.

➪ COWBOYS OF THE PAMPAS. Cattle are herded by gauchos, the Argentine term for cowboys. The country's extensive grass-covered plains support grain and cattle production on ranches called *estancias*.

➪ FORBIDDING MOUNTAINS. Rising to icy heights above Chile's narrow southern coast, the Cordillera de Paine lies about 1,500 miles (2,414 km) south of the capital, Santiago, in the Chilean part of Patagonia. The mountain is part of a national park that was made a world heritage site in 1978.

GLOBAL BEEF EXPORTS

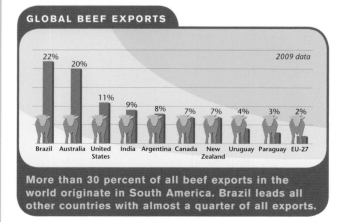

2009 data

Brazil	Australia	United States	India	Argentina	Canada	New Zealand	Uruguay	Paraguay	EU-27
22%	20%	11%	9%	8%	7%	7%	4%	3%	2%

More than 30 percent of all beef exports in the world originate in South America. Brazil leads all other countries with almost a quarter of all exports.

⇐ INCA TREASURE. Near the frozen summit of Argentina's Cerro Llullaillaco, second highest active volcano in the world, archaeologists excavated Inca ruins and uncovered well-preserved mummies and 20 clothed statues, such as the one at left.

⇑ DESERT RICHES. Molten copper is poured into molds at a refinery near Chuquicamata, the world's largest copper deposit, located in northern Chile's Atacama Desert. Chile accounts for about 35 percent of the world's copper production.

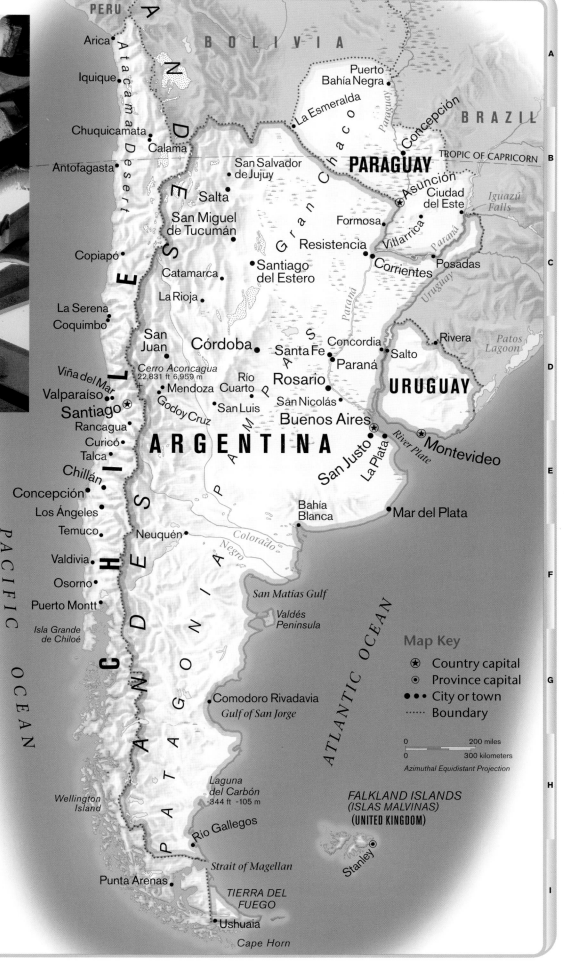

PERU

BOLIVIA

BRAZIL

PARAGUAY

TROPIC OF CAPRICORN

Arica
Iquique
Chuquicamata
Calama
Antofagasta

Atacama Desert

A   N   D   E   S

Puerto
Bahía Negra
La Esmeralda
Concepción
San Salvador
de Jujuy
Salta
San Miguel
de Tucumán
Copiapó
Catamarca
La Rioja
La Serena
Coquimbo

Gran Chaco

Asunción
Ciudad
del Este
Formosa
Resistencia
Villarrica
Corrientes
Posadas

Iguazú
Falls

Paraná

Santiago
del Estero

Paraná

Uruguay

Rivera

Patos
Lagoon

San
Juan
Córdoba
Santa Fe
Concordia
Salto
Paraná

Cerro Aconcagua
22,831 ft 6,959 m
Viña del Mar
Valparaíso
Santiago
Rancagua
Curicó
Talca
Chillán
Concepción
Los Ángeles
Temuco
Valdivia
Osorno
Puerto Montt

Mendoza
Río
Cuarto
Godoy Cruz
San Luis
Rosario
San Nicolás
Buenos Aires

URUGUAY

Montevideo

C   H   I   L   E

A   R   G   E   N   T   I   N   A

P A M P A S

San Justo
La Plata

River Plate

Bahía
Blanca
Mar del Plata

Neuquén
Colorado

Negro

PACIFIC OCEAN

San Matías Gulf

Valdés
Peninsula

Isla Grande
de Chiloé

P   A   T   A   G   O   N   I   A

A   N   D   E   S

Comodoro Rivadavia
Gulf of San Jorge

ATLANTIC OCEAN

Wellington
Island

Laguna
del Carbón
-344 ft -105 m

FALKLAND ISLANDS
(ISLAS MALVINAS)
(UNITED KINGDOM)

Río Gallegos

Stanley

Strait of Magellan

Punta Arenas

TIERRA DEL
FUEGO

Ushuaia
Cape Horn

Map Key

✪ Country capital
◉ Province capital
●●● City or town
⋯⋯ Boundary

0 ___ 200 miles
0 ___ 300 kilometers

Azimuthal Equidistant Projection

THE CONTINENT:
EUROPE

3,841,000 sq mi (9,947,000 sq km)

PHYSICAL

Land area 3,841,000 sq mi (9,947,000 sq km)	**Lowest point** Caspian Sea -92 ft (-28 m)	**Largest lake** **entirely in Europe** Ladoga, Russia 6,853 sq mi (17,703 sq km)
Highest point El'brus, Russia 18,510 ft (5,642 m)	**Longest river** Volga, Russia 2,290 mi (3,685 km)	

POLITICAL

Population 737,725,000	**Largest country entirely in Europe** Ukraine 233,090 sq mi (603,700 sq km)	**Economy** Farming: vegetables, fruit, grains
Largest metropolitan area Moscow, Russia Pop. 10,495,000	**Most densely populated country** Monaco 45,455 people per sq mi (17,500 per sq km)	Industry: chemicals, machinery Services

Europe

EUROPE

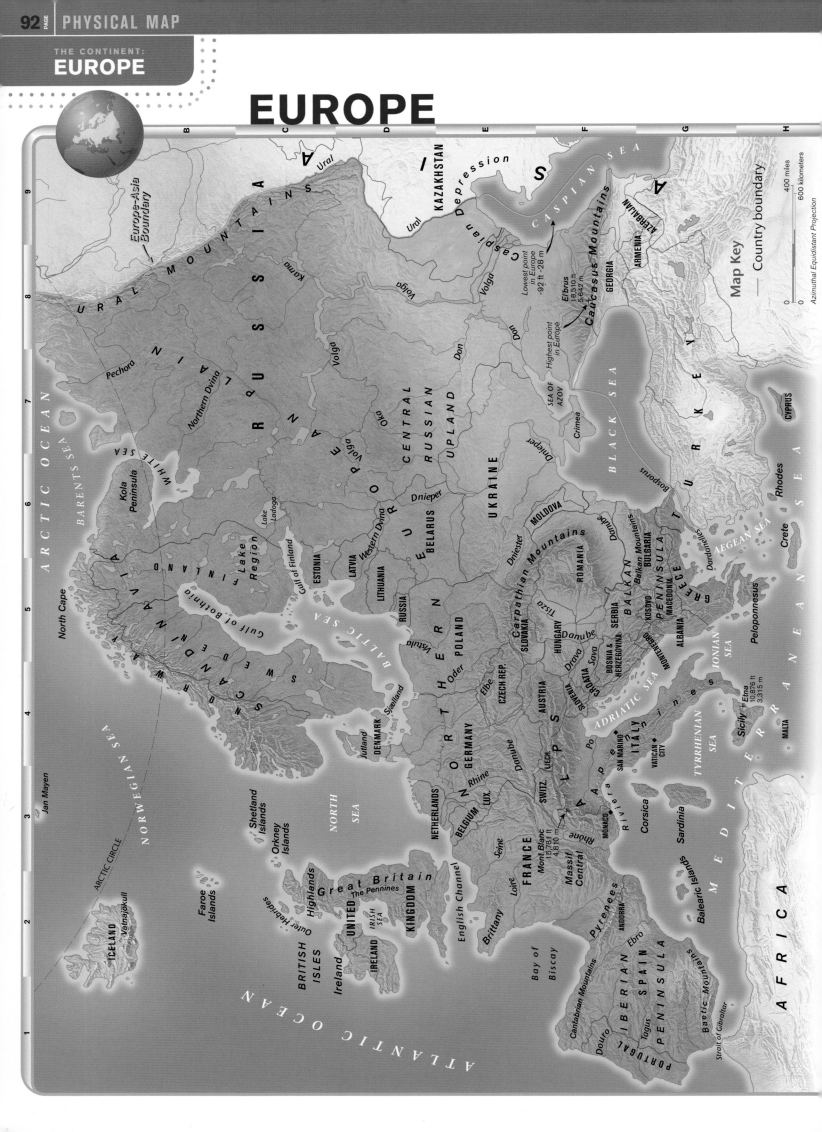

Map Key

— Country boundary

400 miles
600 kilometers

Azimuthal Equidistant Projection

ARCTIC OCEAN

BARENTS SEA

WHITE SEA

Europe-Asia Boundary

Ural

Ural

KAZAKHSTAN

Caspian Depression

CASPIAN SEA

Lowest point in Europe -92 ft -28 m

Highest point in Europe

El'brus 18,510 ft 5,642 m

Caucasus Mountains

AZERBAIJAN

GEORGIA

ARMENIA

U R A L   M O U N T A I N S

R U S S I A

Pechora

Kama

Volga

Volga

Northern Dvina

Don

Don

Volga

P L A I N

Kola Peninsula

North Cape

SCANDINAVIA

ARCTIC CIRCLE

Vatnajökull

ICELAND

Jan Mayen

NORWEGIAN SEA

NORWAY

SWEDEN

FINLAND

Lake Region

Lake Ladoga

Gulf of Bothnia

Gulf of Finland

Oka

Volga

Psel

CENTRAL RUSSIAN UPLAND

SEA OF AZOV

Crimea

Dnieper

BLACK SEA

Bosporus

TURKEY

CYPRUS

Rhodes

Crete

AEGEAN SEA

Dardanelles

ESTONIA

LATVIA

LITHUANIA

Western Dvina

Dnieper

BELARUS

UKRAINE

RUSSIA

MOLDOVA

Dniester

Carpathian Mountains

ROMANIA

Don

Danube

BALKAN PENINSULA

Balkan Mountains

BULGARIA

MACEDONIA

KOSOVO

SERBIA

MONTENEGRO

ALBANIA

GREECE

IONIAN SEA

Peloponnesus

BALTIC SEA

POLAND

Vistula

Oder

N O R T H E R N

SLOVAKIA

Tisza

HUNGARY

Drava

Sava

Danube

CROATIA

BOSNIA & HERZEGOVINA

SLOVENIA

CZECH REP.

AUSTRIA

Elbe

Po

A L P S

ADRIATIC SEA

Apennines

ITALY

SAN MARINO

VATICAN CITY

TYRRHENIAN SEA

Sicily   Etna 10,876 ft 3,315 m

MALTA

Sardinia

Corsica

MEDITERRANEAN SEA

GERMANY

Danube

Rhine

LIECH.

SWITZ.

Mont Blanc 15,781 ft 4,810 m

Riviera

MONACO

Massif Central

FRANCE

Rhône

NETHERLANDS

BELGIUM

LUX.

Seine

Loire

Brittany

English Channel

NORTH SEA

DENMARK

Jutland

Sjælland

Shetland Islands

Orkney Islands

Outer Hebrides

Highlands

The Pennines

Great Britain

UNITED KINGDOM

IRISH SEA

Ireland

IRELAND

BRITISH ISLES

Faroe Islands

Bay of Biscay

Pyrenees

ANDORRA

SPAIN

PORTUGAL

Douro

Tagus

Ebro

IBERIAN PENINSULA

Cantabrian Mountains

Baetic Mountains

Balearic Islands

Strait of Gibraltar

AFRICA

ATLANTIC OCEAN

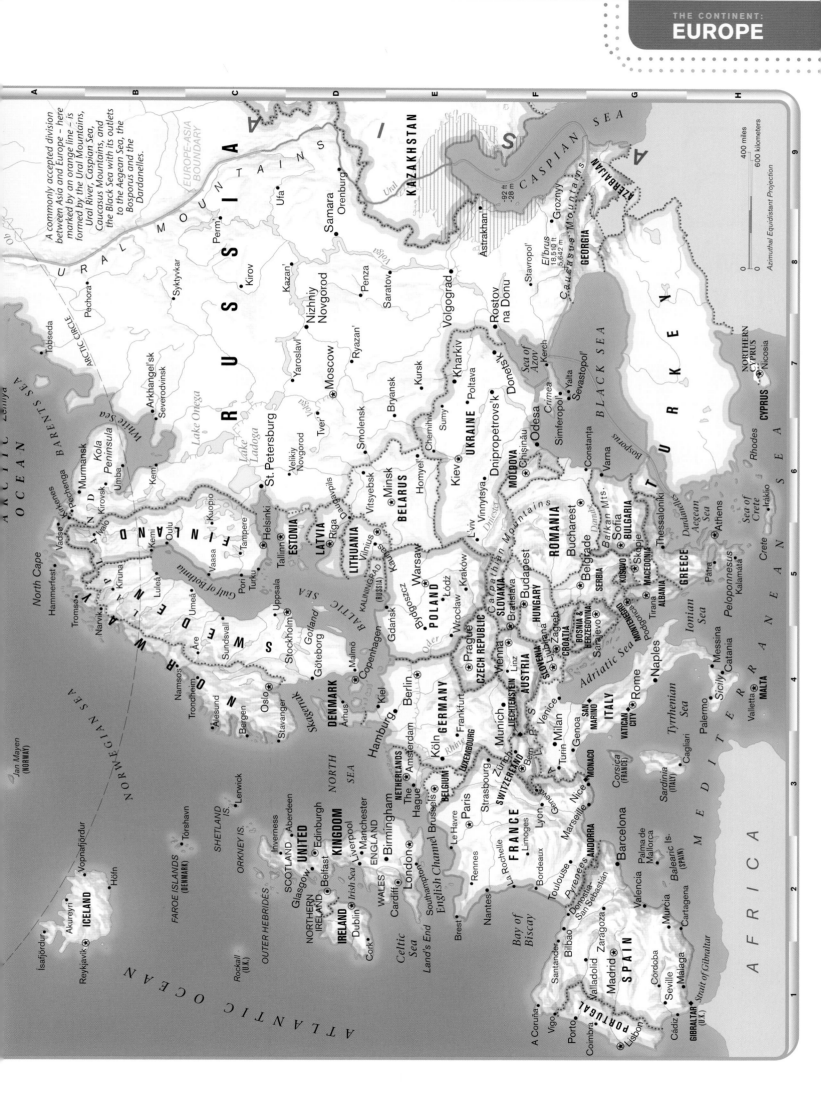

A commonly accepted division between Asia and Europe – here marked by an orange line – is formed by the Ural Mountains, Ural River, Caspian Sea, Caucasus Mountains, and the Black Sea with its outlets to the Aegean Sea, the Bosporus and the Dardanelles.

EUROPE-ASIA BOUNDARY

400 miles
600 kilometers
Azimuthal Equidistant Projection

Europe
SMALL SPACES, DIVERSE PLACES

⇑ WIND POWER.
A traditional windmill stands silent in Spain, calling to mind scenes from the classic Spanish novel *Don Quixote*. Modern windmills are used to generate electricity and to pump water.

A cluster of islands and peninsulas jutting west from Asia, Europe is bordered by two oceans and more than a dozen seas, which are linked to inland areas by canals and navigable rivers such as the Rhine and Danube. The continent boasts a bounty of landscapes. Sweeping west from the Urals is the fertile Northern European Plain. Rugged uplands form part of Europe's western coast, while the Alps shield Mediterranean lands from frigid northern winds. Here, first Greek and then Roman civilizations laid Europe's cultural foundation. Its colonial powers built wealth from vast empires, while its inventors and thinkers revolutionized world industry, economy, and politics. Today, the 27-member European Union seeks to unite the continent's diversity.

⇓ CHEERY GREETINGS. Laughing children clown for the camera in Klaipeda, Lithuania. Klaipeda is the northernmost ice-free port on the eastern coast of the Baltic Sea.

⇐ ROCKY SENTINEL. Towering 14,693 feet (4,478 m) in elevation, the Matterhorn, on the border between Switzerland and Italy, is one of Europe's most famous mountains. Frequent avalanches on its steep slopes pose challenges for mountain climbers.

⇑ WATCHFUL GUARDIAN. A gargoyle stares out across the Paris skyline from a ledge of Notre Dame Cathedral. Gargoyles were first used in Gothic architecture as waterspouts but later were decorative additions meant to ward off evil spirits.

⇓ DAY'S END. The glow of sunset falls on buildings overlooking Strandvagen (Beach Street) in Stockholm, Sweden. This broad avenue has historic buildings dating from the late 1800s on one side and boat docks on the other.

more about EUROPE

⬆ AGELESS TIME. The famous astronomical clock, built in 1410 in Prague, Czech Republic, has an astronomical dial on top of a calendar dial. Together they keep track of time as well as the movement of the sun, moon, and stars.

⇨ CLIFF DWELLERS. The town of Positano clings to the rocky hillside along Italy's Amalfi coast. In the mid-19th century, more than half the town's population emigrated, mainly to the United States. The economy today is based on tourism.

⬇ SEABIRDS OF THE NORTH. Colorful Atlantic puffins perch on a grass-covered cliff in Iceland, Europe's westernmost country. These unusual birds are skilled fishers but have difficulty becoming airborne and often crash upon landing.

⬆ CITY AT NIGHT. A winged victory statue atop the Metropolis Building, a classic example of early 20th-century architecture, appears to watch the evening traffic on the Gran Via in Madrid, Spain.

⇩ GLIMPSE OF THE PAST. Rome's Colosseum is a silent reminder of a once powerful empire that stretched from the British Isles to Persia (now Iran). The concrete, stone, and brick structure combined classic Greek and Roman architectural styles and could seat as many as 50,000 people.

WHERE THE PICTURES ARE

Reindeer herd p. 98
Strandvagen pp. 94–95
Viking burial marker p. 99
Waterfront scene p. 98

Puffins p. 96
Rotterdam harbor p. 100
Bagpipers p. 100
Stonehenge p. 101

Gargoyle p. 95
Goat cheese p. 97

Matterhorn pp. 94–95

Madrid at night p. 96

Windmill p. 94
Cathedral p. 100

Colosseum pp. 96–97
Amalfi Coast p. 97

Folk dancers p. 98
Chess players p. 106
Russian caviar p. 107

Children p. 94
St. Basil's church pp. 106–107

National Day celebrations p. 97
Astronomical clock p. 96

Scythian gold p. 103
Shoveling salt p. 103

Széchenyi Baths p. 102
Smoked meats p. 102

Thracian helmet p. 105

Cat p. 104
Village scene p. 104
Wedding festival p. 104

⇦ LUNCHTIME! Varieties of creamy, fresh goat cheese are displayed in a market in the Brittany region of northern France.

⇩ NATIONAL PRIDE. Young women carry banners in a parade marking Poland's National Day. Celebrated each year on May 3, it is the anniversary of the 1997 proclamation of the Polish Constitution.

THE CONTINENT:
EUROPE

THE BASICS

STATS

Largest country
Sweden 173,732 sq mi (449,964 sq km)

Smallest country
Denmark 16,640 sq mi (43,098 sq km)

Most populous country
Sweden 9,288,000

Least populous country
Iceland 321,000

Predominant languages
Russian, Polish, Swedish, Danish, Finnish, Norwegian, Lithuanian, Latvian, Estonian, Icelandic

Predominant religion
Christianity (Lutheran, Roman Catholic, Orthodox)

Highest GDP per capita
Norway $59,300

Lowest GDP per capita
Latvia $14,500

Highest life expectancy
Iceland, Sweden
81 years

Highest literacy rate
Estonia, Finland, Iceland, Latvia, Lithuania, Norway
100%

GEO WHIZ

Finland has more than 185,000 lakes. In fact, the southeastern part of the country is called the Lake Region.

The national symbol of Denmark is a statue of Hans Christian Andersen's Little Mermaid, in Copenhagen's harbor.

Vatnajokull, in Iceland, is the largest glacier in Europe.

According to Finnish folklore, Father and Mother Christmas live with their helpers on a mountain called Korvatunturi, in the country's Lapland region.

During Iceland's Thorrablot winter festival, locals celebrate by eating a Viking dish of rotten Greenland shark meat.

Legoland theme park, in Billund, Denmark, features miniature cities, models of famous landmarks such as the Taj Mahal, Statue of Liberty, Mount Rushmore, and more—all made from some 33 million Lego blocks.

⇨ COLORFUL TRADITION. Costumed folk dancers perform traditional dances at an open-air museum in Tallinn, Estonia.

NORTHERN EUROPE

This entire region lies in latitudes similar to Canada's Hudson Bay, but the warm North Atlantic Drift current moderates temperatures in western parts of the region, from volcanically active Iceland to Denmark and Norway. The area's better farmlands lie in southern Sweden and the breezy lowlands of Denmark. Lightly populated but mostly urban, Northern Europe is home to slightly more than 32 million people. Sweden is the largest and most populous country. Forested, lake-dotted Finland shares a long border with Russia. Estonia, Latvia, and Lithuania—the so-called Baltic States—were republics of the Russian-dominated Soviet Union, which ceased to exist in 1991.

⇧ NORDIC HERDERS. The Sami, indigenous people of northern Europe, herd their reindeer across the borders of Norway, Sweden, Finland, and Russia. Some use snowmobiles instead of horses.

⇧ LINK TO THE PAST. Rainbow colored buildings line the canal in Nyhavn, Denmark. Dating back to the 12th century, it is part of Copenhagen's original harbor.

NORTHERN FISHERIES

Norway	Iceland	Denmark	Sweden	Lithuania	Finland	Latvia	Estonia
2,378,950*	1,399,167	653,023	238,253	187,513	164,381	155,276	97,836

*Figures are in millions of tons, 2007

Large schools of fish thrive in the cold waters off northern Europe. Norway harvests the most, bringing in more than 2.3 million tons of fish annually.

◁ MARKER FROM THE PAST. A stone memorial marks the burial site of Viking warriors in Sweden. Although their main activities were farming and trade, Vikings are better known for their ships and fierce raids on towns across Europe.

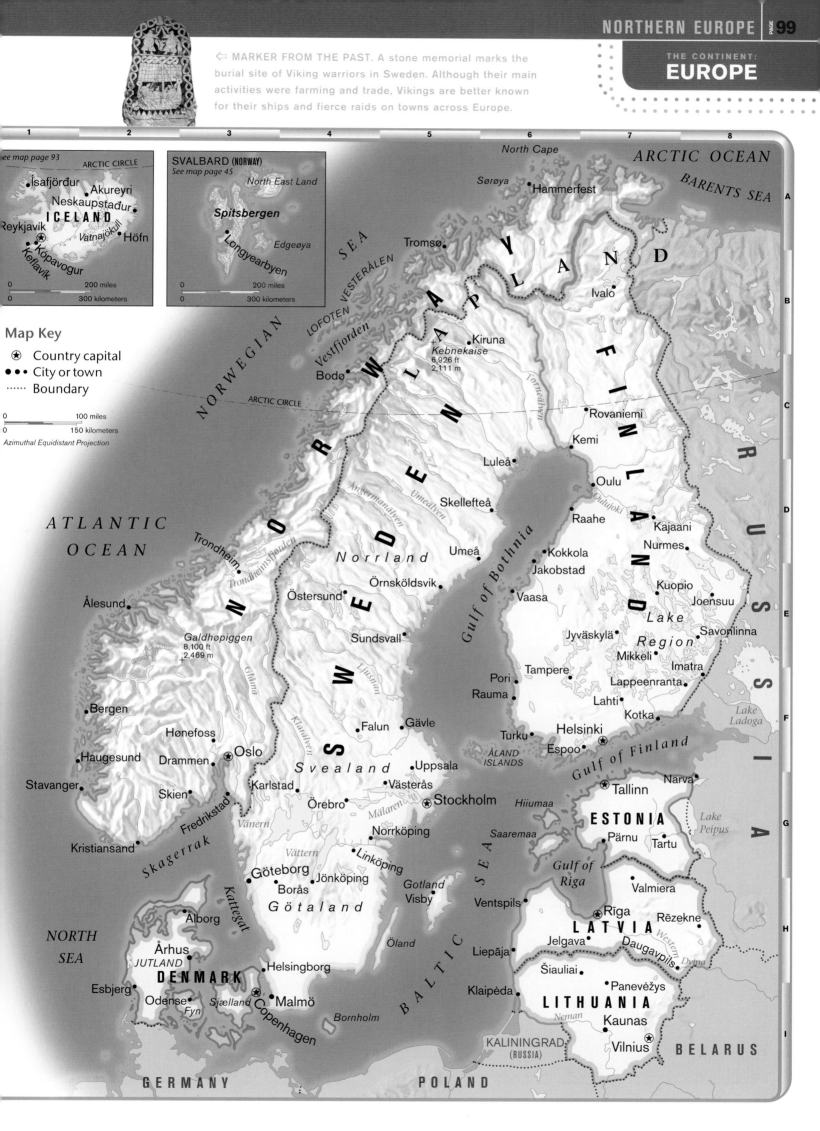

See map page 93

ARCTIC CIRCLE

Ísafjörður • Akureyri
Neskaupstaður
ICELAND
Reykjavík • Vatnajökull • Höfn
Kópavogur
Keflavík

0 ——— 200 miles
0 ——— 300 kilometers

SVALBARD (NORWAY)
See map page 45

North East Land

Spitsbergen
• Longyearbyen Edgeøya

0 ——— 200 miles
0 ——— 300 kilometers

Map Key

⊛ Country capital
••• City or town
····· Boundary

0 ——— 100 miles
0 ——— 150 kilometers
Azimuthal Equidistant Projection

North Cape

ARCTIC OCEAN

BARENTS SEA

Søroya • Hammerfest

NORWEGIAN SEA

Tromsø •

L A P L A N D

LOFOTEN VESTERÅLEN

Vestfjorden

• Kiruna
+ Kebnekaise
6,926 ft
2,111 m

• Ivalo

F I N L A N D

R U S S I A

Bodø •

ARCTIC CIRCLE

Tornedälven

• Rovaniemi

• Kemi

ATLANTIC OCEAN

Trondheim •

Trondheimsfjorden

N O R R L A N D

Ångermanälven Umeälven

• Luleå

• Skellefteå

• Oulu Oulujoki

• Raahe

• Kajaani

• Nurmes

Ålesund •

Östersund •

• Umeå

Gulf of Bothnia

• Kokkola
Jakobstad •

• Kuopio

• Joensuu

Lake Region

Norrland

• Örnsköldsvik

• Vaasa

• Jyväskylä

• Savonlinna

Galdhøpiggen
8,100 ft
+ 2,469 m

Sundsvall •

• Mikkeli

• Imatra

Bergen •

Gläma

S W E D E N

Ljusnan

• Pori

• Tampere

• Lappeenranta

• Rauma

• Lahti

• Kotka

Hønefoss •

• Falun • Gävle

Klarälven

Haugesund •

Drammen • ⊛ Oslo

• Turku

Helsinki ⊛

Lake Ladoga

Svealand

• Uppsala

Åland Islands

Espoo •

Stavanger •

Karlstad •

• Västerås

Skien •

Vänern

• Örebro

Mälaren

⊛ Stockholm

Hiiumaa

Narva •

⊛ Tallinn

Fredrikstad •

Vättern

Norrköping •

• Linköping

ESTONIA

Saaremaa

• Pärnu

Lake Peipus

• Tartu

Kristiansand •

Skagerrak

Göteborg • • Jönköping
Borås •

Gotland
• Visby

B A L T I C   S E A

Gulf of Riga

• Valmiera

Götaland

• Ventspils

⊛ Rīga
Jelgava •

• Rēzekne

NORTH SEA

Ålborg •

Kattegat

Öland

Daugavpils

Western Dvina

Helsingborg •

• Liepāja

LATVIA

Århus •
JUTLAND

DENMARK

Esbjerg •

Odense • Fyn

Malmö •
Sjælland
⊛ Copenhagen

Bornholm

Šiauliai •

• Panevėžys

Neman

• Klaipėda

LITHUANIA

KALININGRAD
(RUSSIA)

• Kaunas

• Vilnius

BELARUS

GERMANY

POLAND

THE CONTINENT:
EUROPE

THE BASICS

STATS

Largest country	France 210,026 sq mi (543,965 sq km)
Smallest country	Vatican City 0.2 sq mi (0.4 sq km)
Most populous country	Germany 81,980,000
Least populous country	Vatican City 798
Predominant languages	German, French, English, Italian, Spanish, Dutch, Portuguese
Predominant religion	Christianity (Roman Catholic, Protestant)
Highest GDP per capita	Liechtenstein $122,100
Lowest GDP per capita	Malta $23,800
Highest life expectancy	Andorra 83 years
Highest literacy rate	Andorra, Liechtenstein, Luxembourg, Vatican City 100%

GEO WHIZ

 Fossil hunters discovered a new species of dinosaur in northern Spain in 2006. Measuring up to 120 feet (37 m) and weighing 48 tons (44 t), *Turiasaurus riodevemsis* is the largest dinosaur ever found in Europe.

The catacombs of Paris, which date from Roman times, contain the skeletons of some six million people, including some victims of the French Revolution.

Antwerp, Belgium, is the center of the world's diamond industry.

The ears on several rhinoceros images in France's Chauvet cave look so much like a certain fast-food chain's Golden Arches that researchers have nicknamed them McEars.

Portugal is the world's leading producer of cork.

Mount Etna, on Italy's island of Sicily, is known as the home of Zeus, ruler of all Greek gods. It is Europe's highest active volcano.

WESTERN EUROPE

Eighteen countries crowd this diverse region, which has enjoyed a central role in world affairs for centuries while suffering the results of devastating wars. The past half-century has seen bitter rivals become wiser allies, with today's European Union growing out of the need to rebuild economic and political stability after World War II. Fertile soil in the many river valleys, across the Northern European Plain, and on Mediterranean hillsides gives rise to abundant harvests of a wide variety of crops grown on rich farmland. France leads in agricultural production and area, while Germany is the most populous. These and other countries here face a population problem unlike most other regions: a decline in numbers.

⇧ MONUMENT TO FAITH. The towering spires of La Sagrada Familia (The Holy Family) rise above Barcelona, Spain. This massive Roman Catholic church has been under construction for more than a century.

⇩ HIGHLAND TUNE. Bagpipers in formal dress parade through the streets of Edinburgh, Scotland. Bagpipes may have arrived with Roman invaders, but today they are most associated with the Scottish Highlands.

⇧ MODERN SPAN. Tall red arches support the Willem Bridge across the Maas River in Rotterdam, Netherlands. The Maas, which flows into the North Sea, is a major trade and transport artery, linking the Netherlands to the rest of Europe.

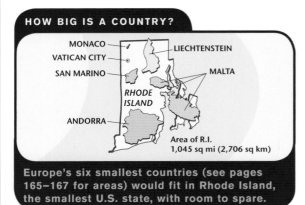

HOW BIG IS A COUNTRY?

MONACO
VATICAN CITY
SAN MARINO
LIECHTENSTEIN
MALTA
RHODE ISLAND
ANDORRA

Area of R.I.
1,045 sq mi (2,706 sq km)

Europe's six smallest countries (see pages 165–167 for areas) would fit in Rhode Island, the smallest U.S. state, with room to spare.

← CELTIC POWER. These rock pillars are part of Stonehenge, a puzzling arrangement of stones on the plains of southern England. Erected more than 5,000 years ago, Stonehenge is believed to be associated with sun worship.

0 — 200 miles
0 — 300 kilometers
Azimuthal Equidistant Projection

Map Key
★ Country capital
⊙ Province capital
• City or town
.... Boundary

FINLAND

ESTONIA

NORWAY

SWEDEN

Shetland Islands

Orkney Islands

Rockall (UNITED KINGDOM)

Outer Hebrides

Inner Hebrides

Inverness

SCOTLAND
Aberdeen
Perth • Dundee
Glasgow • Edinburgh
Londonderry
NORTHERN IRELAND
Belfast

NORTH SEA

DENMARK

BALTIC SEA

POLAND

IRELAND
Limerick • Dublin
Waterford
Cork

IRISH SEA
Isle of Man

UNITED
Newcastle
Sunderland
Leeds
KINGDOM
Liverpool • Kingston upon Hull
Sheffield
Manchester • Nottingham
Birmingham
WALES ENGLAND
Cardiff • London
Bristol
Plymouth
Southampton

CELTIC SEA

Kiel
Rostock
Lübeck
Hamburg
Bremen • Berlin
Hannover
Oldenburg
Groningen
NETHERLANDS
The Hague • Amsterdam
Utrecht
Rotterdam
Brugge • Antwerp
Brussels
BELGIUM
Lille • Charleroi
Luxembourg
LUXEMBOURG

Bielefeld • Magdeburg
Dortmund • Leipzig
Essen • Erfurt
Köln • Dresden
GERMANY • Chemnitz
Bonn
Frankfurt
Mainz
Mannheim
Karlsruhe • Nürnberg
Stuttgart
Augsburg

CZECH REPUBLIC

SLOVAKIA

ATLANTIC OCEAN

ENGLISH CHANNEL
Strait of Dover
Channel Islands (U.K.)

Amiens
Le Havre
Caen • Rouen • Reims
Paris
Rennes • Le Mans
Brest • Orléans
Angers • Tours
Nantes

Metz • Nancy
Strasbourg
Mulhouse
Besançon • Basel
Dijon
Freiburg

Linz
Salzburg • Vienna
Munich AUSTRIA
Innsbruck • Graz

HUNGARY

FRANCE

BAY OF BISCAY

Limoges
Vichy
Clermont-Ferrand
Lyon
St.-Étienne
MASSIF CENTRAL
Nîmes
Montpellier

Zürich
Lausanne
Geneva
Bern SWITZERLAND
LIECHTENSTEIN
Mont Blanc 15,781 ft 4,810 m
Matterhorn 14,691 ft 4,478 m

Bolzano
Trento
Verona • Trieste
Padova • Venice
Milan
Turin
Modena • Ferrara
Genoa • Bologna
Florence
Pisa

SLOVENIA
CROATIA
SERBIA
BOSNIA & HERZEGOVINA

MONTENEGRO
ALBANIA

A Coruña
Gijón
Vigo
Santiago de Compostela
Braga
Porto
Viseu
oimbra
PORTUGAL
Lisbon
Setúbal

Oviedo
Santander
Bilbao
Donostia-San Sebastián
León • Vitoria-Gasteiz
Burgos
Valladolid
Salamanca
Zaragoza
Madrid
Toledo
SPAIN

Badajoz
SIERRA MORENA
Córdoba
Huelva
Seville
Jerez
Cádiz
Algeciras • GIBRALTAR (U.K.)
Ceuta (SPAIN)
ALBORAN SEA
Melilla (SPAIN)
Strait of Gibraltar

Pamplona
ANDORRA
Andorra
Lleida • Sabadell
Martaró
Tarragona
Barcelona
Castelló de la Plana
Valencia
Albacete
Murcia
Jaén
Granada
Alicante
Cartagena
Almería

PYRENEES
Toulouse
Perpignan
Marseille
Toulon

Avignon
Aix-en-Provence
Nice
MONACO

LIGURIAN SEA
Bastia

CORSICA
Ajaccio

Perugia
Terni
SAN MARINO
VATICAN CITY
Rome
Naples
Vesuvius 4,203 ft 1,281 m

ITALY
Ancona
Pescara

ADRIATIC SEA

Foggia
Bari
Taranto
Lecce
Gulf of Taranto

BALEARIC SEA
Palma de Mallorca
Minorca
Majorca
BALEARIC ISLANDS

Sassari
SARDINIA
Cagliari

TYRRHENIAN SEA

Cosenza
Messina
Palermo
Marsala
SICILY
Taormina
Catania
Syracuse

Reggio di Calabria

IONIAN SEA

MEDITERRANEAN SEA

MOROCCO
ALGERIA
TUNISIA
MALTA • Valletta

MORROCO

THE CONTINENT:
EUROPE

EASTERN EUROPE

1   2   3

THE BASICS

STATS

Largest country
Ukraine 233,090 sq mi (603,700 sq km)

Smallest country
Moldova 13,050 sq mi (33,800 sq km)

Most populous country
Ukraine 46,030,000

Least populous country
Moldova 4,133,000

Predominant languages
Ukrainian, Russian, Polish, Hungarian, Czech, Belarusian, Slovak, Moldovan

Predominant religions
Christianity (Roman Catholic, Orthodox, Protestant), Judaism, Islam

Highest GDP per capita
Czech Republic $25,100

Lowest GDP per capita
Moldova $2,400

Highest life expectancy
Czech Republic 75 years

Highest literacy rate
Poland, Slovakia, Belarus 100%

GEO WHIZ

The Wieliczka salt mine has been in operation since the 13th century. Known as the underground salt cathedral of Poland, it features historical, religious, and mythical figures, chambers, chapels, and an exhibit about how salt is mined, all carved in salt.

The Pinsk Marshes, one of Europe's largest wetlands, covers thousands of square miles in southern Belarus and northwestern Ukraine. In 1970 the area was chosen as the site of the Chornobyl' Nuclear Power Plant, largely because few people lived there and it had ready access to water. An explosion closed the power plant in 1986, and much of the area is still uninhabitable due to radioactive contaminants.

Budapest did not become a united city until 1873. Until that time there were two cities—Buda on the west bank of the Danube and Pest on the east. The first bridge between the cities was built in the mid-1800s by Count Istvan Széchenyi.

The so-called Velvet Revolution was the non-violent uprising against the communist government of Czechoslovakia in 1989 that led to the creation of two new countries: the Czech Republic and Slovakia.

⇨ HEALING WATERS. Budapest's Széchenyi Baths, built in 1909–1913, are famous for their medicinal thermal waters, discovered in 1879. A total of 15 baths, as well as saunas and steam rooms, are housed in buildings decorated with sculptures and mosaics by Hungary's leading artists.

⇧ TIME TO EAT. Smoked sausages and bacon, ready for purchase in the market, are an important part of the diet in the countries of eastern Europe.

Eastern Europe stretches from the Baltic Sea southeast to the Black Sea. Before 1991, Ukraine, Belarus, and Moldova were part of the Soviet Union, with the region's other countries largely under its control. A small, separated segment of Russia is still nearby: Kaliningrad. Much of the region has a continental climate similar to that of the U.S. Midwest. Nearly the size of Texas, Ukraine is the region's largest country in both population and area. Like Poland, it holds rich agricultural and industrial resources. Warsaw is the region's largest city, while the historic charms of Prague and Budapest make them popular tourist stops. With the exceptions of Hungary and Moldova, branches of Slavic language and ethnicity link most people in these lands.

BALTIC SEA

Gdynia
Koszalin   Gdańsk
Szczecin
Bydgoszcz
Gorzów   To
Wielkopolski   Vistula
Poznań
Oder   Zielona
Góra   POLA
GERMANY   Kalisz
Wałbrzych   Legnica   Łó
Wrocław
Liberec   Częstochowa
Opole
Prague   Byt
Katowice
Pilsen   CZECH   Tychy
REPUBLIC   Ostrava
Olomouc   Kral
České
Budějovice   Brno   C
Danube   SLOV
Bratislava
AUSTRIA
Győr
Székesfehérvár   Budapest   HUN
SLOVENIA
Drava   Pécs   Szeged
CROATIA   SERB
Danube

⇐ ANCIENT GOLD. This skillfully crafted gold collar, called a pectoral, was found in a Scythian burial mound in Ukraine. The Scythians occupied the area from modern Ukraine into Russia from the eighth century B.C. to the second century A.D.

THE CONTINENT:
EUROPE

COMMUNICATION CHALLENGE

West Slavic 20%
South Slavic 10%
East Slavic 70%

Polish (40.0 million speakers)
Czech (9.5 million speakers)
Slovak (5.0 million speakers)

Bulgarian (9.1 million speakers)
Bosnian (2.2 million speakers)
Serbian (7.0 million speakers)
Slovenian (2.0 million speakers)
Macedonian (2.1 million speakers)
Croatian (5.5 million speakers)

Balarusan (8.6 million speakers)
Russian (144.0 million speakers)
Ukrainian (37.0 million speakers)

Slavic languages of Eastern Europe share a common origin, but they have evolved into a dozen distinctly different languages.

LATVIA

LITHUANIA

KALININGRAD (RUSSIA)

Western Dvina

Vitsyebsk
Orsha
Barysaw
Mahilyow
⊛ Minsk

B E L A R U S

Olsztyn
Hrodna
Białystok
Baranavichy
Babruysk
Homyel'

⊛ Warsaw
Brest
Pinsk
Pinsk Marshes
Mazyr
Dnieper

RUSSIA

dom
Lublin

Kielce
Vistula

Chernihiv

Chernobyl'

Sumy

Luts'k
Rivne

Zhytomyr ⊛ Kiev
Bila Tserkva

Kharkiv

Rzeszów

Tarnów

L'viv
Ternopil'
Dniester

U K R A I N E

Poltava

ATHIAN
Khmel'nyts'kyy
Ivano-Frankivs'k
Kam'yanets'-Podil's'kyy

Vinnytsya
Cherkasy
Kremenchuk

Slov''yans'k
Kramators'k
Kostyantynivka

Lysychans'k
Kadivka
Luhans'k

Košice
Uzhhorod
Chernivtsi

Oleksandriya
Kirovohrad
Dniprodzerzhyns'k

Alchevs'k
Krasnyy Luch

skolc

MOUNTAINS

Dnipropetrovs'k

Horlivka
Yenakiyeve
Makiyivka

Donets'k

Nyíregyháza

Bălți
Dniester

Kryvyy Rih
Zaporizhzhya

Debrecen

MOLDOVA
Chişinău ⊛

Nikopol'
Melitopol'

Mariupol'
Berdyans'k

Prut

Mykolayiv
Dnieper
Kherson

W

R O M A N I A

Tiraspol

Odesa

SEA OF AZOV

Danube

Kerch

C R I M E A

Yevpatoriya

Simferopol'

Sevastopol'
Yalta

B L A C K   S E A

Map Key
⊛ Country capital
••• City or town
...... Boundary

0   200 miles
0   300 kilometers

Azimuthal Equidistant Projection

⇨ MOUNTAIN OF SALT. These men shovel salt at a storage depot in Crimea, Ukraine. Salt is a traditional symbol of friendship in Ukraine.

THE CONTINENT:
EUROPE

THE BASICS

STATS

Largest country
Romania 92,043 sq mi (238,391 sq km)

Smallest country
Cyprus 3,572 sq mi (9,251 sq km)

Most populous country
Romania 21,474,000

Least populous country
Montenegro 628,000

Predominant languages
Romanian, Greek, Serbian, Croatian, Bulgarian, Albanian, Turkish, English

Predominant religions
Christianity (various Orthodox, Roman Catholic), Islam

Highest GDP per capita
Greece $32,100

Lowest GDP per capita
Bosnia and Herzegovina $6,300

Highest life expectancy
Greece 80 years

Highest literacy rate
Slovenia
100%

GEO WHIZ

Along the coast of Croatia there are huge fish farms where bluefin tuna are raised, making the country an important supplier of this highly edible, very popular fish.

The Dalmatian, a popular breed of dog, is named for its region of origin: Dalmatia, along the Adriatic coast of the Balkan peninsula.

Dracula tours abound in Romania, home of Vlad Dracula (also known as Vlad the Impaler), who ruled the region between the Danube and the Transylvanian Alps in the 15th century.

The famous Lipizzan horses of the Spanish Riding School in Vienna, Austria, trace their ancestry and their name back more than 400 years to a horse farm in Lipica, Slovenia.

Lefkosia is the capital of both the independent Republic of Cyprus and the Rebublic of Northern Cyprus, which is under Turkish control.

BALKANS & CYPRUS

The Balkans—named for a Bulgarian mountain range—make up a rugged land with a rough history. Ethnic and religious conflict have long troubled the area. Since 1991, seven new countries have emerged from the breakup of Yugoslavia (see inset on page 105). Kosovo is the most recent. The storied Danube River winds east across the Balkans, separating Bulgaria and Romania, the region's largest country in both area and population. Rimmed by four seas—the Black, Aegean, Ionian, and Adriatic—the Balkans, particularly Greece, have a long maritime history. With more than three million people, Greece's capital, Athens, is the largest city in the region. In 2004, Cyprus, which has been uneasily divided for three decades into Turkish and Greek sections, joined Greece as a member of the European Union.

⇧ TRADITIONAL LIFE. Villagers walk down a cobbled street in Gusinje, a rural town in northeastern Montenegro. A place of rugged mountains, Montenegro is one of the countries that emerged from the former Yugoslavia.

⇩ LAZY DAYS. A cat stretches out along a whitewashed wall on the Greek island of Thira. The blue dome in the background is part of a Greek Orthodox church.

⇧ JOYFUL SOUNDS. Young boys playing traditional instruments participate in a wedding festival in Crnomelj, Slovenia. Engaged couples, dancers, and musicians celebrate for four days. Then couples take their vows in a mass ceremony—an old Slovene wedding custom. Slovenia sponsors these festivals to preserve tradition in a fast changing world.

← ANCIENT WARRIORS. Soldiers and horsemen from Thrace, an ancient territory in present-day Bulgaria and Greece, wore masks as they rode into battle. Often serving as paid fighters in other armies, the Thracians were allies of Troy in Homer's *Iliad*.

SLOVAKIA
UKRAINE
CARPATHIAN MTS.
AUSTRIA
Dniester

• Satu Mare
• Botoşani
• Baia Mare
• Suceava
HUNGARY
• Zalău
• Iaşi
TRANSYLVANIA
• Piatra
• Oradea
Neamţ
MOLDOVA
• Cluj-Napoca
• Târgu-Mureş
• Bacău
Maribor •
• Arad
ROMANIA
Prut
SLOVENIA
• Deva
• Alba Iulia
Ljubljana ⊛
Sava
⊛ Zagreb
Subotica •
• Timişoara
• Sibiu
• Braşov
Galaţi
Drava
• Zrenjanin
Transylvanian Alps
Brăila
CROATIA
• Rijeka
Novi
• Reşiţa
• Râmnicu
• Ploieşti
Buzău
Tulcea
Gulf of
Osijek •
Sad
Vâlcea
Venice
Danube
Iron Gate
• Piteşti
Pula •
Prijedor •
Doboj •
Sava
Šabac
Pančevo
Dam
Drobeta-
⊛ Bucharest
Constanţa
Banja Luka •
• Tuzla
⊛ Belgrade
• Smederevo
Turnu
BOSNIA AND
Zenica •
SERBIA
Severin
• Craiova
DINARIC
Danube
Zadar •
HERZEGOVINA
Sarajevo ⊛
• Kragujevac
• Ruse
Dobrich
Split •
Čačak •
• Kruševac
Pleven •
Shumen
• Varna
Mostar •
Kraljevo •
• Niš
Teteven
BULGARIA
ADRIATIC
ALPS
Leskovac •
Dryanovo •
BLACK
Priština
Tryavna •
Sliven
Burgas
Dubrovnik •
MONTENEGRO
• Peja
KOSOVO
Sofia ⊛
Stara Zagora
SEA
DALMATIA
Podgorica ⊛
• Prizren
BALKAN
ITALY
• Ferizaj
Plovdiv •
SEA
Shkodër •
BALKAN MOUNTAINS
RHODOPE MTS.
Tetovo •
⊛ Skopje
Durrës •
MACEDONIA
Bosporus
Tirana ⊛
PENINSULA
Elbasan •
• Bitola
Kavála •
ALBANIA
Thessaloníki •
Sea of
• Vlorë
Olympus
Marmara
9,570 ft
Halkidíki
Límnos
2,917 m
TURKEY
Strait of Otranto
Dardanelles
Corfu
• Lárissa
AEGEAN
IONIAN
Vólos •
Lesbos
ISLANDS
(Mitilíni)
IONIAN
GREECE
Chios
SEA
SEA
Sámos
• Pátra
Pireás •
Athens ⊛
Corinth •
⊛ Kallithéa
Ikaría
Olympia
PELOPONNÉSUS
CYCLADES
Náxos
• Sparta
DODECANESE
Gulf of Messinía
Thíra
Rhodes
(Santoríni)
Rhodes
SEA OF CRETE
MEDITERRANEAN
Iráklio •
Crete
SEA

Map Key

⊛ Country capital
••• City or town
····· Boundary

0 ——————— 100 miles
0 ——————— 100 kilometers
Azimuthal Equidistant Projection

See map page 93 for position

NORTHERN CYPRUS
(recognized only by Turkey)

CYPRUS ⊛ Lefkosía
• Lemesos

Same Scale as Main Map

REGION IN TURMOIL

Former Yugoslavia
Border (1991) ———

AUSTRIA
HUNGARY
SLOVENIA
CROATIA
ROMANIA
BOSNIA
AND
HERZEGOVINA
SERBIA
Adriatic Sea
ITALY
MONTENEGRO
KOSOVO
BULGARIA
ALBANIA
MACEDONIA
GREECE
TURKEY

Political and social change brought an end to the southern Slavic country of Yugoslavia. Seven new countries emerged, but peace has been fragile.

EUROPEAN RUSSIA

THE BASICS

STATS*

Area
6,592,850 sq mi (17,075,400 sq km)

Population
141,839,000

Predominant languages
Russian, minority languages

Predominant religions
Christianity (Russian Orthodox), Islam

GDP per capita
$15,200

Life expectancy
66 years

Literacy rate
99%

*Note: These figures are for all of Russia. For Asian Russia, see pages 116–117.

GEO WHIZ

St. Petersburg's many canals and hundreds of bridges have earned it the nickname Venice of the North.

The fertile Northern European Plain, which stretches west from the Urals, is home to most of Russia's population and industry, while most of its mineral resources lie east of the Urals in the Asian portion of the country.

Two of the world's most famous ballet companies are in Russia: the Kirov in St. Petersburg and the Bolshoi in Moscow.

Arkhangel'sk, founded in 1584, is Russia's oldest Arctic port. The rich timber resources that surround it and make up the bulk of its exports have been nicknamed "green gold."

The official residence of the President of Russia is inside a walled fortress known as the Kremlin in downtown Moscow. The site on which the Kremlin stands has been continuously occupied since 2000 B.C.

During the Soviet era (1920–1991), the city Nizhniy Novgorod was named Gorky after author Maxim Gorky. "Gorky" is a Russian word meaning "bitter."

Soviet dictator Josef Stalin used the GUM department store, located on Moscow's Red Square, to display propaganda posters and the body of his wife, who committed suicide in 1932.

⇧ CHECKMATE! Bystanders watch intently as one player prepares to make his move in this chess game in a park in St. Petersburg. In Russia, chess is a national pastime, popular with people from all walks of life.

Home to four-fifths of Russia's 142 million people, European Russia contains most of the world's largest country's agriculture and industry. Here also is Moscow, its capital and Europe's largest city. Far to the north, Murmansk provides a year-round seaport—a gift of the warming currents of the North Atlantic Drift. This large, funnel-shaped portion of Russia, which spans 1,600 miles (2,575 km) from the icy Arctic to the imposing Caucasus Mountains, is home to the Volga, Europe's longest river, and Mount El'brus (18,510 ft/5,642 m), its highest peak. The Caucasus together with the mineral-rich Urals form a natural boundary between Europe and Asia. Although parts of Azerbaijan and Georgia in the south and Kazakhstan in the east span the continental boundary, only Russia is counted as part of Europe. To read about Asian Russia, see pages 116–117.

⇨ CATHEDRAL ON THE SQUARE. The onion-dome-topped towers of St. Basil's are a key landmark on Moscow's Red Square. Built between 1555 and 1561 to commemorate successful military campaigns by Ivan the Terrible, the building is rich in Christian symbolism.

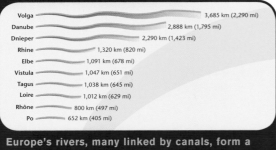

EUROPE'S GREAT RIVERS

Volga	3,685 km (2,290 mi)
Danube	2,888 km (1,795 mi)
Dnieper	2,290 km (1,423 mi)
Rhine	1,320 km (820 mi)
Elbe	1,091 km (678 mi)
Vistula	1,047 km (651 mi)
Tagus	1,038 km (645 mi)
Loire	1,012 km (629 mi)
Rhône	800 km (497 mi)
Po	652 km (405 mi)

Europe's rivers, many linked by canals, form a transportation network that connects its people and places to each other and the world beyond.

⇐ RUSSIAN DELICACY. Caviar, a distinctly Russian luxury food item, is the eggs (called roe) of sturgeon fish caught in the Caspian Sea. The eggs are aged in a salty brine before being packaged in cans (left) for shipment around the world.

ARCTIC OCEAN

NOVAYA ZEMLYA

KARA SEA

Yamal Peninsula

Gulf of Ob

NORWAY

BARENTS SEA

Kolguyev I.

Vorkuta

LAPLAND

Murmansk

ARCTIC CIRCLE

SWEDEN

Kola Peninsula

Usinsk

Kanin Peninsula

Pechora

See pages 116–117 for Asian part of Russia

FINLAND

Gulf of Bothnia

WHITE SEA

Pechora

Ukhta

Sosnogorsk

URAL

Severodvinsk

Arkhangel'sk

Northern Dvina

Zheleznodorozhnyy

SIBERIA

Petrozavodsk

Syktyvkar

Lake Ladoga

Lake Onega

Kotlas

Gulf of Finland

Sukhona

Bereezniki

R

MOUNTAINS

EUROPE-ASIA BOUNDARY

BALTIC SEA

St. Petersburg

ESTONIA

Lake Peipus

Cherepovets

Vologda

U

Perm'

Pskov

Velikiy Novgorod

Rybinsk Reservoir

Kirov

Izhevsk

Kama

LATVIA

Velikiye Luki

Rybinsk

Kostroma

S

KALININGRAD (RUSSIA)

Tver'

Yaroslavl'

Ivanovo

Nizhniy Novgorod

Kazan'

Naberezhnyye Chelny

Ufa

LITHUANIA

Volga

Moscow

Vladimir

R

Ural

POLAND

Smolensk

Oka

Cheboksary

Magnitogorsk

N

Kaluga

Ryazan'

Volga

Ul'yanovsk

Sterlitamak

BELARUS

Tula

Saransk

Tol'yatti

CENTRAL

Bryansk

Oka

Syzran'

Samara

Belaya

Orel

Lipetsk

Penza

Orenburg

Novotroitsk

RUSSIAN

Kursk

Tambov

Balakovo

Orsk

Voronezh

Saratov

Belgorod

Engels

UPLAND

Kamyshin

KAZAKHSTAN

UKRAINE

Don

Ural

MOLDOVA

Donets

Volgograd

Volzhskiy

Shakhty

CASPIAN DEPRESSION

Dnieper

Don

Volga

Rostov na Donu

Taganrog

Astrakhan'

SEA OF AZOV

Krasnodar

Stavropol'

CASPIAN SEA

Novorossiysk

Maykop

Pyatigorsk

BLACK SEA

El'brus 18,510 ft 5,642 m

Sochi

CHECHNYA

Groznyy

Makhachkala

CAUCASUS MOUNTAINS

Vladikavkaz

GEORGIA

TURKEY

ARMENIA

AZERBAIJAN

Map Key

⊛ Country capital

••• City or town

······ Boundary

0 — 200 miles
0 — 300 kilometers

Azimuthal Equidistant Projection

THE CONTINENT:
ASIA

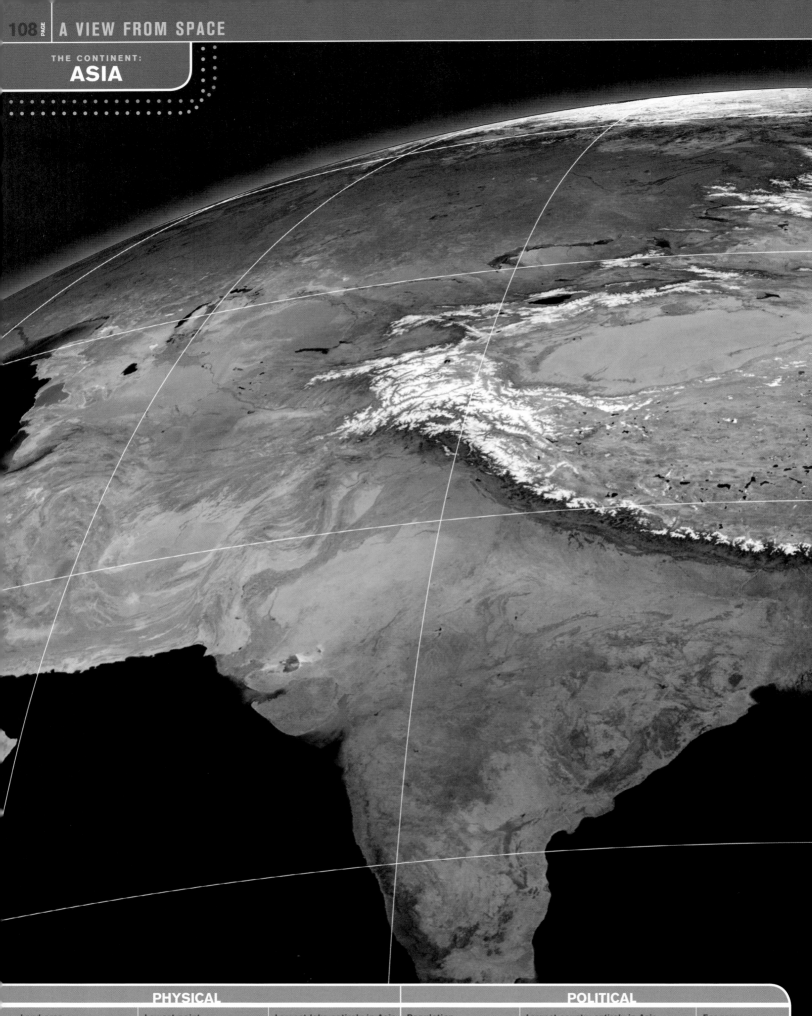

PHYSICAL

Land area 17,208,000 sq mi (44,570,000 sq km)	**Lowest point** Dead Sea, Israel-Jordan -1,380 ft (-421 m)	**Largest lake entirely in Asia** Lake Baikal 12,200 sq mi (31,500 sq km)
Highest point Mount Everest, China-Nepal 29,035 ft (8,850 m)	**Longest river** Yangtze (Chang), China 3,964 mi (6,380 km)	

POLITICAL

Population 4,117,435,000	**Largest country entirely in Asia** China 3,705,405 sq mi (9,596,960 sq km)	**Economy** Farming: rice, wheat
Largest metropolitan area Tokyo, Japan Pop. 36,094,000	**Most densely populated country** Singapore 19,000 people per sq mi (7,335 per sq km)	Industry: petroleum, electronics Services

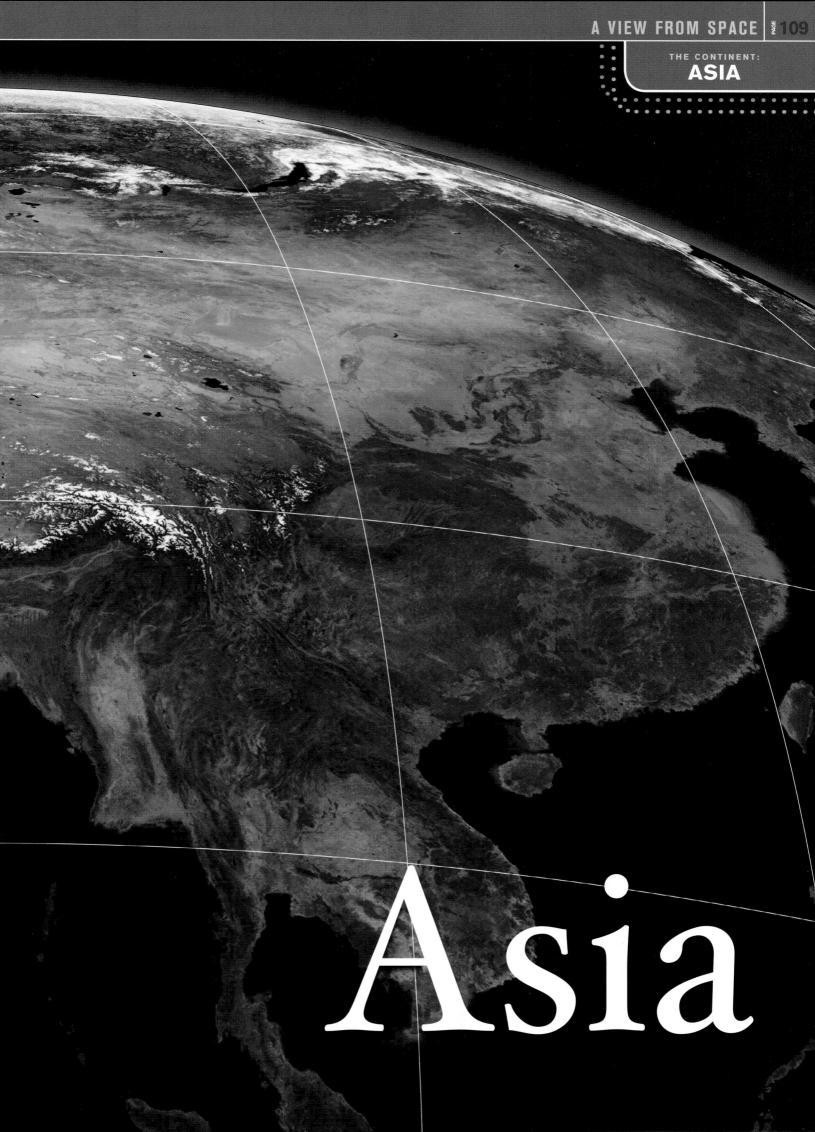

Asia

ASIA

Map Key
— Country boundary

1,000 miles
1,500 kilometers

A commonly accepted division
between Asia and Europe – here marked
by an orange line – is formed by the
Ural Mountains, Ural River, Caspian Sea,
Caucasus Mountains, and the Black Sea
with its outlets to the Aegean Sea,
the Bosporus, and the Dardanelles.

The People's Republic of China claims Taiwan
as its 23rd province. Taiwan maintains
that there are two political entities.

ARCTIC OCEAN

PACIFIC OCEAN

INDIAN OCEAN

EUROPE

AFRICA

AUSTRALIA

RUSSIA
SIBERIA

CHINA
DONGBEI
MONGOLIA
SINKIANG
TIBET
GOBI
ALTAY MOUNTAINS
KUNLUN SHAN
TIEN SHAN

KAZAKHSTAN
UZBEKISTAN
TURKMENISTAN
KYRGYZSTAN
TAJIKISTAN
AFGHANISTAN
PAKISTAN
IRAN
IRAQ
SYRIA
TURKEY
SAUDI ARABIA
YEMEN
OMAN
UNITED ARAB EMIRATES
QATAR
BAHRAIN
KUWAIT
JORDAN
ISRAEL
LEBANON
GEORGIA
ARMENIA
AZERBAIJAN

INDIA
NEPAL
BHUTAN
BANGLADESH
MYANMAR (BURMA)
SRI LANKA
MALDIVES
KASHMIR

JAPAN
NORTH KOREA
SOUTH KOREA
TAIWAN
PHILIPPINES
VIETNAM
LAOS
THAILAND
CAMBODIA
MALAYSIA
BRUNEI
SINGAPORE
INDONESIA

PACIFIC OCEAN

Two-Point Equidistant Projection

1,000 miles
1,500 kilometers

Asia
WORLD CHAMPION

From Turkey to the eastern tip of Russia, Asia sprawls across nearly 180 degrees of longitude—almost half the globe! It boasts the highest (the Himalaya) and lowest (the Dead Sea) places on Earth's surface. Then there are Asia's people—more than four billion of them. That's more people than live on all the other continents put together. Asia has both the most farmers and the most million-plus cities. The world's first civilization arose in Sumer, in what is now southern Iraq. Rich cultures also emerged along rivers in present-day India and China, strongly influencing the world ever since.

⇧ TASTY SNACK. This black and white giant panda, native to China, munches on a stalk of bamboo, the mainstay of its diet.

⇩ NEW VS. OLD. An Afghan woman, completely covered by a traditional burka, sits among young girls dressed in Western clothes in Kabul.

⇐ LUNAR NEW YEAR.
Young men carry a
writhing paper dragon
on poles in this Chinese
New Year's parade in Singapore.

⇐ NEON AVENUE.
Bright lights and
neon signs highlight
bustling Nanjing Lu,
Shanghai's main
shopping street.
With a population of
more than 15 million,
Shanghai is China's
largest city.

⇒ WINGED HUNTER.
A Kazakh falconer sits
astride his pony as he
releases his golden eagle to
pursue prey on the dry Mongolian steppe.

more about
ASIA

⇧ EASTERN BELIEF. From its origins in the foothills of the Himalaya, Buddhism has spread across much of eastern Asia. Statues of the Buddha, such as this one in Bangkok, Thailand, appear frequently in the landscape.

⇩ UP AND DOWN. Traditional dress and a modern motorized walkway create sharp contrast in this mall in Doha, Qatar.

⇩ A FINAL TOUCH. Silk kimono and perfectly applied makeup are part of the tradition of a *maiko*, or apprentice geisha, in Kyoto, Japan.

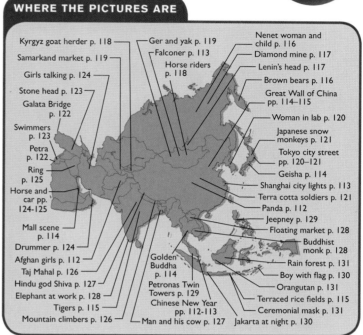

⇩ STONE BARRIER. Construction on China's Great Wall began in 220 B.C. as a defense against invasion from the north and continued until the A.D. 1600s. Extending in sections for almost 4,000 miles (6,436 km), the wall attracts tourists from around the world.

WHERE THE PICTURES ARE

Kyrgyz goat herder p. 118
Samarkand market p. 119
Girls talking p. 124
Stone head p. 123
Galata Bridge p. 122
Swimmers p. 123
Petra p. 122
Ring p. 125
Horse and car pp. 124-125
Mall scene p. 114
Drummer p. 124
Afghan girls p. 112
Taj Mahal p. 126
Hindu god Shiva p. 127
Elephant at work p. 128
Tigers p. 115
Mountain climbers p. 126

Ger and yak p. 119
Falconer p. 113
Horse riders p. 118

Golden Buddha p. 114
Petronas Twin Towers p. 129
Chinese New Year pp. 112-113
Man and his cow p. 127

Nenet woman and child p. 116
Diamond mine p. 117
Lenin's head p. 117
Brown bears p. 116
Great Wall of China pp. 114-115
Woman in lab p. 120
Japanese snow monkeys p. 121
Tokyo city street pp. 120-121
Geisha p. 114
Shanghai city lights p. 113
Terra cotta soldiers p. 121
Panda p. 112
Jeepney p. 129
Floating market p. 128
Buddhist monk p. 128
Rain forest p. 131
Boy with flag p. 130
Orangutan p. 131
Terraced rice fields p. 115
Ceremonial mask p. 131
Jakarta at night p. 130

⇩ MOUNTAIN STAIRWAY. Terraces cut into a steep mountainside create fields for rice on the island of Bali, in Indonesia. Rice is the staple grain crop in much of eastern Asia. In the foreground, a man nimbly climbs a palm tree to harvest coconuts.

⇧ MOTHER KNOWS BEST. A Bengal tiger gently moves her cub to a safe hiding place before stalking her prey in India's Bandhavgarh National Park. Tigers are an endangered species.

ASIAN RUSSIA

THE BASICS

STATS*

Area
6,592,850 sq mi (17,075,400 sq km)

Population
141,839,000

Predominant languages
Russian, minority languages

Predominant religions
Christianity (Russian Orthodox), Islam

GDP per capita
$15,200

Life expectancy
66 years

Literacy rate
99%

*These figures are for all of Russia. For European Russia, see pages 106–107.

GEO WHIZ

The name "Siberia" comes from the Turkic language and means "Sleeping Land."

 Trophy hunting, oil and gas exploration, and gold mining have reduced the brown bear population on the Kamchatka Peninsula from 20,000 during the Soviet era, when the peninsula was restricted to military use, to about 12,500.

A region of northern coniferous forest called taiga stretches across northern Russia as far west as Norway. It covers an area that is more than 11 times the size of Texas.

It takes at least six days to travel 6,000 miles (9,656 km) on the Trans-Siberian Railroad from Moscow to the Pacific port of Vladivostok. The trip crosses eight time zones.

Russia produces more natural gas than the next six countries combined. More than a quarter of the world's proven reserves are in Russia, mainly in Siberia, the Urals, and the region around the Volga River.

Lake Baikal, nicknamed Siberia's "blue eye," is home to 1,500 unique species of plants and animals, including the nerpa, the world's only freshwater seal.

The Chukchi, the largest group of native people in Siberia, take their name from a word that means "rich in reindeer." They share their name with their homeland, a peninsula that borders the Arctic and Pacific Oceans.

⇧ NOMADIC HERDERS. A Nenet woman and her grandson prepare to follow the family reindeer herd into northern Siberia for spring and summer grazing.

Forming more than half of gigantic Russia, this region stretches from the Ural Mountains east to the Pacific, and from the Arctic Ocean south to mountains and deserts along borders with Central Asia and China. Siberia, as this region is commonly known, has limited croplands but bountiful forests (the taiga) and rich mineral resources such as natural gas, oil, and gold. The Trans-Siberian Railroad, built between 1891 and 1905, opened up the region for settlement—but not too much. Only about one-sixth of Russia's population—fewer than 25 million people—lives in sprawling Siberia.

NORWAY
SWEDEN
FINLAND
BALTIC SEA
ESTONIA
RUSSIA
LATVIA
POLAND LITHUANIA
BELARUS

See page 107 for European part of Ru...

★ Moscow

UKRAINE

R

Nizhniy Tag...
Yekaterinbur...
Kamensk Ural...
Chelyabinsk
Magnitogorsk

Volga
BLACK SEA
EUROPE-ASIA BOUNDARY
Ural
Orsk

CAUCASUS MTS.
Caspian Depression
KAZ...
TURKEY
GEORGIA
ARMENIA
AZERBAIJAN
CASPIAN SEA

⇨ FISHING FOR A MEAL. A brown bear and her cubs hunt for fish in a river below the snow-laced slopes of a volcano on Russia's Kamchatka Peninsula. Part of the Pacific Ring of Fire, this peninsula in far eastern Russia has 29 active volcanoes.

← REVOLUTIONARY LEADER. Vladimir Ilyich Lenin, a founder of the Soviet Union, was honored with statues throughout the former Communist union and beyond. This one in Ulan Ude, in Siberia, is the largest still standing in Russia.

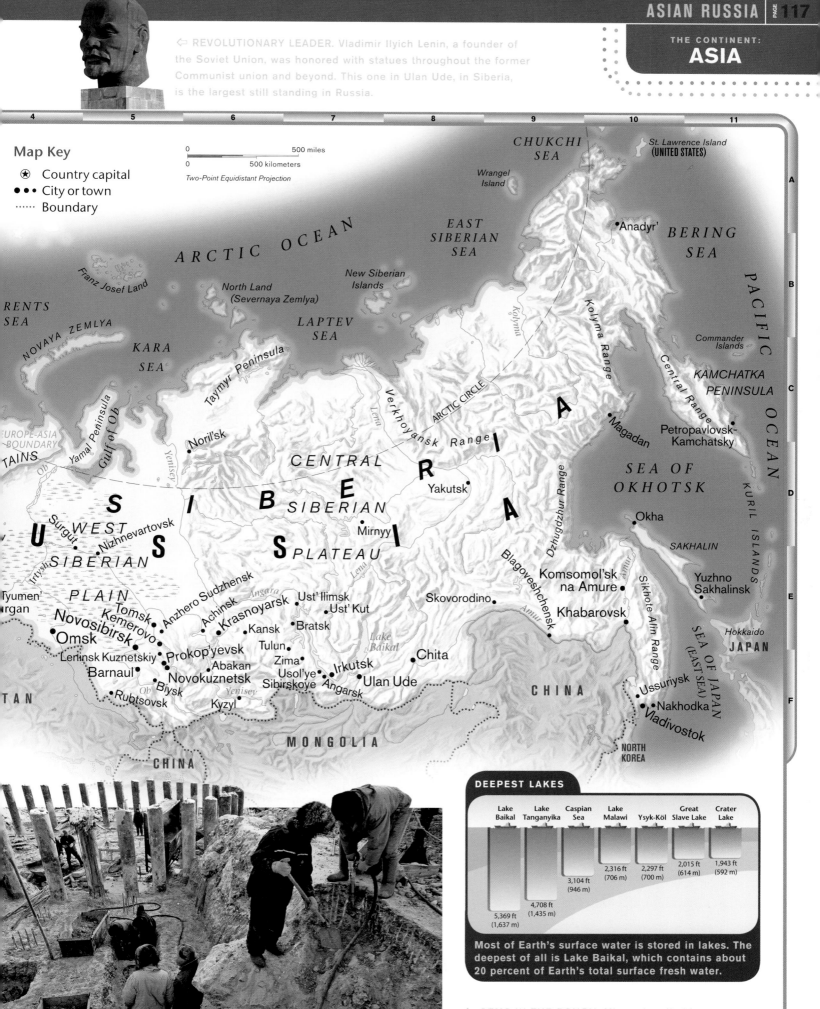

Map Key

- ★ Country capital
- ●● City or town
- ····· Boundary

0 ─── 500 miles
0 ─── 500 kilometers

Two-Point Equidistant Projection

CHUKCHI SEA

St. Lawrence Island (UNITED STATES)

Wrangel Island

ARCTIC OCEAN

EAST SIBERIAN SEA

•Anadyr' BERING SEA

Franz Josef Land

NOVAYA ZEMLYA

BARENTS SEA

North Land (Severnaya Zemlya)

New Siberian Islands

LAPTEV SEA

KARA SEA

Taymyr Peninsula

Kolyma

Kolyma Range

Commander Islands

KAMCHATKA PENINSULA

EUROPE-ASIA BOUNDARY

MOUNTAINS

Yamal Peninsula

Gulf of Ob

Noril'sk

Lena

Verkhoyansk Range

ARCTIC CIRCLE

CENTRAL SIBERIAN PLATEAU

Yakutsk•

Mirnyy•

Lena

Magadan•

Central Range

Petropavlovsk-Kamchatsky

SEA OF OKHOTSK

Okha•

SAKHALIN

Dzhugdzhur Range

KURIL ISLANDS

PACIFIC OCEAN

Ob

Yenisey

WEST SIBERIAN PLAIN

Surgut•

Nizhnevartovsk•

Irtysh

Tyumen'
rgan

Tomsk•

Novosibirsk•

Kemerovo•

Omsk•

Lerinsk Kuznetskiy•

Barnaul•

Anzhero Sudzhensk•

Achinsk•

Prokop'yevsk•

Abakan•

Biysk•

Ob

Angara

Krasnoyarsk•

Kansk•

Tulun•

Zima•

Novokuznetsk•

Usol'ye Sibirskoye•

Rubtsovsk•

Kyzyl•

Yenisey

Ust' Ilimsk•

Ust' Kut•

Bratsk•

Lake Baikal

Irkutsk•

Angarsk•

Ulan Ude•

Chita•

Skovorodino•

Blagoveshchensk•

Komsomol'sk na Amure•

Amur

Khabarovsk•

Sikhote Alin Range

SIBERIA

Komsomol'sk na Amure

Yuzhno Sakhalinsk•

SEA OF JAPAN (EAST SEA)

Hokkaido

JAPAN

Ussuriysk•

Nakhodka•

Vladivostok•

CHINA

MONGOLIA

CHINA

NORTH KOREA

DEEPEST LAKES

Lake Baikal	Lake Tanganyika	Caspian Sea	Lake Malawi	Ysyk-Köl	Great Slave Lake	Crater Lake
			2,316 ft (706 m)	2,297 ft (700 m)	2,015 ft (614 m)	1,943 ft (592 m)
		3,104 ft (946 m)				
	4,708 ft (1,435 m)					
5,369 ft (1,637 m)						

Most of Earth's surface water is stored in lakes. The deepest of all is Lake Baikal, which contains about 20 percent of Earth's total surface fresh water.

← GEMS IN THE ROUGH. Miners bundled in warm clothing cut through permafrost in the Mir diamond mine in northern Siberia. Although mined out and closed in 2004, it once produced two million carats a year.

THE BASICS

STATS

Largest country
**Kazakhstan 1,049,155 sq mi
(2,717,300 sq km)**

Smallest country
Tajikistan 55,251 sq mi (143,100 sq km)

Most populous country
Uzbekistan 27,562,000

Least populous country
Mongolia 2,708,000

Predominant languages
**Russian, Kazakh, Uzbek, Kyrgyz, Tajik,
Mongol, Turkmen**

Predominant religions
Islam, Christianity (Orthodox), Buddhism

Highest GDP per capita
Kazakhstan $11,400

Lowest GDP per capita
Tajikistan $1,800

Highest life expectancy
Uzbekistan 72 years

Highest literacy rate
**Kazakhstan, Tajikistan
100%**

GEO WHIZ

The main instrument of the steppes
in Kazakhstan is the dombra, a
long-necked lute with two strings.

Uzbekistan is among the top ten
gold-producing countries, and the
world's largest open-pit gold mine is at
Muruntau in the Qizilqum Desert some
250 miles (400 km) from Tashkent.

The world's only surviving breed of
wild horse, the *takh,* or Prezewalski,
was "discovered" in southwestern
Mongolia in the 1880s by Count
Prezewalski. The largest number—some 300—now live in zoos
around the world, but a select few
that have been reintroduced in the
wild graze on the steppe in Mongolia's
Hustai National Park.

Kazakhstan's Baikonur Cosmodrome,
site of most space flights launched by the
Soviet Union from the late 1950s to the
1980s, is the world's oldest space-launch
facility. It is still managed by the Russian
Federal Space Agency.

The Pamir and the Tian Shan are among
the mountain ranges that cover more
than 90 percent of Tajikistan.

⇨ SKILLED RIDERS.
Young people ride their
horses across the steppe
in Darhad Valley, a region
of nomadic herders in
northern Mongolia. From
the time of Genghis Khan's
13th-century armies,
Mongolians have been
known for their skill
on horseback.

CENTRAL ASIA

1   2

Mongolia and five *stans*—"homelands"—make up Central
Asia. Kazakhs, Turkmen, Uzbeks, Tajiks, and Kyrgyz
outnumber others in
their largely Muslim
countries. Russians
are still present in
each, a result of
decades of Soviet
efforts to con-
trol these lands.
Sparsely settled,
largely Buddhist
Mongolia consists

⇧ BEST FRIENDS. A boy carries
his goat in mountainous Kyrgyzstan
where almost half the land is used
for pasture and hay to support
herds of goats and sheep.

of valley grasslands and dry basins beneath
towering peaks. Kazakhstan's short-grass
steppes give way to deserts, arid plateaus, and
rugged mountains to the south. Irrigation provides
water for wheat, cotton, and fruit crops. Though far from
any ocean, this region possesses several inland seas, including
the salty Caspian. Beneath its floor lie huge oil deposits, both tapped
and undeveloped, which will add to the region's future importance.

⇐ HOME ON THE STEPPE. A ger, made of a wooden frame overlaid with felt, is the traditional Mongolian dwelling. The cowlike yak works as a pack animal and is a source of milk. Its waste is burned as fuel.

Map Key
⊛ Country capital
●●● City or town
⋯⋯ Boundary

0   500 miles
0   500 kilometers
Two-Point Equidistant Projection

EUROPE-ASIA
BOUNDARY

Qostanay
• Rŭdnyy
Petropavlovsk
mirtaū
Kökshetaū
Ekibastuz   Pavlodar
Astana ⊛   *Irtysh*
Ertis
Kasakh
STEPPES
Temirtaū   Semey
HSTAN
Qaraghandy
Uplands   Öskemen
KONUR
SMODROME

Qyzylorda
Lake
Balkhash

Taldyqorghan

Shymkent
Chirchiq Angren Taraz
Namangan Bishkek • Almaty
shkent   *Ysyk-köl*
A N   KYRGYZSTAN
zax   Andijon
• Osh
Khujand Farg'ona
         Qo'qon
TAJIKISTAN *Victory Peak*
amarqand   24,406 ft
• Dushanbe 7,439 m
Pamirs
+ *Communism Peak*
24,590 ft 7,495 m

STAN   PAKISTAN

RUSSIA

Yenisey

DARHAD
VALLEY ▪

Selenga   • Darhan
Ulaanbaatar ⊛
HUSTAI
NATIONAL PARK ▪

Hovd •
         Uliastay •   *Hangayn*
                       Mountains   MONGOLIA

A L T A Y M O U N T A I N S

T I A N   S H A N

C H I N A

Lake Baikal

• Choybalsan
Herlen

Mongolian
Saynshand •
Plateau

G O B I

Yellow

Ertix

⇨ WHERE BARGAINING IS AN ART. Two men haggle over the price of cherries in a bazaar in Samarkand, Uzbekistan. Located on the fabled Silk Road, the country relies on agriculture, especially cotton production, to support its economy.

VANISHING SEA

KAZAKHSTAN

Extent of Aral ──
Sea in 1965
Dry/Salt Lake ▒▒

*Aral
Sea*   *Syr Darya*

Amu Darya

UZBEKISTAN

The Aral Sea has lost more than 60 percent of its area due to water from feeder rivers being used to irrigate millions of acres of cotton and rice.

EAST ASIA

1   2   3

China takes up most of this region, with the Koreas and Japan lining the Pacific edge. With more than 1.3 billion people, China's population is unrivalled in size. Rich river valleys have nourished Chinese civilization for more than four millennia. The Tibetan Plateau, dry basins, and the hulking Himalaya border China's western regions. Rugged uplands limit living space in Japan and the Koreas. Japan's economic success—especially in technology and manufacturing—has made it a global powerhouse. South Korea has followed similar economic paths, while North Korea's dictator prefers to isolate his country. A gradual move to capitalism has led communist China near the top of the global marketplace.

⇦ HIGH TECH. This young South Korean woman works in a laboratory that makes microcircuits in a semiconductor plant in Seoul.

⇨ NIGHTLIGHTS. Tokyo's Shinjuku is both a shopping center and a theater district as well as the the city's busiest train station. It serves more than two million passengers daily.

THE BASICS

STATS

Largest country
China 3,705,405 sq mi (9,596,960 sq km)

Smallest country
South Korea 38,321 sq mi (99,250 sq km)

Most populous country
China 1,362,069,000

Least populous country
North Korea 22,665,000

Predominant languages
Standard Chinese or Mandarin, Japanese, Korean, local dialects

Predominant religions
Daoism, Buddhism, Shintoism, Christianity, Confucianism

Highest GDP per capita
Japan $32,600

Lowest GDP per capita
North Korea $1,800

Highest life expectancy
Japan 82 years

Highest literacy rate
Japan, North Korea 99%

GEO WHIZ

The Seikan Tunnel, the world's longest railroad tunnel, links Japan's two largest islands: Honshu and Hokkaido.

Roughly 900 square miles (2,300 sq km) of farmland in northern China are blown away by the wind each year. Huge dust plumes travel hundreds of miles to Beijing and other cities. The clouds are often so thick that they hide the sun, slow traffic, and close airports.

Each year on October 9, people in South Korea celebrate their alphabet, which was created in 1446 to increase literacy.

Construction of the Three Gorges Dam across the Yangtze River created a reservoir that caused more than a million people to have to find new homes.

Kim Il-sung, who ruled North Korea from its founding in 1948 to his death in 1994, is referred to in the country's constitution as the Eternal President. Both his birthday and the anniversary of his death are public holidays.

Only about 18 percent of Japan's land is suitable for people to live on. Most of the people choose to live in cities along the narrow coastal plain.

AUTO GIANTS

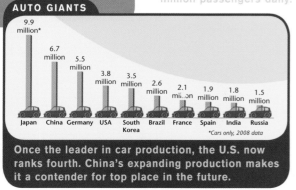

Japan	China	Germany	USA	South Korea	Brazil	France	Spain	India	Russia
9.9 million*	6.7 million	5.5 million	3.8 million	3.5 million	2.6 million	2.1 million	1.9 million	1.8 million	1.5 million

*Cars only, 2008 data

Once the leader in car production, the U.S. now ranks fourth. China's expanding production makes it a contender for top place in the future.

KAZAKHSTAN

KYRGYZSTAN

TAJIKISTAN

AFGHANISTAN

PAKISTAN

KASHMIR

Boundary claimed by India

Boundary claimed by China

RUSS

ALTA

Altay

Yining   Karamay
Changji

S H A N   Ürün

Aksu   Turpan Depression
-505 ft
-154 m

Tarim   Korla

Kashi

SINKIANG
TARIM BASIN
Taklimakan Desert

Hotan   ALTUN SHA

K U N L U N   S

PLATEAU OF TIBE

T I B E T

Mt. Everest
29,035 ft
8,850 m   Lha

Yarlung Za

BHUTAN

Ganges   A   Brahma

BANGLADESH

NEPAL

I N D I A

H   M   A   L   A   Y

⇐ STANDING GUARD. Lifelike terra cotta statues formed part of the "army" buried in 141 B.C. with Han Dynasty emperor Jing Di. The emperor believed the army, arranged in battle formation and facing enemy territory, would protect him after death.

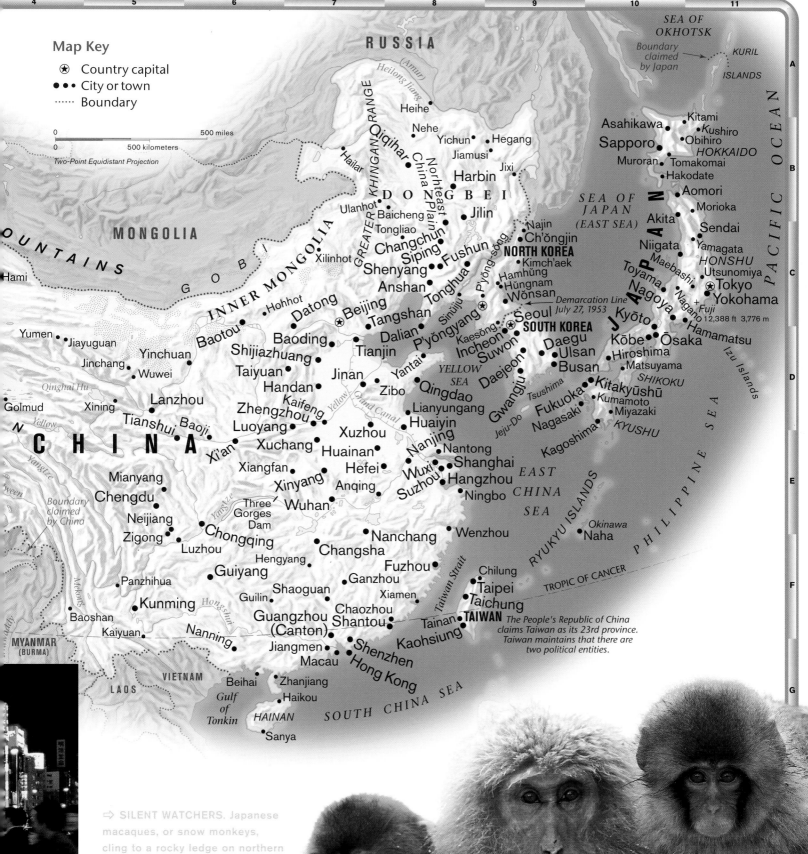

Map Key

⊛ Country capital
● ● ● City or town
······ Boundary

0 ——— 500 miles
0 ——— 500 kilometers
Two-Point Equidistant Projection

RUSSIA

SEA OF OKHOTSK
Boundary claimed by Japan → KURIL ISLANDS

Heilong Jiang (Amur)

Heihe
Nehe
Yichun
Hegang
Jiamusi
Hailar
Jixi
Harbin

GREATER KHINGAN RANGE
QIQIHAR
Qiqihar

Northeast China Plain

D O N G B E I

Kitami
Asahikawa
Kushiro
Sapporo
Obihiro
HOKKAIDO
Muroran
Tomakomai
Hakodate

MONGOLIA

Ulanhot
Baicheng
Jilin
Tongliao
Changchun
Siping
Fushun
Najin
Ch'ŏngjin

Xilinhot
Shenyang
Tonghua
Pyŏngsong
Anshan
Hamhŭng

Hami

INNER MONGOLIA

GOBI

Hohhot
Datong
Beijing
Tangshan
Sinŭiju
Pyŏngyang
Seoul
Kaesŏng
SOUTH KOREA
Incheon
Suwon

Baotou
Baoding
Dalian
Yantai

NORTH KOREA
Kimch'aek
Hŭngnam
Wŏnsan
Demarcation Line July 27, 1953

SEA OF JAPAN (EAST SEA)

Aomori
Morioka
Akita
Sendai
Niigata
Yamagata
Maebashi
HONSHU
Utsunomiya
Toyama
Nagano
Tokyo
Nagoya
Yokohama
+Fuji 12,388 ft 3,776 m
Kyōto
Kōbe
Ōsaka
Hamamatsu

Yumen
Jiayuguan
Yinchuan
Jinchang
Wuwei
Hohhot

Shijiazhuang
Taiyuan
Jinan
Zibo
Qingdao

Qinghai Hu

Golmud
Xining
Lanzhou
Handan
Kaifeng
Zhengzhou

N
CHINA

Yellow

Tianshui
Baoji
Luoyang
Xuzhou

Xi'an
Xuchang
Huainan
Huaiyin
Nanjing

Grand Canal

Lianyungang
Huaiyin
Nantong

YELLOW SEA

Daejeon
Gwangju
Ulsan
Busan
Daegu

Jeju-Do
Tsushima
Fukuoka
Kitakyūshū
SHIKOKU
Matsuyama

Hiroshima
Nagasaki
Kumamoto
Miyazaki
Kagoshima
KYUSHU

Izu Islands

Mianyang
Xiangfan
Hefei
Shanghai
Wuxi
Hangzhou
Ningbo

Boundary claimed by China

Chengdu
Xinyang
Anqing
Suzhou

Neijiang
Three Gorges Dam
Wuhan

Yangtze

EAST CHINA SEA

Zigong
Chongqing
Nanchang
Wenzhou

Luzhou
Changsha
Hengyang
Fuzhou

RYUKYU ISLANDS

Okinawa
Naha

PHILIPPINE SEA

Panzhihua
Guiyang
Ganzhou

Guilin
Shaoguan
Xiamen
Chaozhou

TROPIC OF CANCER

Kunming
Hongshui
Chilung
Taipei
Taichung

Baoshan
Guangzhou (Canton)
Shantou
Tainan
TAIWAN

Kaiyuan
Nanning
Kaohsiung

The People's Republic of China claims Taiwan as its 23rd province. Taiwan maintains that there are two political entities.

MYANMAR (BURMA)

Jiangmen
Shenzhen
Macau
Hong Kong

VIETNAM
LAOS

Beihai
Zhanjiang
Haikou

Gulf of Tonkin
HAINAN

SOUTH CHINA SEA

Sanya

Mekong

⇒ SILENT WATCHERS. Japanese macaques, or snow monkeys, cling to a rocky ledge on northern Honshu. Macaques live farther north than any other species of monkey. In winter they bathe in hot springs to stay warm. Japanese macaques are an endangered species.

THE BASICS

STATS

Largest country
Turkey 300,948 sq mi (779,452 sq km)

Smallest country
Lebanon 4,036 sq mi (10,452 sq km)

Most populous country
Turkey 74,816,000

Least populous country
Armenia 3,097,000

Predominant languages
Turkish, Arabic, Azeri, Hebrew, Armenian, Azerbaijani, Georgian, English, Kurdish

Predominant religions
Islam, Judaism, Christianity

Highest GDP per capita
Israel $28,400

Lowest GDP per capita
Georgia $4,500

Highest life expectancy
Israel 81 years

Highest literacy rate
**Georgia
99%**

GEO WHIZ

A 1.75-million-year-old skull recently discovered in the Republic of Georgia is forcing scientists to rethink humankind's first great migration.

Nagorno-Karabakh is an Armenian Christian enclave surrounded by Muslim Azerbaijan that has been the focus of bitter conflict between Armenians and Azeris for decades.

Mount Ararat, near Turkey's border with Iran and Armenia, is believed by some to be the resting place for the ark that—according to the Bible—Noah built to survive the great flood.

To capture Tyre, capital of ancient Phoenicia and now a port in Lebanon, Alexander the Great destroyed the mainland portion of the city, then used the rubble to build a causeway to the island fortress.

Israelis capture runoff from seasonal rains to support crops in the Negev, a desert region that extends across more than half their country.

EASTERN MEDITERRANEAN

This region forms a bridge between Europe and Asia, from the Caucasus Mountains to the desert lands of Jordan. Turkey, framed by the Black, Aegean, and Mediterranean Seas, leads the region in population and area. The historic and life-giving Tigris and Euphrates Rivers begin in Turkey and flow southeast through arid Syria and Iraq. Israel, Lebanon, and Syria share the Mediterranean shore. While Islam claims the majority of followers across these lands, Jewish, Christian, and other faiths are present. Indeed, the holiest places to Christians and Jews occupy Israeli soil in Jerusalem, adjacent to the third-holiest site for Muslims, a situation that continues to cause tension and conflict.

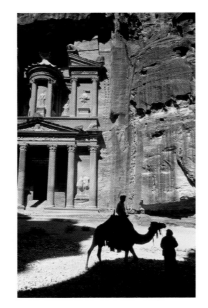

⇧ ANCIENT MYSTERY. A camel walks before El-Khazneh in Petra, a World Heritage site in Jordan. Carved out of the mountainside more than 2,500 years ago, Petra was the capital of the Nabateans.

WEST BANK & GAZA STRIP
Captured by Israel in the 1967 Six Day War, areas of the West Bank and Gaza have limited Palestinian self rule under a 1993 peace agreeme The future for these areas and four million Palestin is subject to Israeli-Palestinian negotiations.

BELOW SEA LEVEL

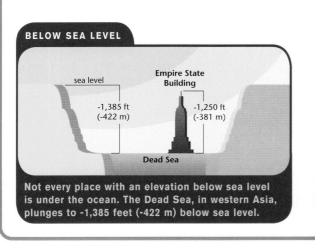

sea level

Empire State Building

-1,385 ft (-422 m)

-1,250 ft (-381 m)

Dead Sea

Not every place with an elevation below sea level is under the ocean. The Dead Sea, in western Asia, plunges to -1,385 feet (-422 m) below sea level.

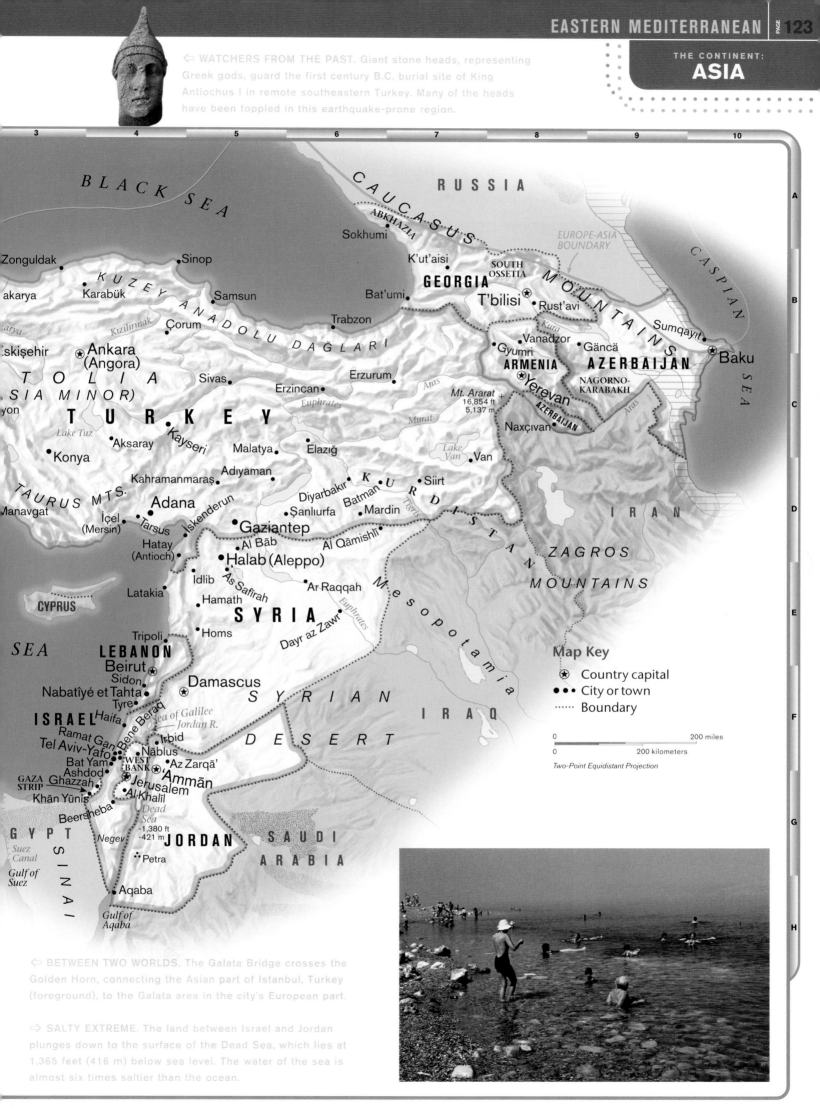

← WATCHERS FROM THE PAST. Giant stone heads, representing Greek gods, guard the first century B.C. burial site of King Antiochus I in remote southeastern Turkey. Many of the heads have been toppled in this earthquake-prone region.

BLACK SEA

RUSSIA

CAUCASUS MOUNTAINS

Zonguldak
Sinop
akarya
Karabük
Samsun
Çorum
KUZEY ANADOLU DAĞLARI
Kızılırmak
Trabzon
Sokhumi
ABKHAZIA
K'ut'aisi
Bat'umi
GEORGIA
SOUTH OSSETIA
T'bilisi
Rust'avi
EUROPE-ASIA BOUNDARY
Sumqayıt
CASPIAN SEA

İskişehir
Ankara
(Angora)
TOLIA
(SIA MINOR)
yon
TURKEY
Sivas
Erzurum
Erzincan
Euphrates
Murat
Aras
Mt. Ararat 16,854 ft 5,137 m
Gyumri
Vanadzor
Gäncä
ARMENIA
Yerevan
AZERBAIJAN
NAGORNO-KARABAKH
AZERBAIJAN
Baku

Lake Tuz
Aksaray
Kayseri
Konya
Malatya
Elazığ
Lake Van
Van
Naxçıvan
IRAN

TAURUS MTS.
Adana
Kahramanmaraş
Adıyaman
Diyarbakır
Batman
Siirt
KURDISTAN
ZAGROS MOUNTAINS

Manavgat
İçel
(Mersin)
Tarsus
İskenderun
Gaziantep
Şanlıurfa
Mardin
Tigris

Hatay
(Antioch)
Al Bāb
Al Qāmishlī
Halab (Aleppo)
Mesopotamia

CYPRUS
Latakia
Idlib
As Safirah
Ar Raqqah
Euphrates

Hamath
SYRIA
Homs
Dayr az Zawr

SEA
Tripoli
LEBANON
Beirut
Sidon
Nabatîyé et Tahta
Tyre
Damascus
SYRIAN
IRAQ

Map Key
⊛ Country capital
••• City or town
······ Boundary

0   200 miles
0   200 kilometers
Two-Point Equidistant Projection

ISRAEL
Haifa
Bene Beraq
Sea of Galilee
Jordan R.
Ramat Gan
Tel Aviv-Yafo
Bat Yam
Ashdod
GAZA STRIP
Ghazzah
Khān Yūnis
Beersheba
Nāblus
WEST BANK
Jerusalem
Al-Khalīl
Irbid
Az Zarqā'
Ammān
DESERT

EGYPT
SINAI
Suez Canal
Gulf of Suez
Negev
Dead Sea
-1,380 ft
-421 m
JORDAN
Petra
Aqaba
Gulf of Aqaba
SAUDI ARABIA

← BETWEEN TWO WORLDS. The Galata Bridge crosses the Golden Horn, connecting the Asian part of Istanbul, Turkey (foreground), to the Galata area in the city's European part.

⇨ SALTY EXTREME. The land between Israel and Jordan plunges down to the surface of the Dead Sea, which lies at 1,365 feet (416 m) below sea level. The water of the sea is almost six times saltier than the ocean.

THE BASICS

STATS

Largest country
Saudi Arabia 756,985 sq mi
(1,960,582 sq km)

Smallest country
Bahrain 277 sq mi (717 sq km)

Most populous country
Iran 73,244,000

Least populous country
Bahrain 1,217,000

Predominant languages
Arabic, Farsi (modern-day Persian),
Kurdish

Predominant religion
Islam

Highest GDP per capita
Qatar $121,400

Lowest GDP per capita
Yemen $2,500

Highest life expectancy
Kuwait 78 years

Highest literacy rate
Kuwait
93%

GEO WHIZ

Rub' al Khali (Empty Quarter),
the world's largest sand desert,
covers 225,000 square miles
(583,000 sq km), an area larger
than France.

More than 4,000 years ago, the Sumerians
built the first cities in the world on the plain
between the Tigris and Euphrates Rivers in
what is now Iraq.

The ancient Romans called Yemen
"Arabia Felix," meaning "Happy Arabia."

Five times a day, every day, Muslims
all over the world face the city of
Mecca, in Saudi Arabia, to pray.
Mecca is the birthplace of the prophet
Muhammad, the founder of Islam.

Iran drilled the first oil wells in the
region in 1908.

Causeways connect Bahrain Island—the
largest of the 35 islands that make up
the country of Bahrain—to two others
and to the mainland of Saudi Arabia.

SOUTHWEST ASIA

This region, made up largely of deserts and mountains, includes the countries of the Arabian Peninsula and those that border the Persian Gulf. Islam is the dominant religion in each, and the two holiest places for Muslims—Mecca and Medina—are here. Arabic is the principal language everywhere but Iran, where most people speak Farsi. While water has been the most important natural resource here for millennia, global attention has focused in recent decades on the region's oil wealth. With the majority of the world's reserves found here, oil has brought outside influences and military conflict. Long a cradle of civilization, Southwest Asia continues to hold the world's gaze.

⇧ GIRL TALK. Young Iranian girls get together at a film festival in Tehran. The scarves they are wearing are part of the Islamic dress code *hijab*, which says that women and girls must cover their heads and dress modestly.

⇧ HE'S GOT THE BEAT. This Omani drummer plays at a dance in the Arabian Sea port of Qurayyat. Though modernizing in many ways, Oman works hard to preserve its traditional culture.

⇨ DIFFERENT WORLDS. A contrast between horse and horsepower, this roadside meeting in Qatar also displays both traditional Arab and Western clothing styles. This Persian Gulf country preserves a rich history of Arabian horse breeding and continues to produce champions.

REGIONAL OIL RESERVES

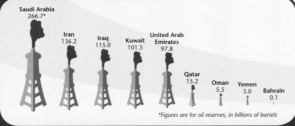

Saudi Arabia
266.7*

Iran
136.2

Iraq
115.0

Kuwait
101.5

United Arab
Emirates
97.8

Qatar
15.2

Oman
5.5

Yemen
3.0

Bahrain
0.1

*Figures are for oil reserves, in billions of barrels

Saudi Arabia leads the region and the world in oil reserves and production, but four other countries in Southwest Asia also rank near the top.

← LOST AND FOUND. Thousands of treasures dating from ancient Mesopotamia were destroyed, lost, or stolen during the invasion of Iraq in April 2003. This ring is among the few items recovered.

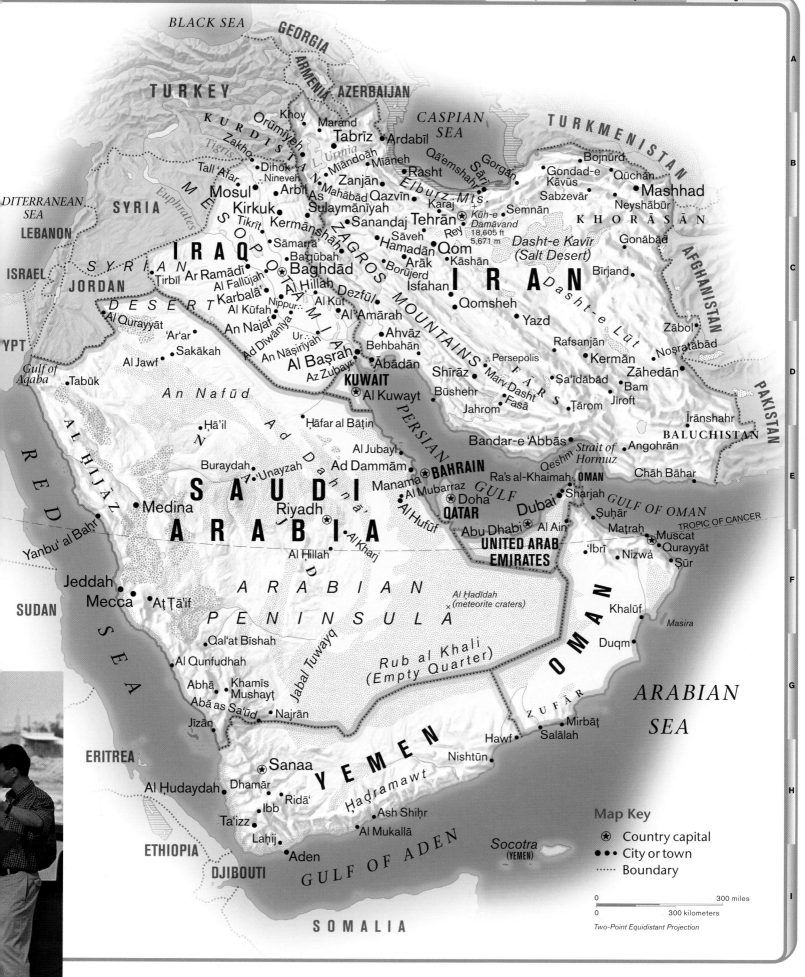

BLACK SEA

GEORGIA

ARMENIA

AZERBAIJAN

TURKEY

KURDISTAN

Khoy
Marand
Orūmīyeh
Tabrīz
Ardabīl

CASPIAN SEA

TURKMENISTAN

Zakhō
Tigris
Tall 'Afar
Dihōk
Nineveh
Miāndoāb
Mīāneh
Rasht
Gorgān
Qā'emshahr
Sārī
Bojnūrd
Gondad-e Kāvūs
Qūchān

SYRIA

Mosul
Arbīl
Zanjān
Qazvīn
Karaj
Semnān
Sabzevār
Neyshābūr
Mashhad

Kirkuk
As Sulaymānīyah
Mahābād
Kuh-e Damāvand 18,605 ft 5,671 m
Elburz Mts.
KHORĀSĀN

MEDITERRANEAN SEA

Euphrates

Tikrīt
Kermānshāh
Sanandaj
Tehrān
Rey
Dasht-e Kavīr (Salt Desert)
Gonābād

LEBANON

Sāmarrā'
Hamadān
Sāveh
Qom
Kāshān

ISRAEL

IRAQ
Baqūbah
Baghdad
Arāk
Isfahan
Birjand

JORDAN

MESOPOTAMIA
SYRIAN
Tirbīl
Ar Ramādī
Al Fallūjah
Karbalā'
Al Hillah
Nippur
Al Kūfah
Borūjerd
Qomsheh
IRAN
Dasht-e Lūt
Zābol

Al Qurayyāt
'Ar'ar
Sakākah
Al Jawf
DESERT
An Najaf
Ad Dīwānīya
Ur
An Nāşirīyah
Dezfūl
Al Kūt
Al 'Amārah
Ahvāz
Behbahān
Yazd
Rafsanjān
Persepolis
Kermān
Nosratābād

EGYPT

Gulf of Aqaba

Tabūk

An Nafūd

Al Başrah
Az Zubayr
Abādān
Shīrāz
Marv Dasht
FĀRS
Sa'īdābād
Zāhedan

ZAGROS MOUNTAINS

Būshehr
Jahrom
Fasā
Tārom
Bam
Jīroft

KUWAIT
Al Kuwayt

Īrānshahr

BALUCHISTAN

PAKISTAN

AFGHANISTAN

Medina

AL HIJĀZ

Hā'il

Hāfar al Bātin

PERSIAN

Bandar-e 'Abbās
Qeshm
Strait of Hormuz
Angohrān
Chāh Bāhar

SAUDI ARABIA

Buraydah
'Unayzah
Al Jubayl
Ad Dammām
BAHRAIN
Manama
Al Mubarraz
Ra's al-Khaimah
OMAN

Ad Dahnā'

RED SEA

Yanbu' al Bahr

Riyadh
Al Kharj
Al Hufūf
GULF
Doha
QATAR
Abu Dhabi
UNITED ARAB EMIRATES
Dubai
Al Ain
Sharjah
Suhār
Matrah
'Ibrī
Nizwā
Muscat
Qurayyāt
Şūr

Jeddah
Mecca
At Tā'if

Al Hillah

ARABIAN PENINSULA

GULF OF OMAN

TROPIC OF CANCER

SUDAN

Qal'at Bīshah
Jabal Tuwayq

Al Hadīdah (meteorite craters)

OMAN
Khalūf

ZUFĀR

ARABIAN SEA

Al Qunfudhah

Rub al Khali (Empty Quarter)

Masira
Duqm

Abhā
Khamīs Mushayt
Abā as Sa'ūd
Najrān
Jīzān

YEMEN

Mirbāt
Salālah

ERITREA

Sanaa
Dhamār
Ridā'
Hadramawt
Hawf
Nishtūn

Al Hudaydah
Ibb
Ash Shihr

Ta'izz
Al Mukallā

ETHIOPIA

Lahij
Aden

Socotra (YEMEN)

Map Key
⊛ Country capital
••• City or town
····· Boundary

DJIBOUTI

GULF OF ADEN

0   300 miles
0   300 kilometers

Two-Point Equidistant Projection

SOMALIA

SOUTH ASIA

This region is home to the world's highest peaks, and three of the world's storied rivers—the Indus, Ganges, and Brahmaputra—support the hundreds of millions of people who live here. India is at the center, with greater area than the other countries combined and three times their population. Born in India, Hinduism and Buddhism were spread to other places by traders, teachers, and priests. Muslims form the majority in Afghanistan, Pakistan, and Bangladesh, while there are large numbers of Buddhists in Bhutan, Nepal, Sri Lanka, and Myanmar.

Poverty and prosperity live side by side across the region, with streams of migrants flowing from rural areas to mushrooming cities.

⇧ TAJ MAHAL. In 1631 in Agra, India, the Mughal emperor Shah Jehan began construction of this magnificent marble memorial to his deceased wife.

THE BASICS

STATS

Largest country
India 1,269,221 sq mi (3,287,270 sq km)

Smallest country
Maldives 115 sq mi (298 sq km)

Most populous country
India 1,171,000,000

Least populous country
Maldives 315,000

Predominant languages
Hindi, English, Punjabi, Bangla, Dari, Burmese, Pashtu, Urdu, Sinhala, Nepali, Dzongkha

Predominant religions
Hindu, Islam, Buddhism

Highest GDP per capita
Bhutan $6,200

Lowest GDP per capita
Nepal, Myanmar $1,200

Highest life expectancy
Sri Lanka 75 years

Highest literacy rate
Maldives
96%

GEO WHIZ

India's rail system transports four billion passengers each year across nearly 38,000 miles (61,155 km) of track.

Bhutan, a Himalayan country known as Land of the Thunder Dragon, is the world's only Buddhist kingdom.

Nepal has the only national flag that is not a rectangle or a square. Its shape evokes the high Himalayan peaks that dominate its landscape (see page 168).

Mountains of the Hindu Kush in northeastern Afghanistan have been a source of rubies, silver, and other mineral wealth for thousands of years. The lapis lazuli that adorns the golden funeral mask of Egypt's King Tutankhamun was mined in this region.

Beaches along the southern and western coasts of Sri Lanka are nesting sites for five species of endangered sea turtle. The December 2004 tsunami wiped out several hatcheries, but the devastation has not kept the turtles from returning to their traditional nesting areas.

⇨ TOP OF THE WORLD. Climbers make their way through Nepal's treacherous Khumbu Icefall on their approach to Mount Everest.

TOP OF THE WORLD

Everest, *Asia*
Aconcagua, *South America*
McKinley, *North America*
Kilimanjaro, *Africa*
El'brus, *Europe*
Vinson Massif, *Antarctica*
Kosciusko, *Australia*

sea level   * For elevations, see page 174.

Each continent has its highest mountain, but Asia's Mount Everest, in the Himalaya on the Nepal-China border, towers above all others.

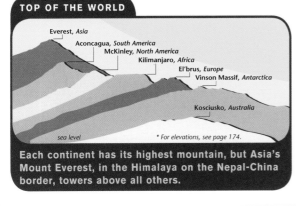

TUR
He
Hariru
AFGH
IRAN
Helmo
BALUCHIST
•Turbat
TROPIC OF CANCE
ARABIA
SEA

⟵ EASTERN BELIEF. The god Shiva is part of the Hindu trinity, which also includes the gods Brahma and Vishnu. With more than 900 million followers, Hinduism is the world's third largest religion, after Christianity and Islam.

Map Key

⊛ Country capital
●●● City or town
⋯⋯ Boundary

0 ——————— 300 miles
0 ——————— 300 kilometers
Two-Point Projection

UZBEKISTAN
TAJIKISTAN

Balkh
Feyzabad
Kondoz
-e Sharif
Baghlan
Bamian
HINDU KUSH
Charikar
Jalalabad
Ghazni
Kabul ⊛
Peshawar
Mardan
Gardiz
Khost
Kandahar
Kohat
Rawalpindi
Islamabad ⊛
Srinagar
Chakwal
Sialkot
Jammu
Jhelum
Pathankot
Dera Ismail Khan
Gujranwala
Amritsar
Simla
STAN
Quetta
Faisalabad
Lahore
Jalandhar
Chandigarh
Ludhiana
Multan
Khanewal
abad
Bahawalpur
Khanpur
karpur
Sadiqabad
Meerut
New Delhi ⊛
ana
Khairpur
GREAT INDIAN
DESERT
Delhi
Nawabshah
Jaipur
Agra
Tando Adam
Ajmer
Etawah
Hyderabad
Jodhpur
Gwalior
Pali
Udaipur
Kota
Karachi
Gandhinagar
Ahmadabad
Jamnagar
Rajkot
Vadodara
Indore
Bhuj
Bharuch
SATPURA RANGE
Bhopal
Jabalpur
rbandar
Bhavnagar
Nasik
Akola
Surat
Aurangabad
Amravati
Nagpur
Raipur
Kalyan
DECCAN
Chandrapur
Mumbai
(Bombay)
Pune
Sholapur
Vijayawada
Kolhapur
Hyderabad
PLATEAU
Belgaum
Rajahmundry
Hubli
Chitradurga
Bangalore
Mangalore
Mysore
Chittoor
Lakshadweep
(INDIA)
Kozhikode
(Calicut)
Salem
Puducherry (Pondicherry)
Coimbatore
Tiruchchirappalli
Kochi
(Cochin)
Dindigul
Madurai
Minicoy
(INDIA)
Rajapalaiyam
Jaffna
Thiruvananthapuram
(Trivandrum)
Nagercoil
Tuticorin
SRI LANKA
(CEYLON)
Cape Comorin
Colombo
Kandy

Boundary claimed by India
K2
(Godwin Austen)
28,250 ft
8,611 m
KARAKORAM Range
KUNLUN SHAN
KASHMIR
Indus
CHINA
Salween
TIBET
Boundary claimed by China
HIMALAYA
Brahmaputra
Mt. Everest
29,035 ft
8,850 m
Dehra Dun
Bareilly
Kathmandu ⊛
Thimphu ⊛
Budaun
Lucknow
NEPAL
Gangtok
BHUTAN
Dibrugarh
Mathura
Gorakhpur
Lalitpur
Shiliguri
Jorhat
Kanpur
Biratnagar
Purnia
Guwahati
Kohima
Fatehpur
Patna
Rangpur
Shillong
Imphal
Jhansi
Varanasi
(Benares)
Munger
BANGLADESH
Silchar
Allahabad
Mirzapur
Asansol
Dhaka ⊛
Agartala
Alzawl
Sagar
BANDHAVGARH
NAT. PARK
Ranchi
Haora
Khulna
Chittagong
Bilaspur
Raurkela
Kolkata
(Calcutta)
Monywa
Mandalay
LAOS
Jamshedpur
Mouths
of the Ganges
Bagan
Taunggyi
Sambalpur
Kharagpur
Sittwe
MYANMAR
Puri
Bhubaneshwar
Nay Pyi Taw ⊛
Pyinmana
Brahmapur
(administrative capital)
Vizianagaram
(BURMA)
Vishakhapatnam
Bago
Eluru
Kakinada
Pathein
Insein
Guntur
Machilipatnam
Yangon (Rangoon) ⊛
Ongole
BAY OF BENGAL
(legislative capital)
Mawlamyine
Nellore
THAILAND
Cuddapah
Dawei
Chennai (Madras)
ANDAMAN
ISLANDS
(INDIA)
Myeik
ANDAMAN
SEA
Isthmus
of Kra
Malay Peninsula
NICOBAR
ISLANDS
(INDIA)

INDIAN OCEAN

Male ⊛
MALDIVES

Maldive Islands

EQUATOR
Fua Mulaku
Gan

⟹ GOLDEN GRAIN. A man leads his cow past a field of rice south of Rangpur, Bangladesh. Rice is the staple food for 162 million Bangladeshis and provides employment for almost half the rural population.

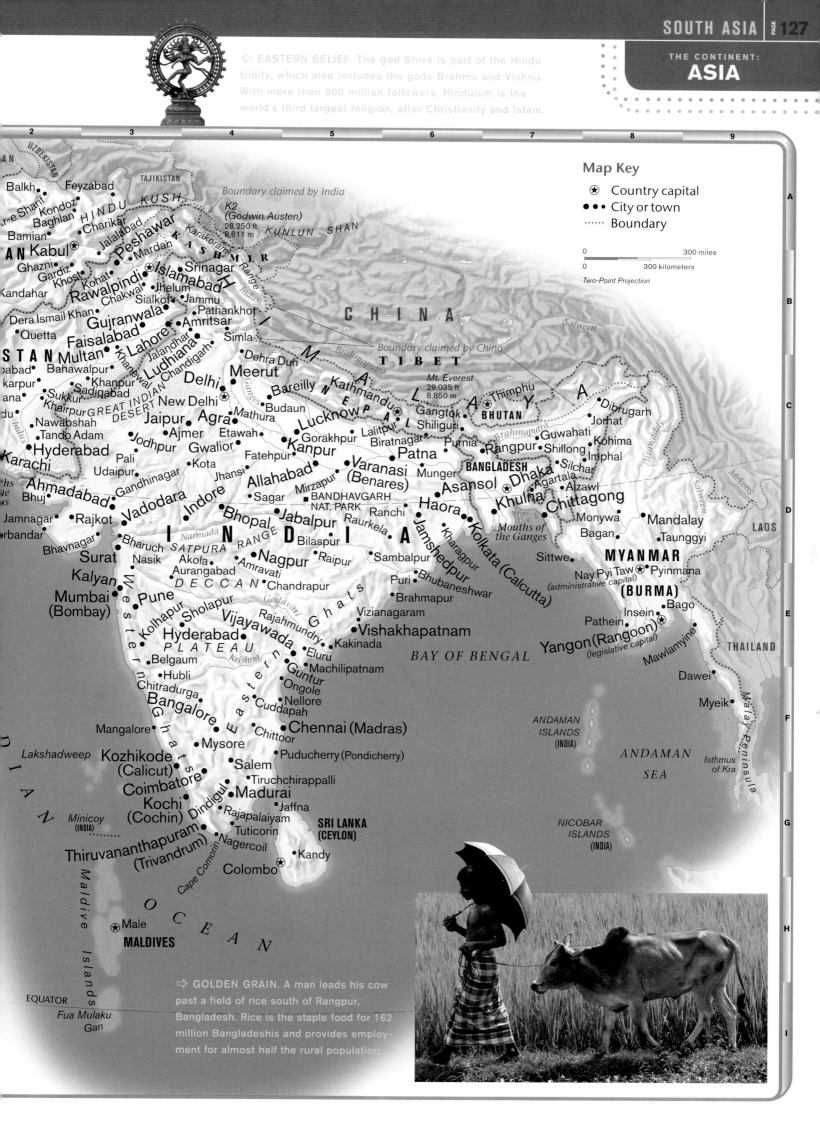

THE BASICS

STATS

Largest country
Thailand 198,115 sq mi (513,115 sq km)

Smallest country
Singapore 255 sq mi (660 sq km)

Most populous country
Philippines 92,227,000

Least populous country
Brunei 383,000

Predominant languages
Filipino (based on Tagalog), English, Vietnamese, Thai, Khmer, Lao, French, Malay, Bahasa Melayu, Mandarin

Predominant religions
Christianity, Buddhism, Islam

Highest GDP per capita
Singapore $50,300

Lowest GDP per capita
Cambodia $1,900

Highest life expectancy
Singapore 82 years

Highest literacy rate
Thailand, Singapore, Philippines 93%

GEO WHIZ

Cambodia's Mekong Fish Conservation Project pays fishermen more than the market price to release any giant fish they catch. Catfish as long as 10 feet (3 m) weigh up to 600 pounds (270 kg).

The Philippines has one of the highest rates of deforestation in the world. Based on the current rate of removal, studies estimate that the country's virgin forests are in danger of disappearing as soon as 2025.

The Cathedral of Notre Dame in Ho Chi Minh City, capital of predominantly Buddhist Vietnam, was built in the late 1800s during French colonial times, when the city was named Saigon.

The Plain of Jars, in northern Laos, takes its name from hundreds of huge stone urns spread across the ground. Archaeologists believe the jars were made by Bronze Age people who used them to hold the cremated remains of their dead.

"Thailand" means "Land of the Free." It is the only country in Southeast Asia that has never been ruled by a colonial power.

Singapore is a melting pot of cultures. Its name comes from the Sanskrit *Singha Pura* (Lion City), its national anthem is sung in Malay, and English is the lingua franca.

SOUTHEAST ASIA

The countries of Southeast Asia have long been influenced by neighboring giants India and China. The result is a dazzling mix of cultures, rich histories, terrible conflicts, and future promise. Cambodia's spectacular 12th-century Angkor temple complex provides a glimpse of former greatness. Colonial rule brought division and change, while struggles for independence took a heavy toll, as in Vietnam. Mainland countries are largely Buddhist, while peninsular Malaysia is mostly Muslim, and Christians dominate the Philippines. All but Laos have ocean access, with fisheries providing jobs and food for millions. Rivers like the Chao Phraya and the mighty Mekong provide transport and water-rich croplands dominated by rice growing. Tiny Singapore has gained global importance with its bustling port operations and high-tech focus.

⇧ SMILING BUDDHA. A Buddhist monk admires a sculpture on a temple wall near Siem Reap, Cambodia. Built between A.D. 800 and 1200 by the Khmer, the Angkor complex includes Buddhist and Hindu temples.

⇧ WILLING WORKER. Smaller and more easily tamed than the African variety, Asian elephants have been a part of the workforce for centuries. They are found from India to Indonesia.

⇨ FLOATING MARKET. This market scene in Laos is typical of much of Southeast Asia. People in small boats move about selling or trading goods and produce.

⇐ FLASHY RIDE. Colorful Philippine taxis, called jeepneys, are a common sight on the streets of Manila. Originally rebuilt WWII jeeps, these wildly decorated vehicles offer inexpensive, but crowded, transportation.

CHINA

TROPIC OF CANCER

Map Key

⍟ Country capital
●●● City or town
······ Boundary

0 ———————— 400 miles
0 ———————— 400 kilometers
Two-Point Equidistant Projection

MYANMAR (BURMA)

Louangphrabang

Thai Nguyen

Hanoi

Cam Pha

Nam Dinh

Hong Gai

Haiphong

Chiang Mai

LAOS

Vientiane

Vinh

Gulf of Tonkin

Hainan

THAILAND

Udon Thani

Khon Kaen

Savannakhét

Hue

Nakhon Sawan

Ratchasima

Nakhon Ratchasima

Ubon Ratchathani

Da Nang

Nonthaburi

Saraburi

Chao Phraya

Dangrek Range

VIETNAM

Bangkok

Samut Prakhan

Chon Buri

Siem Reap

Tonle Sap

Qui Nhon

Rayong

Battambang

CAMBODIA

Buon Me Thuot

Nha Trang

Isthmus of Kra

Gulf of Thailand

Phnom Penh

Da Lat

Cam Ranh

Surat Thani

Long Xuyen

Bien Hoa

Ho Chi Minh City (Saigon)

Nakhon Si Thammarat

Rach Gia

Can Tho

My Tho

Vung Tau

Songkhla

Bac Lieu

Hat Yai

Alor Setar

Sungai Petani

George Town

Taiping

MALAY PENINSULA

Kota Baharu

Ipoh

Kuala Terengganu

Kuala Lumpur

Kelang

Kuantan

MALAYSIA

Seremban

Malacca

Johor Baharu

Natuna Islands

Anambas Islands

Strait of Malacca

SINGAPORE

Kuching

Sibu

SARAWAK

EQUATOR

BORNEO

SUMATRA

INDONESIA

GREATER SUNDA ISLANDS

SOUTH CHINA SEA

Batan Islands

Babuyan Islands

Laoag

LUZON

Baguio

Dagupan

Tarlac

Cabanatuan

Angeles

Quezon City

Olongapo

Manila

San Pablo

Batangas

Lucena

Naga

Lipa

Legazpi

Mindoro

Calbayog

Roxas

Ormoc

Samar

Panay

Cadiz

Tacloban

Iloilo

Cebu

Leyte

Bacolod

Cebu

San Carlos

Bohol

Surigao

PALAWAN

Negros

Butuan

Puerto Princesa

Cagayan de Oro

Gingoog

SULU SEA

Pagadian

MINDANAO

Iligan

Davao

Kota Kinabalu

Zamboanga

Cotabato

SABAH

Sandakan

General Santos

Bandar Seri Begawan

BRUNEI

Tawau

Sulu Archipelago

CELEBES SEA

PHILIPPINES

PHILIPPINE SEA

⇓ REACH FOR THE SKY. The Petronas Twin Towers dominate the skyline of Kuala Lumpur, Malaysia's capital city.

DUELING SKYSCRAPERS

2,717 ft (828 m)
Burj Khalifa (Dubai)

1,667 ft (508 m)
Taipei 101 (Taipei)

1,614 ft (492 m)
Shanghai World Financial Center (Shanghai)

1,483 ft (452 m)
Petronas Towers (Kuala Lumpur)

Four of the world's tallest buildings are in Asia. The 2,717-foot (828-m) Burj Khalifa, in the United Arab Emirates, was completed in 2008.

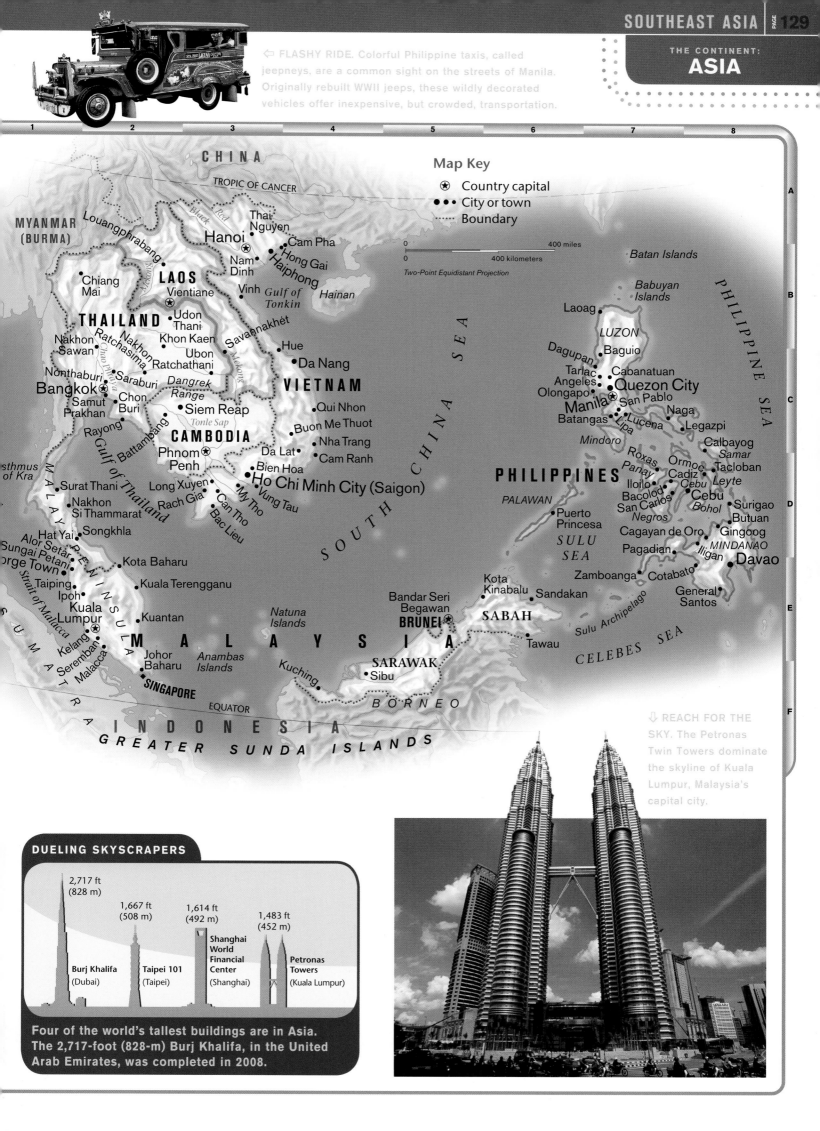

THE BASICS

STATS

Largest country
Indonesia 742,308 sq mi (1,922,570 sq km)

Smallest country
Timor-Leste 5,640 sq mi (14,609 sq km)

Most populous country
Indonesia 243,306,000

Least populous country
Timor-Leste 1,134,000

Predominant languages
Indonesian, English, Dutch, Javanese, Tetum, Portuguese

Predominant religions
Islam, Christianity

Highest GDP per capita
Indonesia $4,000

Lowest GDP per capita
Timor-Leste $2,400

Highest life expectancy
Indonesia 71 years

Highest literacy rate
Indonesia
90%

GEO WHIZ

Two species of sharks that use their fins to "walk" on coral reefs were discovered off the northwestern coast of Indonesia's Papua province in 2006. Scientists believe they might be similar to the first vertebrates that moved from sea to land.

In an effort to reduce crowding on Java, the government adopted a program of relocating landless people to more remote islands, a policy that has created tensions and that helped lead to Timor-Leste's independence in 2002.

With a length of 10 feet (3 m) and weighing more than 300 pounds (135 kg), the Komodo dragon is Earth's heaviest lizard. This meat eater lives only on Indonesia's Lesser Sunda Islands where it eats all types of prey—sometimes people!

When seen from the air, Timor Island resembles a crocodile. According to local legend, a crocodile turned itself into the island as a way of saying thank you to a boy who saved its life.

In December 2004 an earthquake off the coast of Sumatra, measuring 9.1 on the Richter scale, triggered a massive tsunami that killed hundreds of thousands of people and left millions homeless in countries around the Indian Ocean, from Indonesia to Africa's east coast.

⇨ CITY ON THE MOVE. Skyscrapers and a busy freeway are just one face of Jakarta, Indonesia. In this city of almost 10 million people—national capital and center of trade and industry—the modern and traditional, the rich and poor, live side by side. Just like Indonesia as a whole, the city has a very diverse population.

INDONESIA & TIMOR-LESTE

Stretching more than 2,200 miles (3,520 km) from Sumatra to New Guinea, Indonesia is the world's largest island nation and the fourth most populous country. Most of its 243 million people live on the volcanically active island of Java. Indonesia shares rainforested Borneo with Malaysia and Brunei. Most Indonesians are of Malay ethnicity, though there are large numbers of Melanesians, Chinese, and East Indians. Arab traders brought Islam to the islands in the 13th century, and today six of seven Indonesians are Muslim. Timor-Leste gained independence from Indonesia in 2002. It and the Philippines are Asia's only predominantly Catholic countries.

⇧ NEWLY INDEPENDENT. A young boy smiles broadly as he waves Timor-Leste's flag in Dili, the capital city. The country is also known as East Timor.

⇐ SPIRIT WORLD. Hand-carved masks, such as this one from Bali, Indonesia, were probably first created for traditional dance and storytelling rituals. Later, they incorporated Hindu and Islamic beliefs as well.

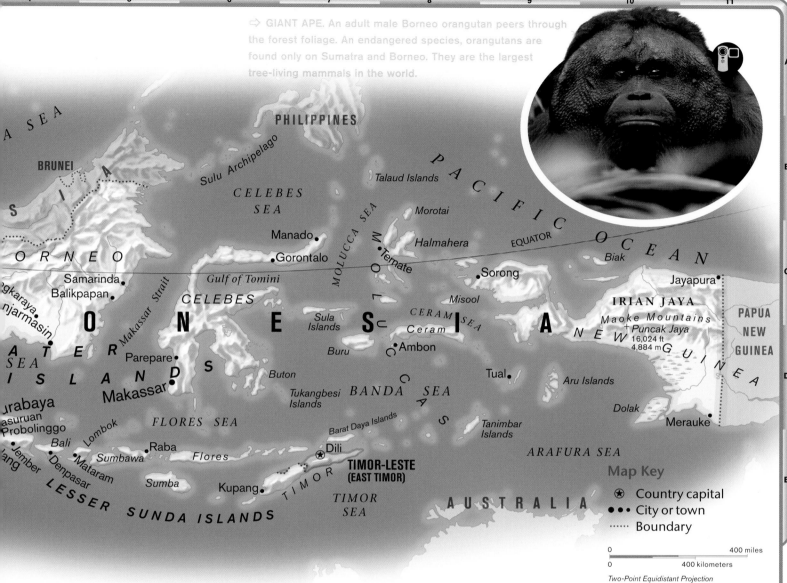

⇒ GIANT APE. An adult male Borneo orangutan peers through the forest foliage. An endangered species, orangutans are found only on Sumatra and Borneo. They are the largest tree-living mammals in the world.

Map Key
- ⊛ Country capital
- ••• City or town
- ····· Boundary

0 — 400 miles
0 — 400 kilometers
Two-Point Equidistant Projection

FOLLOWERS OF ISLAM

Country	Millions
Indonesia	202.9*
Pakistan	174.1
India	160.9
Bangladesh	145.3
Egypt	78.5
Nigeria	78.1
Iran	73.8
Turkey	73.6
Algeria	34.2
Morocco	32.0

*Figures are in millions, 2009

Islam's origins trace to southwestern Asia, but the religion has spread around the world. The country with the largest Muslim population is Indonesia.

⇒ GENETIC STOREHOUSE. About 75 percent of Indonesia's Kalimantan Province in eastern Borneo remains covered in rain forest that is home to 221 different types of mammals and 450 different species of birds. The forest and its inhabitants are at risk due to widespread logging and mining.

THE CONTINENT:
AFRICA

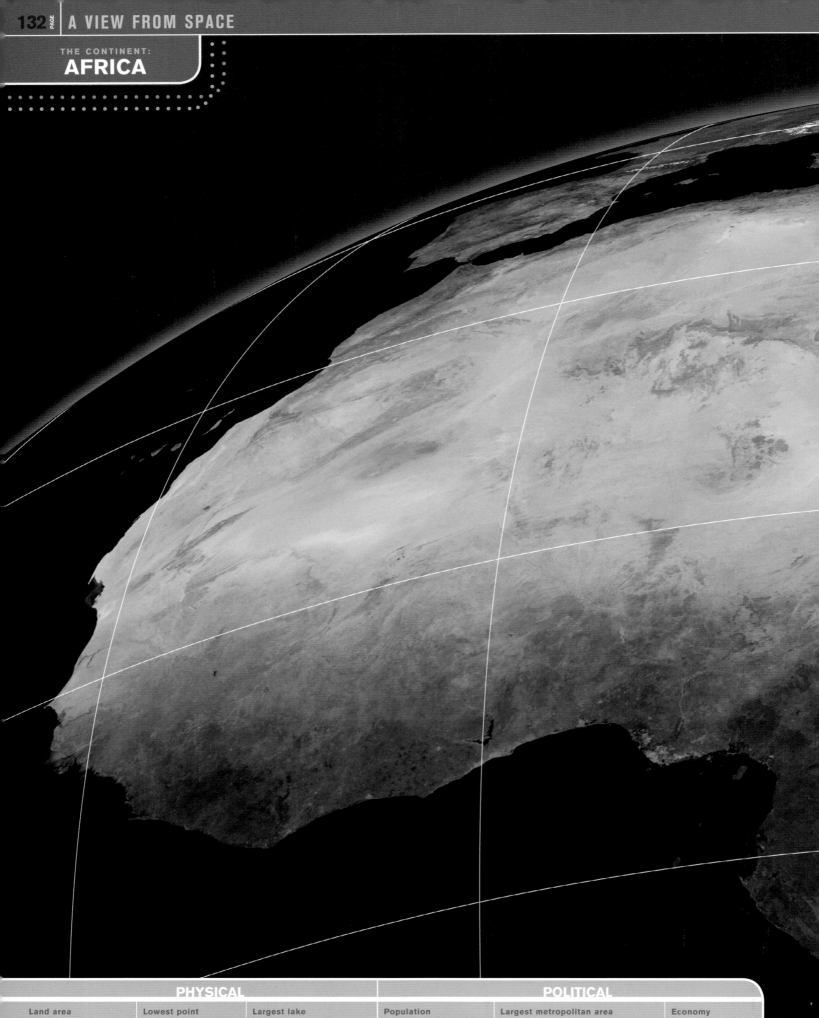

PHYSICAL

Land area	Lowest point	Largest lake
11,608,000 sq mi (30,065,000 sq km)	Lake Assal, Djibouti -512 ft (-156 m)	Victoria 26,800 sq mi (69,500 sq km)
Highest point Kilimanjaro, Tanzania 19,340 ft (5,895 m)	**Longest river** Nile 4,241 mi (6,825 km)	

POLITICAL

Population	Largest metropolitan area	Economy
998,705,000	Cairo, Egypt Pop. 12,503,000	Farming: fruit, grains
Largest country Sudan 967,500 sq mi (2,505,813 sq km)	**Most densely populated country** Mauritius 1,620 people per sq mi (625 per sq km)	Industry: chemicals, mining, cement Services

Africa

AFRICA

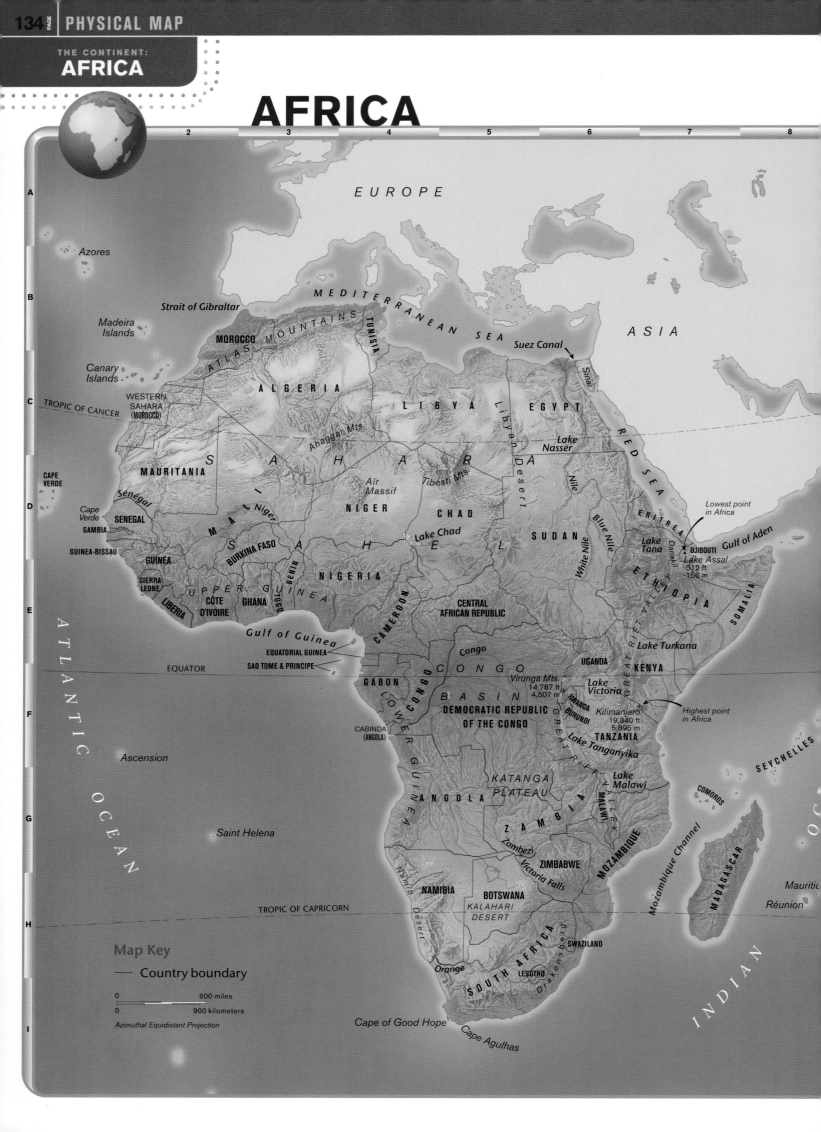

EUROPE

ASIA

MEDITERRANEAN SEA

Azores

Strait of Gibraltar

*Madeira
Islands*

MOROCCO

TUNISIA

ATLAS MOUNTAINS

Suez Canal

Sinai

*Canary
Islands*

ALGERIA

LIBYA

EGYPT

TROPIC OF CANCER

WESTERN
SAHARA
(MOROCCO)

Ahaggar Mts.

Libyan Desert

*Lake
Nasser*

RED SEA

**CAPE
VERDE**

MAURITANIA

S A H A R A

*Aïr
Massif*

Tibesti Mts.

Nile

*Lowest point
in Africa*

Sénégal

*Cape
Verde*

SENEGAL

MALI

Niger

NIGER

CHAD

Lake Chad

SUDAN

White Nile

Blue Nile

*Lake
Tana*

Danakil

DJIBOUTI

ERITREA

Gulf of Aden

*Lake Assal
-512 ft
-156 m*

GAMBIA

GUINEA-BISSAU

GUINEA

BURKINA FASO

S A H E L

NIGERIA

**CENTRAL
AFRICAN REPUBLIC**

ETHIOPIA

SOMALIA

**SIERRA
LEONE**

BENIN

LIBERIA

**CÔTE
D'IVOIRE**

GHANA

TOGO

UPPER GUINEA

CAMEROON

Congo

UGANDA

KENYA

Lake Turkana

Gulf of Guinea

EQUATOR

EQUATORIAL GUINEA

SAO TOME & PRINCIPE

C O N G O

*Virunga Mts.
14,787 ft
4,507 m*

*Lake
Victoria*

GREAT RIFT VALLEY

GABON

B A S I N

RWANDA

BURUNDI

*Highest point
in Africa*

LOWER GUINEA

CONGO

**DEMOCRATIC REPUBLIC
OF THE CONGO**

*Kilimanjaro
19,340 ft
5,895 m*

**CABINDA
(ANGOLA)**

GREAT RIFT VALLEY

TANZANIA

Lake Tanganyika

SEYCHELLES

Ascension

ANGOLA

*KATANGA
PLATEAU*

*Lake
Malawi*

MALAWI

COMOROS

ATLANTIC
OCEAN

Saint Helena

ZAMBIA

Zambezi

MOZAMBIQUE

Mozambique Channel

MADAGASCAR

INDIAN OCEAN

ZIMBABWE

Victoria Falls

Mauritius

Réunion

Namib Desert

NAMIBIA

BOTSWANA

*KALAHARI
DESERT*

TROPIC OF CAPRICORN

Orange

SOUTH AFRICA

SWAZILAND

LESOTHO

Drakensberg

Cape of Good Hope

Cape Agulhas

Map Key

—— Country boundary

| 0 | 600 miles |
| 0 | 900 kilometers |

Azimuthal Equidistant Projection

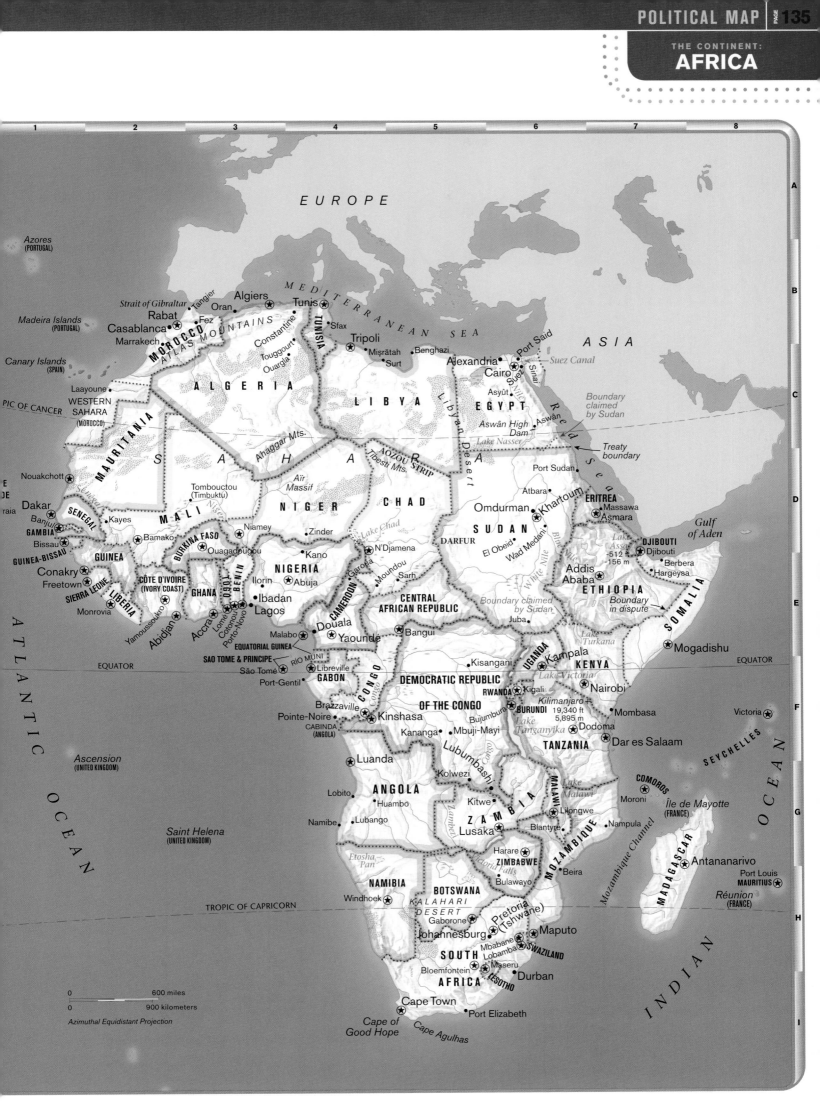

EUROPE

Azores
(PORTUGAL)

Madeira Islands
(PORTUGAL)

Canary Islands
(SPAIN)

MEDITERRANEAN SEA

ASIA

Strait of Gibraltar
Tangier
Oran · Algiers · Tunis
Rabat · Fez · TUNISIA · Sfax
Casablanca · MOROCCO · Constantine · Tripoli
Marrakech · ATLAS MOUNTAINS · Touggourt · Mişrātah · Benghazi
Laayoune · Ouargla · Surt
WESTERN · ALGERIA · LIBYA
SAHARA
(MOROCCO)
Port Said
Alexandria · Suez Canal
Cairo · Suez
Asyût · Sinai

TROPIC OF CANCER
MAURITANIA · S A H A R A · Ahaggar Mts. · Aozou Strip · EGYPT
Aïr · Tibesti Mts. · Aswân High Dam · Aswân
Nouakchott · Massif · NIGER · CHAD · Lake Nasser
Dakar · Tombouctou (Timbuktu) · Libyan Desert · Boundary claimed by Sudan
Banjul · SENEGAL · Kayes · MALI · Niamey · Zinder · Port Sudan · Treaty boundary
GAMBIA · Bamako · Lake Chad · N'Djamena · Atbara · ERITREA
Bissau · BURKINA FASO · Kano · SUDAN · Omdurman · Khartoum · Massawa
GUINEA-BISSAU · Ouagadougou · NIGERIA · Maroua · DARFUR · El Obeid · Wad Medani · Asmara
Conakry · GUINEA · Abuja · Moundou · Sarh · White Nile · Lake Assal · DJIBOUTI
Freetown · CÔTE D'IVOIRE · Ilorin · Blue Nile · -512 ft · Djibouti
SIERRA LEONE · (IVORY COAST) · GHANA · TOGO · BENIN · Ibadan · CAMEROON · CENTRAL · Juba · -156 m · Berbera
Monrovia · LIBERIA · Accra · Lagos · AFRICAN REPUBLIC · Boundary claimed · Addis · Hargeysa
LIBERIA · Yamoussoukro · Lomé · Cotonou · Malabo · Douala · Bangui · by Sudan · Ababa · ETHIOPIA
Abidjan · Porto-Novo · Yaoundé · Boundary · SOMALIA
EQUATORIAL GUINEA · in dispute
SAO TOME & PRINCIPE · RIO MUNI · Lake Turkana
São Tomé · Libreville · CONGO · DEMOCRATIC REPUBLIC · UGANDA · Kampala · KENYA · Mogadishu
EQUATOR · Port-Gentil · GABON · Kisangani · Kampala · KENYA
OF THE CONGO · RWANDA · Kigali · Lake Victoria · Nairobi
Brazzaville · Kinshasa · BURUNDI · Kilimanjaro · Mombasa · Victoria
Pointe-Noire · Bujumbura · 19,340 ft · SEYCHELLES
CABINDA · Kananga · Mbuji-Mayi · 5,895 m · Dodoma · Dar es Salaam
(ANGOLA) · Lake Tanganyika · TANZANIA
Luanda · Lubumbashi · Île de Mayotte
Ascension · Kolwezi · MALAWI · COMOROS · (FRANCE)
(UNITED KINGDOM) · Moroni
Lobito · ANGOLA · Kitwe · Lake Malawi · Nampula
Namibe · Lubango · ZAMBIA · Lilongwe
Saint Helena · Blantyre · Mozambique Channel
(UNITED KINGDOM) · Lusaka · MOZAMBIQUE
Etosha · Harare · Beira · MADAGASCAR · Antananarivo
Pan · ZIMBABWE · Port Louis
Victoria Falls · Bulawayo · MAURITIUS
TROPIC OF CAPRICORN · NAMIBIA · BOTSWANA · Réunion
Windhoek · KALAHARI · Pretoria (Tshwane) · (FRANCE)
DESERT · Gaborone · Maputo
Johannesburg · Mbabane · SWAZILAND
SOUTH · Lobamba
Bloemfontein · Maseru · Durban
AFRICA · LESOTHO

ATLANTIC OCEAN

INDIAN OCEAN

Gulf of Aden

Red Sea

0 — 600 miles
0 — 900 kilometers
Azimuthal Equidistant Projection

Cape Town
Port Elizabeth
Cape of Good Hope · Cape Agulhas

Africa
A COMPLEX GIANT

Africa spans nearly as far west to east as it does north to south. The Sahara—the world's largest desert—covers Africa's northern third, while to the south lie bands of grassland, tropical rain forest, and more desert. The East African Rift system marks where shifting plates are splitting off the continent's edge. Africa has a wealth of cultures, speaking some 1,600 languages—more than on any other continent. Though still largely rural, Africans increasingly migrate to booming cities like Cairo, Lagos, and Johannesburg. While rich in natural resources, from oil and coal to gemstones and precious metals, Africa is the poorest continent, long plagued by outside interference, corruption, and disease.

⇧ FASHION STATEMENT. Maasai women in Kenya adorn themselves with distinctive, colorful bead jewelry.

⇩ CHARGE! Sensing danger, an African elephant charges. The world's largest land mammal, African elephants are at risk due to poaching and loss of habitat.

⇧ SEA OF COLOR. Women balance trays of dates on their heads in a Saqqara market in Egypt. By tradition, only unmarried women dress in bright colors.

⇩ AFRICAN SAVANNA. Zebras graze on the tall grasses of the Serengeti Plain, in East Africa. Each year more than 200,000 zebras migrate through Serengeti, following the seasonal rains.

⇩ CRYSTAL WATERS. A snorkeler swims in the clear blue waters off the Seychelles, one of Africa's island countries. Made up of 116 granite and coral islands, it lies about 1,000 miles (1,600 km) east of Kenya.

⇨ FREE RIDE. A woman in Kumasi, Ghana, with her infant wrapped snugly on her back in a colorful cloth, goes about her daily chores.

more about
AFRICA

⇩ **DESERT WORSHIPPERS.** Muslim faithful gather before the Great Mosque in Mopti, Mali. An earthen structure typical of Muslim architecture in Africa's Sahel, the mosque was built between 1936 and 1943.

⇨ **WINDOW ON THE PAST.** Traditional Egyptian sailing vessels called feluccas skim along the Nile River below the ruins at Qubbat al Hawa. Tombs from ancient Egypt's sixth dynasty are carved into the hillside.

⇩ **MODERN SKYLINE.** Established in 1899 as a railway supply depot, Nairobi, Kenya, is now one of Africa's most modern cities. In Maasai, the name means "place of cold water."

⇐ **TALL LOAD.** A woman carries a stack of brightly dyed cotton cloth, called wax prints, through a market in Lomé, Togo.

WHERE THE PICTURES ARE

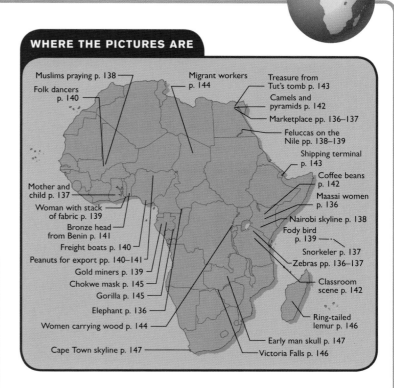

Muslims praying p. 138
Folk dancers p. 140
Migrant workers p. 144
Treasure from Tut's tomb p. 143
Camels and pyramids p. 142
Marketplace pp. 136–137
Feluccas on the Nile pp. 138–139
Shipping terminal p. 143
Coffee beans p. 142
Maasai women p. 136
Mother and child p. 137
Woman with stack of fabric p. 139
Bronze head from Benin p. 141
Freight boats p. 140
Nairobi skyline p. 138
Fody bird p. 139
Peanuts for export pp. 140–141
Snorkeler p. 137
Gold miners p. 139
Zebras pp. 136–137
Chokwe mask p. 145
Classroom scene p. 142
Gorilla p. 145
Elephant p. 136
Ring-tailed lemur p. 146
Women carrying wood p. 144
Early man skull p. 147
Cape Town skyline p. 147
Victoria Falls p. 146

⇓ **DIGGING FOR GOLD.** Miners dig a pit mine near the edge of the rain forest in Gabon. While searching for traces of gold, they expose the fragile soil to erosion. Oil and mineral extraction is an important part of Gabon's economy.

⇑ **TROPICAL JEWEL.** A ruby red fody bird perches on a forest branch on Mahe Island in the Seychelles. Native to neighboring Madagascar, the fody eats seeds and insects.

THE CONTINENT:
AFRICA

THE BASICS

STATS

Largest country
Algeria 919,595 sq mi (2,381,741 sq km)

Smallest country
Cape Verde 1,558 sq mi (4,036 sq km)

Most populous country
Nigeria 152,616,000

Least populous country
Cape Verde 509,000

Predominant languages
Arabic, French, English, Portuguese,
various indigenous languages and dialects

Predominant religions
Islam, Christianity, indigenous beliefs

Highest GDP per capita
Libya $14,600

Lowest GDP per capita
Liberia $500

Highest life expectancy
Libya 77 years

Highest literacy rate
Libya
83%

GEO WHIZ

Nigeria is Africa's largest producer and
exporter of oil. Port Harcourt, in the
Niger River delta, is the center of the
country's oil industry.

Ibn Battuta, who was born in Tangier,
Morocco, in 1304, set off on a pilgrim-
age to Mecca that turned into a 29-year,
75,000-mile (120,675-km) journey that
took him from the Middle East to India,
China, the East Indies, and back home.

For more than 300 years, the Slave
House on Senegal's Gorée Island
served as a holding pen for slaves
before they were sent to the Americas
and elsewhere. Today it is a museum
and a memorial to those slaves.

NORTHWEST AFRICA

This region stretches from the Gulf of Guinea north to the Atlas Mountains, which rise between Mediterranean waters and Sahara

⬆ RIVER TRANSPORT. Traditional river boats are an important link in the movement of cargo and people along the Niger River.

sands. Early kingdoms thrived in Mali, Ghana, and Benin, but European invasions disrupted the social order and took out vast wealth, leaving a colonial legacy of disorder and conflict. Palm oil, rubber, and cacao are produced in tropical areas. Drier lands grow peanuts and cotton, and olives are raised along the Mediterranean Sea.

Energy fuels the economies of several countries: Nigeria, Libya, and Algeria produce great quantities of oil and natural gas. The region's 20 countries are largely poor, with fast-growing populations totaling 379 million people.

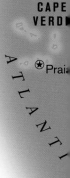

CAPE VERDE

⊛ Praia

ATLANTI

⬅ COLORFUL COSTUMES. Folk dancers perform in a festival in Djenné, Mali. Built as a center for trade between the desert to the north and the rain forest to the south, Djenné is the oldest known city in Sub-Saharan Africa.

⇨ WAITING FOR SHIPMENT. Sacks of peanuts create an artificial mountain in Kano, Nigeria, where they wait for transport to Lagos and then export to world markets. The Kano region produces about half of Nigeria's peanut crop.

⇐ **MASTER ARTISANS.** The ancient African kingdom of Benin produced outstanding bronze work. Sculpted by hand and then cast in bronze by the lost wax method, each piece was created to honor the king.

SPAIN
PORTUGAL
MEDITERRANEAN
ITALY
GREECE
Strait of Gibraltar
Mostaganem
Ceuta (SPAIN)
Algiers
Constantine
Annaba
Bizerte
Tangier
Melilla (SPAIN)
Blida
Skikda
Tunis
Tétouan
Oran
Bejaia
Sétif
Sousse
MALTA
Rabat
Oujda
Saïda
Biskra
Tébessa
Qairouan
SEA
Kenitra
Fez
Tlemcen
TUNISIA
Sfax
Casablanca
Meknès
MOUNTAINS
Gabes
Tripoli
El Jadida
Al Khums
Al Baydā'
Safi
MOROCCO
Zuwārah
Mişrātah
Tobruk
Marrakech
Surt
Benghazi
Agadir
Béchar
Gulf of Sidra
MADEIRA
ISLANDS
(PORTUGAL)
Jebel
Toubkal
13,665 ft
4,165 m
TRIPOLITANIA
CYRENAICA
Santa Cruz
de Tenerife
ATLAS
Great Western Dunes
Great Eastern Dunes
Las Palmas
CANARY
ISLANDS
(SPAIN)
ALGERIA
Sabhā
LIBYA
FEZZAN
Laayoune
WESTERN
SAHARA
(MOROCCO)
TROPIC OF CANCER
Mount
Tahat
9,852 ft
3,003 m
EGYPT
Tamanrasset
MAURITANIA
S A H A R A
Nouakchott
Aïr
Massif
Ténéré
NIGER
SUDAN
Tombouctou
(Timbuktu)
Agadez
CHAD
kar
Thiès
Gao
Sénégal
SENEGAL
Kaolack
Kayes
MALI
Tahoua
Lake
Chad
AMBIA
Gambia
Ségou
Niamey
Zinder
anjul
Bamako
Mopti
Niger
SAHEL
Sokoto
Katsina
Kano
Potiskum
Maiduguri
inchor
Bissau
BURKINA FASO
Gusau
GUINEA-BISSAU
Kankan
Ouagadougou
Kaduna
Zaria
Gombe
Boké
GUINEA
Sikasso
Bobo Dioulasso
Kandi
NIGERIA
Jos
Yola
Fria
Kindia
Kissidougou
Sokodé
Djougou
Parakou
Minna
Bauchi
Conakry
SIERRA
LEONE
Nzérékoré
Korhogo
Lake
Volta
Bida
Abuja
Jalingo
Freetown
Man
CÔTE D'IVOIRE
(IVORY COAST)
Ilorin
Oshogbo
Makurdi
Bo
Bouaké
GHANA
TOGO
BENIN
Ikare
Otukpo
CENTRAL
AFRICAN
REPUBLIC
Kenema
Daloa
Abengourou
Ogbomosho
Ibadan
Enugu
Monrovia
LIBERIA
Gagnoa
Divo
Tema
Abeokuta
Onitsha
Buchanan
Yamoussoukro
(legislative capital)
Abidjan
Kumasi
Accra
Lomé
Porto-Novo
Lagos
Benin City
Aba
(administrative capital)
Ivory Coast
Sekondi-Takoradi
Gold Coast
Cotonou
(seat of government)
Warri
Niger
Port Harcourt
CAMEROON
Grain Coast
Gulf of
Guinea
(constitutional capital) Porto-Novo
Calabar
EQUATORIAL
GUINEA
OCEAN
EQUATOR
SAO TOME &
PRINCIPE
GABON

CHANGING THE LAND

true desert

severe risk of
desertification

moderate to
great risk

Source: UN Food and Agricultural Organization

Overgrazing, removal of vegetation by farmers, and unreliable rainfall are turning some land in Africa into deserts—a process called desertification.

Map Key

⊛ Country capital

••• City or town

····· Boundary

0 ——— 600 miles
0 ——— 900 kilometers

Azimuthal Equidistant Projection

THE CONTINENT:
AFRICA

NORTHEAST AFRICA

THE BASICS

STATS

Largest country
Sudan 967,500 sq mi (2,505,813 sq km)

Smallest country
Djibouti 8,958 sq mi (23,200 sq km)

Most populous country
Ethiopia 82,825,000

Least populous country
Djibouti 864,000

Predominant languages
French, English, Arabic, Swahili, various indigenous languages and dialects

Predominant religions
Christianity, Islam, various indigenous beliefs

Highest GDP per capita
Egypt $6,000

Lowest GDP per capita
Burundi $600

Highest life expectancy
Egypt 72 years

Highest literacy rate
Kenya
85%

GEO WHIZ

Lakes Malawi, Tanganyika, and Albert are part of a chain of lakes that mark where the Somali Plate (see page 19) is breaking away from Africa. Millions of years from now, much of the region from Djibouti to Mozambique could be one big island.

As part of a coming-of-age ritual, each Maasai boy must kill a lion. Read the true-life story of Joseph Lemasolai Lekuton in *Facing the Lion*, published by National Geographic Children's Books.

Lake Nasser, formed by the Aswan High Dam, is the world's third largest reservoir. Built to provide water for farms along the Nile in years of drought, it also produces more than 10 billion kilowatt hours of electricity every year.

In 2006 the 3.3-million-year-old fossilized remains of a child were found in the Danakil area of northern Ethiopia. The find was not far from where the 2.3-million-year-old remains of Lucy, an adult female of the same primitive human species, were found in 1974.

The world's longest river— the Nile—winds through much of this region. Along its banks rose one of Earth's greatest civilizations: Ancient Egypt. Today, more than nine of ten Egyptians live within a few miles of its life-giving water, and Cairo, the region's largest urban area, lies near its delta. Volcanic peaks such as Kilimanjaro—Africa's highest mountain—tower above fertile farmlands in Tanzania and Kenya. Tree-dotted grasslands, called savannas, are home to vast herds of wildlife that attract tourists from across the globe. For more than 50 years, religious and ethnic conflicts have fueled warfare throughout much of the region, especially in Sudan, where millions suffer in refugee camps in Darfur.

⇧ EAGER LEARNERS. Tanzania, a poor country with a literacy rate of only 69 percent, lags in education. Students in this crowded village school compete for the teacher's attention.

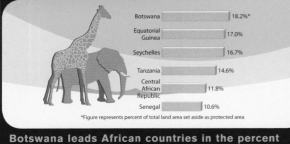

⇦ FROM FIELD TO CUP. A worker on a coffee estate in Kenya holds freshly harvested coffee berries, which will soon be on their way to the world market. Coffee production was introduced to Kenya in 1900. Today, it employs more than six million workers.

⇩ SYMBOLS OF ANCIENT EGYPT. Camels plod through the desert as the sun sets behind the ancient pyramids of Giza. Built 4,500 years ago, the pyramids were monumental tombs of the pharaohs.

PROTECTING THE ENVIRONMENT

Botswana	18.2%*
Equatorial Guinea	17.0%
Seychelles	16.7%
Tanzania	14.6%
Central African Republic	11.8%
Senegal	10.6%

*Figure represents percent of total land area set aside as protected area

Botswana leads African countries in the percent of land set aside as special parks and reserves to protect the habitats of animals.

← SPIRIT OF THE PAST. A gold hawk pendant adorned with semiprecious stones and colored glass may represent the god Horus, one of the oldest Egyptian gods. This treasure was found in the tomb of King Tut.

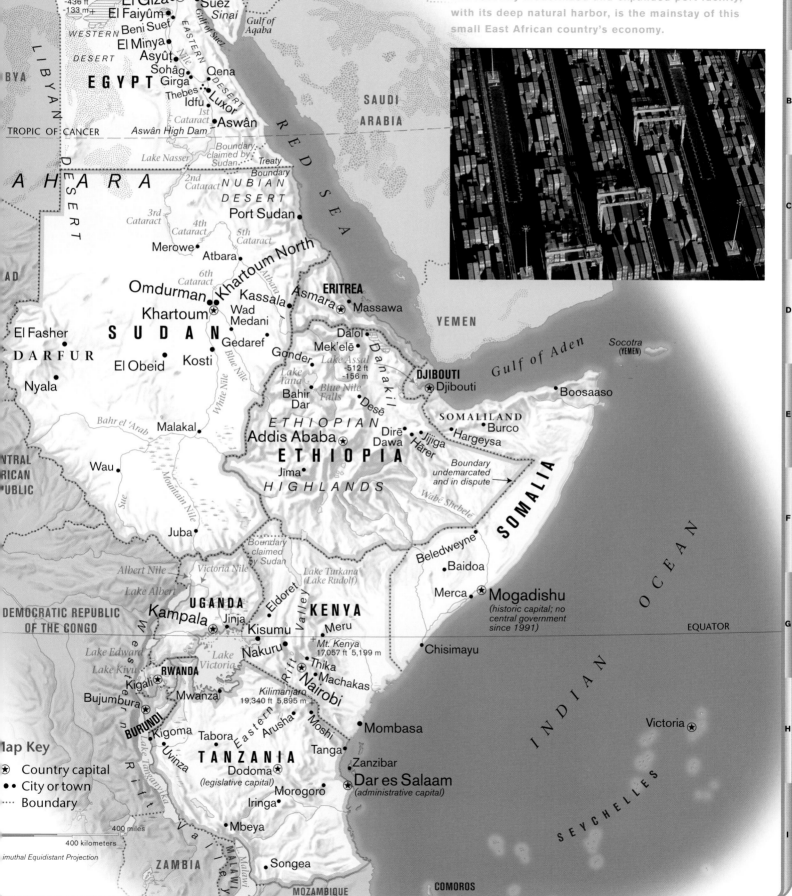

⇩ INTERNATIONAL PORT. Shipping containers look like colorful ribbons at a port terminal in Djibouti. The recently modernized and expanded port facility, with its deep natural harbor, is the mainstay of this small East African country's economy.

MEDITERRANEAN SEA

Alexandria
Port Said
Tanta
Cairo
El Gîza
Suez
El Faiyûm
Sinai
Gulf of Aqaba
Beni Suef
El Minya
Asyût
Eastern
Sohâg
Qena
Girga
Thebes
Luxor
Idfu
1st Cataract
Aswân
Aswân High Dam

Qattara Depression
-436 ft
-133 m

Lake Nasser

WESTERN DESERT
LIBYAN DESERT

EGYPT

LIBYA

TROPIC OF CANCER

SAUDI ARABIA

JORDAN
ISRAEL

RED SEA

Boundary claimed by Sudan
Treaty Boundary

SAHARA

2nd Cataract
3rd Cataract
4th Cataract
5th Cataract
6th Cataract

NUBIAN DESERT

Port Sudan

Merowe
Atbara
Khartoum North
Omdurman
Kassala
Asmara
ERITREA
Massawa
Khartoum
Wad Medani
Gedaref
Dalol
Mek'elē
Danakil
DJIBOUTI
Djibouti

Gulf of Aden
Socotra (YEMEN)
Boosaaso

YEMEN

SUDAN

DARFUR
El Fasher
El Obeid
Kosti
Gonder
Lake Tana
Bahir Dar
Blue Nile Falls
Desē
Lake Assal
-512 ft
-156 m
Dirē
Dawa
Hârer
Jijiga
Hargeysa
SOMALILAND
Burco

Nyala

Bahr el 'Arab
Malakal
ETHIOPIAN
Addis Ababa
ETHIOPIA
Jīma
HIGHLANDS

White Nile
Blue Nile

Boundary undemarcated and in dispute

Wabē Shebele

Wau
Sue
Mountain Nile

CENTRAL AFRICAN REPUBLIC

SOMALIA

Juba

Boundary claimed by Sudan

Albert Nile
Victoria Nile
Lake Turkana (Lake Rudolf)
Lake Albert

Beledweyne
Baidoa

DEMOCRATIC REPUBLIC OF THE CONGO

UGANDA
Kampala
Jinja
Eldoret
Kisumu
KENYA
Meru
Merca
Mogadishu
(historic capital; no central government since 1991)

EQUATOR

Lake Edward
Lake Kivu
RWANDA
Kigali
Nakuru
Mt. Kenya
17,057 ft 5,199 m
Thika
Chisimayu

Bujumbura
Mwanza
Kilimanjaro
19,340 ft 5,895 m
Nairobi
Machakas

Lake Victoria

BURUNDI
Kigoma
Tabora
Arusha
Moshi
Mombasa
Victoria

Eastern Rift Valley

TANZANIA
Uvinza
Dodoma
(legislative capital)
Tanga
Zanzibar
Dar es Salaam
(administrative capital)

Lake Tanganyika
Morogoro

INDIAN OCEAN

SEYCHELLES

Map Key
★ Country capital
• City or town
··· Boundary

Iringa
Mbeya
400 miles
400 kilometers
Azimuthal Equidistant Projection

ZAMBIA
Songea

MALAWI
L. Malawi

MOZAMBIQUE

COMOROS

THE CONTINENT:
AFRICA

CENTRAL AFRICA

French is the official language of most of this region. The Congo, the region's longest river and chief commercial highway, flows through rain forests that, despite efforts to save them, are being cut for timber and palm oil plantations. Oil fields dot the coasts of Gabon and Cameroon, while diamonds and reserves of metals such as copper and chromium are mined for export in the Central African Republic and the Democratic Republic of the Congo. Coffee is grown in highland regions, and Chadians raise livestock as well as cotton and other crops. Extended drought and diversion of water for agriculture have reduced Lake Chad to one-twentieth of its former size.

⇧ CATCHING A RIDE. A big flatbed truck, diesel engine churning, carries people and freight across the dusty brown Sahara. Men from poverty-stricken Chad travel to Libya, along with their belongings, for short-term work, then return home.

⇨ WOMEN'S WORK. Villagers throughout Africa depend on wood as their main source of fuel to cook and heat their homes. This helps cause widespread deforestation. These women carry wood out of Virunga National Park in the Democratic Republic of the Congo.

VANISHING FORESTS

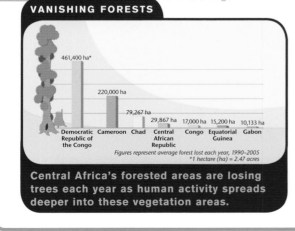

461,400 ha*

220,000 ha

79,267 ha

29,867 ha   17,000 ha   15,200 ha   10,133 ha

| Democratic Republic of the Congo | Cameroon | Chad | Central African Republic | Congo | Equatorial Guinea | Gabon |

Figures represent average forest lost each year, 1990–2005
*1 hectare (ha) = 2.47 acres

Central Africa's forested areas are losing trees each year as human activity spreads deeper into these vegetation areas.

⇐ CELEBRATING A KING. The Chokwe people of Central Africa used masks such as this to celebrate the inauguration of a new king. Considered sacred, the mask could only be worn by the current chief of a group.

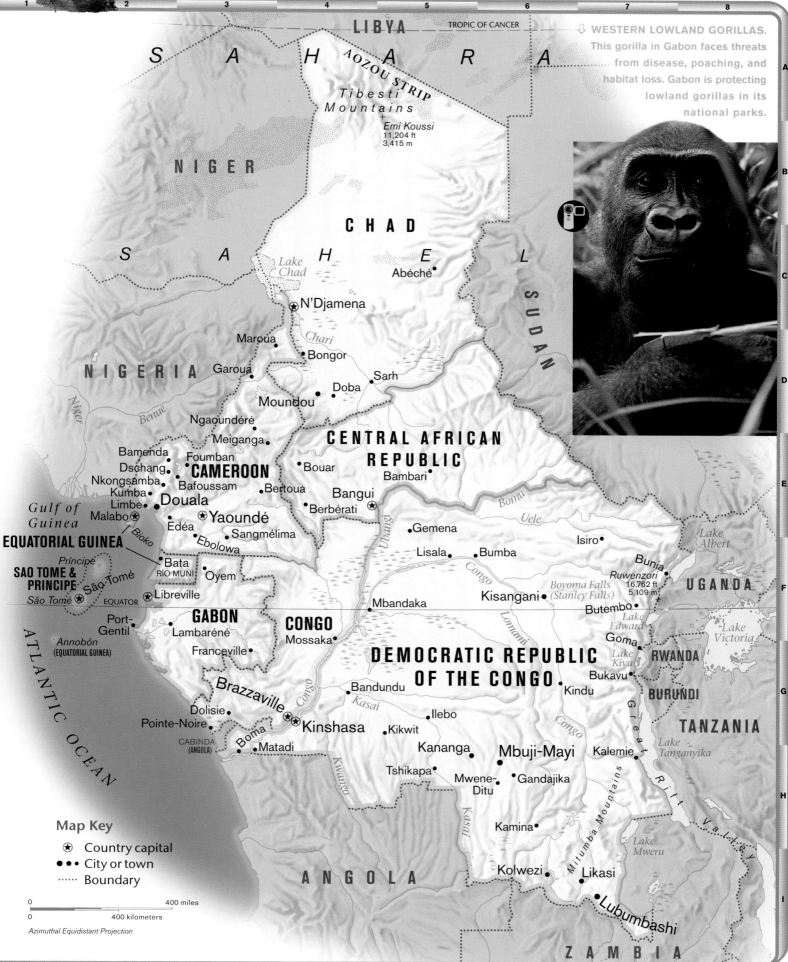

⇩ WESTERN LOWLAND GORILLAS. This gorilla in Gabon faces threats from disease, poaching, and habitat loss. Gabon is protecting lowland gorillas in its national parks.

LIBYA
TROPIC OF CANCER

S A H A R A

AOZOU STRIP

Tibesti Mountains
+ *Emi Koussi*
11,204 ft
3,415 m

N I G E R

C H A D

S A H E L

Lake Chad
Abéché

⍟ N'Djamena

Maroua
Chari
Bongor

NIGERIA
Garoua
Doba
Sarh

Benue
Moundou

Ngaoundéré

Meiganga
CENTRAL AFRICAN REPUBLIC

Bamenda
Foumban
Bouar
Dschang
CAMEROON
Bambari
Nkongsamba
Bafoussam
Bertoua
Kumba
Douala
Bangui ⍟
Limbe
Berbérati
Malabo ⍟
Bioko
⍟ Yaoundé

Gulf of Guinea
Edéa
Sangmélima
Gemena
Isiro
EQUATORIAL GUINEA
Ebolowa
Lisala
Bumba
Príncipe
Bata
Oyem
Bonu
Uele
Bunia
SAO TOME & PRINCIPE
RIO MUNI
Ubangi
Ruwenzori
16,762 ft
5,109 m
São Tomé
São Tomé
Libreville
Congo
Boyoma Falls
(Stanley Falls)
UGANDA
São Tomé
EQUATOR

Lake Albert

Mbandaka
Kisangani
Butembo

Port-Gentil
GABON
CONGO
Lomami
Lake Edward

Annobón
(EQUATORIAL GUINEA)
Lambaréné
Mossaka
Goma
Lake Victoria

Franceville
DEMOCRATIC REPUBLIC
Lake Kivu
RWANDA

OF THE CONGO
Bukavu
BURUNDI

Brazzaville
Bandundu
Kindu

Kasai
TANZANIA
Dolisie
Congo
Ilebo
Pointe-Noire
Kikwit
Lake Tanganyika
CABINDA
(ANGOLA)
Boma
Kananga
Mbuji-Mayi
Kalemie
Matadi
Tshikapa
Mwene-
Gandajika
Ditu
Kwango
Kasai

Kamina
Mitumba Mountains
Lake Mweru

Map Key
⍟ Country capital
••• City or town
······ Boundary

Kasai
Great Rift Valley

Kamina

Kolwezi
Likasi

0   400 miles
0   400 kilometers
Lubumbashi

Azimuthal Equidistant Projection

A N G O L A

Z A M B I A

A
T
L
A
N
T
I
C

O
C
E
A
N

THE CONTINENT:
AFRICA

THE BASICS

STATS

Largest country
Angola 481,354 sq mi (1,246,700 sq km)

Smallest country
Seychelles 176 sq mi (455 sq km)

Most populous country
South Africa 50,674,000

Least populous country
Seychelles 87,000

Predominant languages
English, French, Portuguese, various indigenous languages and dialects

Predominant religions
Christianity, Islam, various indigenous beliefs

Highest GDP per capita
Seychelles $19,400

Lowest GDP per capita
Zimbabwe $200

Highest life expectancy
Seychelles 73 years

Highest literacy rate
Seychelles
92%

GEO WHIZ

South Africa's Kruger National Park, largest in Africa, covers more area than the entire country of Israel. Within its boundary are 14 different ecological zones that provide habitat to a great variety of plants, birds, and other animals, including the "big five": lions, elephants, leopards, rhinos, and buffaloes.

Great Zimbabwe National Monument has the largest ancient stone ruins south of the Sahara. This massive fortress city was the center of an empire that flourished from the 11th to the 15th century.

The Makgadikgadi salt pans in the eastern Kalahari of Botswana are what is left of an immense lake. Each spring, rains flood the area and attract herds of migrating zebras and wildebeests.

Namibia is famed for sand dunes that are reportedly the highest in the world. The largest, Big Daddy, towers 1,200 feet (366 m) above the surrounding land. Along Namibia's northwestern coast, treacherous crosscurrents have caused countless shipwrecks, earning it the nickname Skeleton Coast.

SOUTHERN AFRICA

Ringed by uplands, the region's central basin holds the seasonally lush Okavango Delta and scorching Kalahari Desert. The mighty Zambezi thunders over Victoria Falls on its way to the Indian Ocean, where Madagascar is home to plants and animals found nowhere else in the world. Bantu and San are among the indigenous people who saw their hold on the land give way to Portuguese, Dutch, and British traders and colonists. The region offers a range of mineral resources and a variety of climates and soils that in some places yield bumper crops of grains, grapes, and citrus. Rich deposits of coal, gold, and diamonds have helped make South Africa the continent's economic powerhouse.

⇧ NATURAL WONDER. Victoria Falls, third largest waterfall in the world, is 5,500 feet (1,676 m) wide and 355 feet (108 m) high.

⇦ STARING EYES. This ring-tailed lemur sits on a forest tree branch. The ring-tail, found only in Madagascar, spends time both on the ground and in the trees. It eats fruits, leaves, insects, small birds, and even lizards.

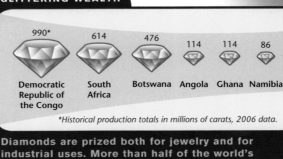

GLITTERING WEALTH

990*	614	476	114	114	86
Democratic Republic of the Congo	South Africa	Botswana	Angola	Ghana	Namibia

*Historical production totals in millions of carats, 2006 data.

Diamonds are prized both for jewelry and for industrial uses. More than half of the world's diamond production comes from mines in Africa.

Map labels:
CONGO
CABINDA (ANGOLA) · Cabinda
DEMOCRATIC OF T[HE]
Cuango
Uíge
Luanda ✪
Malanje
Lobito
Benguela · Kuito
Huambo
ANGOLA
Lubango
Etosha Pan
Okavango
CAPRIVI STRIP
Kaokoland
NAMIB DESERT
NAMIBIA
Swakopmund
Walvis Bay
Windhoek ✪
KA[LAHARI]
ATLANTIC OCEAN
Orange
Worcester
Cape Town ✪
(legislative capital)
Cape of Good Hope
Cape Agulhas

⇐ EARLY MAN. Dating back perhaps 70,000 years, this skull of "Broken Hill Man," found in Zimbabwe, is thought to represent a transitional type between *Homo erectus* and *Homo sapiens*.

4   5   6   7   8   9   10   11

REPUBLIC
ONGO

TANZANIA

Lake Tanganyika

Map Key

★ Country capital
●●● City or town
······ Boundary

0   200 miles
0   300 kilometers

Azimuthal Equidistant Projection

Kasama

Lake Malawi

Mzuzu

Rovuma

SEYCHELLES

Moroni ★

COMOROS

Îles Glorieuses
(FRANCE)

Cap d'Ambre

Mufulira

Chingola

Kitwe

Luanshya

Kabwe

Ndola

Muchinga Mountains

Chipata

Lichinga

Lugenda

Pemba

Île de Mayotte
(FRANCE)

Antsiranana

Zambezi

Mongu

ZAMBIA

Lilongwe ★

Zomba

Blantyre

Tete

Nampula

Nacala

Moçambique

+Maromokotro
9,436 ft
2,876 m

Mahajanga

MALAWI

Lusaka ★

Victoria Falls

Livingstone

Lake Kariba

Harare ★

Chitungwiza

ZIMBABWE

Mutare

Chimoio

Quelimane

Île Juan De Nova
(FRANCE)

Toamasina

MADAGASCAR

Antananarivo ★

Antsirabe

Okavango Delta

Makgadikgadi Pans

Francistown

Gweru

Great Zimbabwe

Bulawayo

Beira

MOZAMBIQUE

Mozambique Channel

Bassas da India
(FRANCE)

Fianarantsoa

INDIAN OCEAN

TSWANA

Serowe

Île Europa
(FRANCE)

TROPIC OF CAPRICORN

Toliara

For Mauritius and Réunion, see maps on pages 134–135.

HARI
ERT

Gaborone ★

Kanye

Polokwane
(Pietersburg)

Limpopo

Pretoria (Tshwane)
(administrative capital)

Inhambane

Johannesburg

Soweto

Klerksdorp

Vereeniging

Xai-Xai

Maputo ★

Mbabane *(administrative capital)*

SWAZILAND ★

Lobamba *(legislative and royal capital)*

Cap Ste. Marie

OUTH

Welkom

Kroonstad

Vaal

Kimberley

Bloemfontein ★
(judicial capital)

Maseru ★

LESOTHO

Richards Bay

Pietermaritzburg

FRICA

Orange

Drakensberg

Durban

Middelburg

Karroo

Queenstown

udtshoorn

East London

Grahamstown

Uitenhage

George

Port Elizabeth

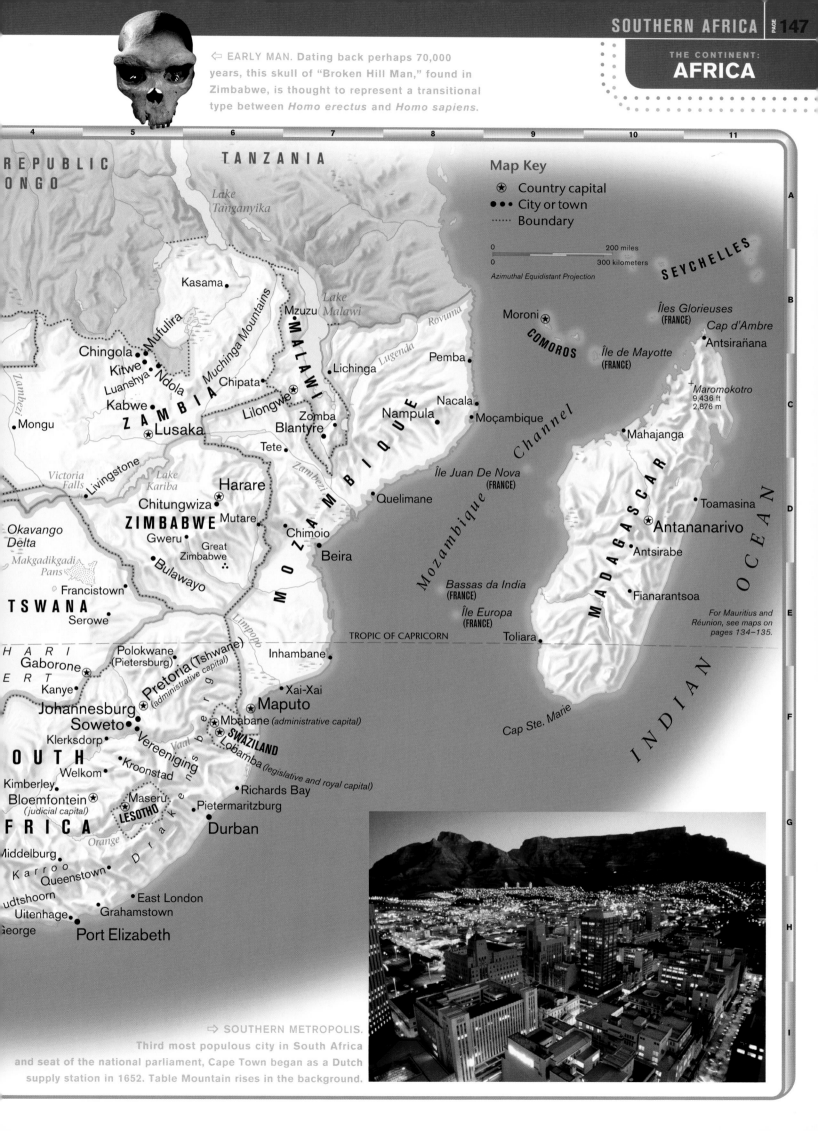

⇒ SOUTHERN METROPOLIS. Third most populous city in South Africa and seat of the national parliament, Cape Town began as a Dutch supply station in 1652. Table Mountain rises in the background.

PHYSICAL

Area and population totals are for the independent countries in the region only.

Land area
3,278,000 sq mi
(8,490,000 sq km)

Highest point
Mount Wilhelm, Papua New Guinea
14,793 ft (4,509 m)

Lowest point
Lake Eyre, Australia
-52 ft (-16 m)

Longest river
Murray-Darling, Australia
2,310 mi (3,718 km)

Largest lake
Lake Eyre, Australia
3,430 sq mi (8,884 sq km)

POLITICAL

Population
35,845,000

Largest metropolitan area
Sydney, Australia
Pop. 4,427,000

Largest country
Australia
2,969,906 sq mi (7,692,024 sq km)

Most densely populated country
Nauru
1,233 people per sq mi (476 per sq km)

Economy
Farming: livestock, wheat, fruit
Industry: mining, wool, oil
Services

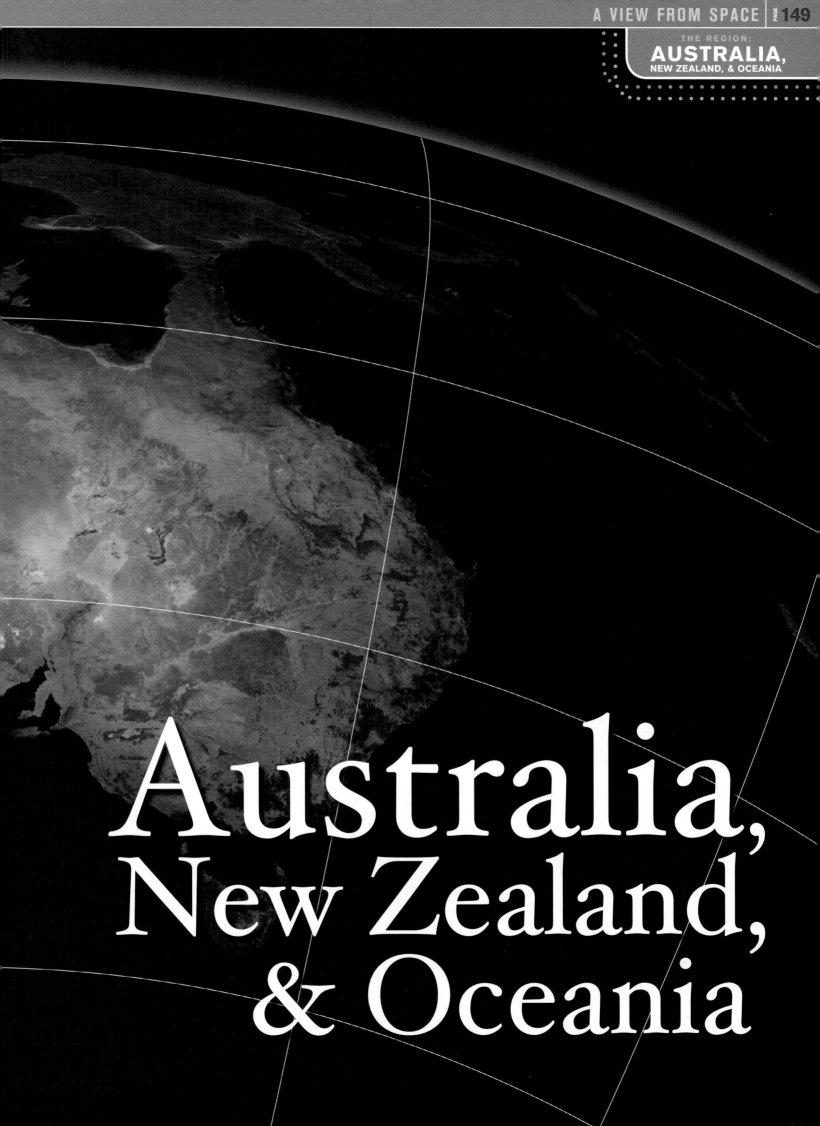

Australia, New Zealand, & Oceania

AUSTRALIA
NEW ZEALAND, & OCEANIA

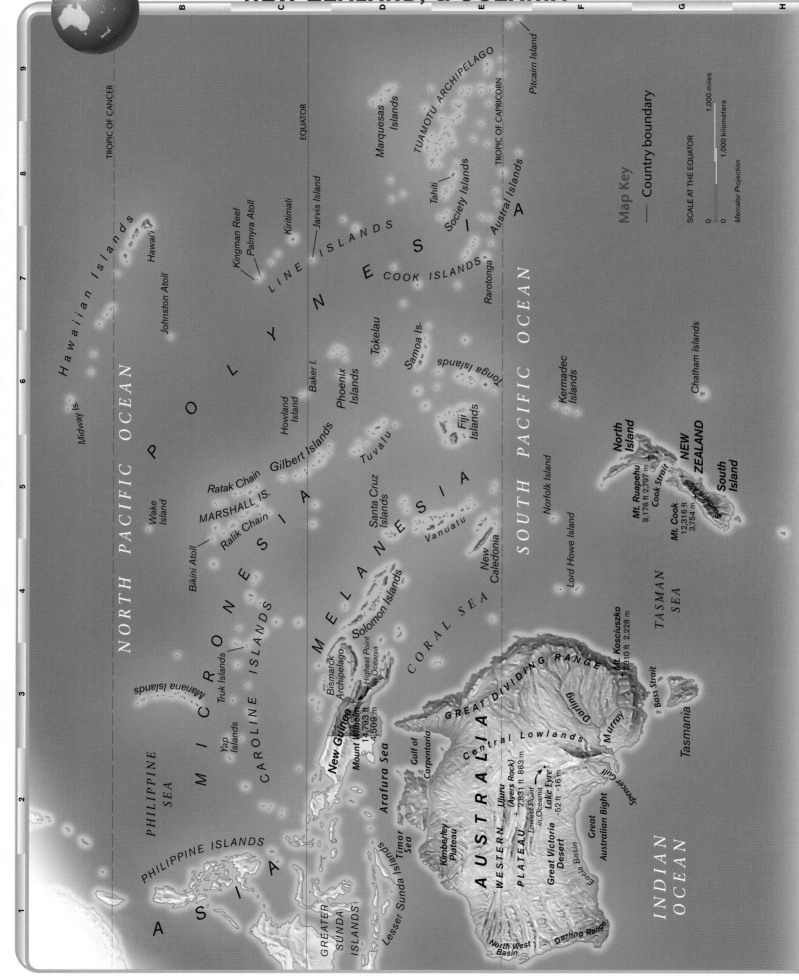

Map Key

—— Country boundary

SCALE AT THE EQUATOR

0   1,000 miles
0   1,000 kilometers

Mercator Projection

TROPIC OF CANCER

EQUATOR

TROPIC OF CAPRICORN

Pitcairn Island

Hawaiian Islands

Hawai'i

Midway Is.

Johnston Atoll

Wake Island

Bikini Atoll

Ralik Chain

Ratak Chain

MARSHALL IS.

Gilbert Islands

Kingman Reef

Palmyra Atoll

Kiritimati

Jarvis Island

LINE ISLANDS

Marquesas Islands

TUAMOTU ARCHIPELAGO

Tahiti

Society Islands

Austral Islands

COOK ISLANDS

Rarotonga

Howland Island

Baker I.

Phoenix Islands

Tokelau

Samoa Is.

Tonga Islands

Tuvalu

Santa Cruz Islands

Fiji Islands

Vanuatu

New Caledonia

Kermadec Islands

Norfolk Island

Lord Howe Island

Chatham Islands

North Island

NEW ZEALAND

Mt. Ruapehu
9,176 ft/2,797 m

Cook Strait

Mt. Cook
12,316 ft
3,754 m

Southern Alps

South Island

NORTH PACIFIC OCEAN

SOUTH PACIFIC OCEAN

P O L Y N E S I A

M I C R O N E S I A

M E L A N E S I A

A S I A

Mariana Islands

Yap Islands

Truk Islands

CAROLINE ISLANDS

PHILIPPINE SEA

PHILIPPINE ISLANDS

GREATER SUNDA ISLANDS

Lesser Sunda Islands

Timor Sea

New Guinea

Mount Wilhelm
14,793 ft
4,509 m
Highest Point in Oceania

Bismarck Archipelago

Solomon Islands

CORAL SEA

Arafura Sea

Gulf of Carpentaria

GREAT DIVIDING RANGE

Mt. Kosciuszko
7,310 ft 2,228 m

Darling

Murray

Bass Strait

Tasmania

TASMAN SEA

AUSTRALIA

Central Lowlands

WESTERN PLATEAU

Uluru (Ayers Rock)
2,831 ft 863 m

Lake Eyre
Lowest Point in Oceania
-52 ft -16 m

Kimberley Plateau

Great Victoria Desert

Eucla Basin

Great Australian Bight

Spencer Gulf

North West Basin

Darling Range

INDIAN OCEAN

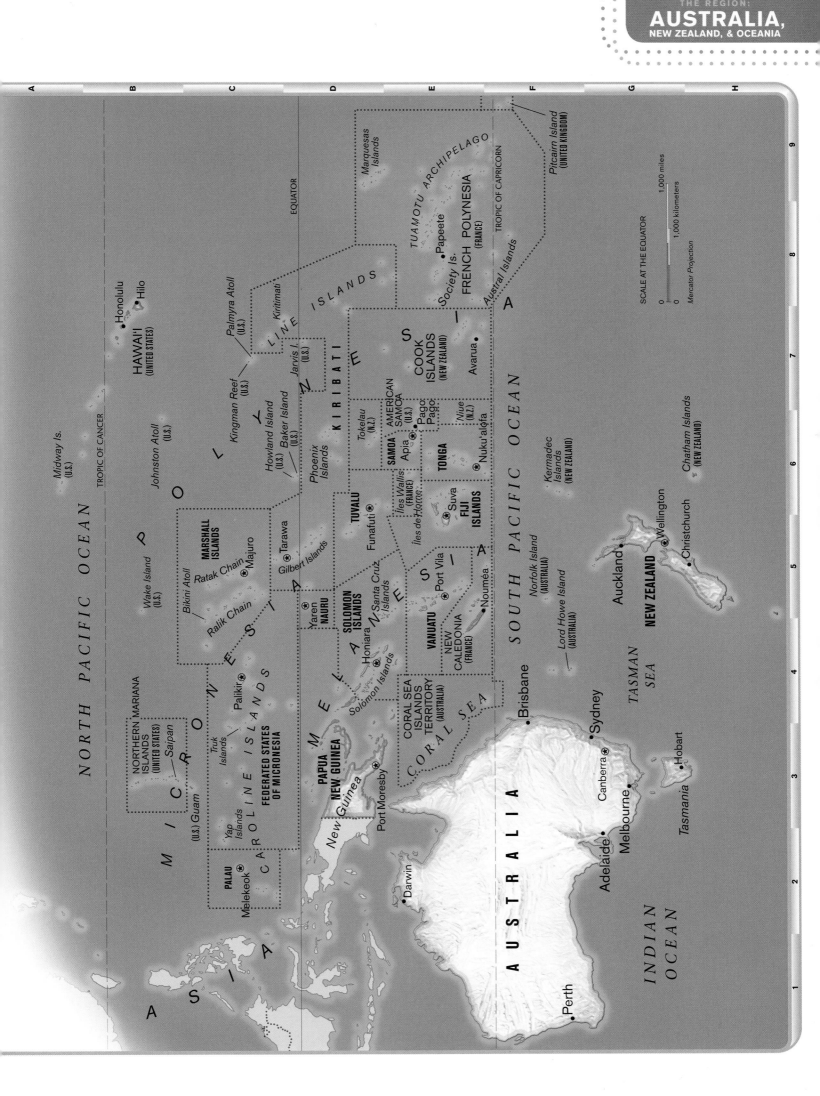

A B C D E F G H

9

8

7

6

5

4

3

2

1

NORTH PACIFIC OCEAN

SOUTH PACIFIC OCEAN

INDIAN OCEAN

ASIA

AUSTRALIA

NEW ZEALAND

TASMAN SEA

CORAL SEA

EQUATOR

TROPIC OF CANCER

TROPIC OF CAPRICORN

MICRONESIA

MELANESIA

POLYNESIA

TUAMOTU ARCHIPELAGO

LINE ISLANDS

Midway Is. (U.S.)

HAWAI'I (UNITED STATES)
Honolulu
Hilo

Johnston Atoll (U.S.)

Wake Island (U.S.)

NORTHERN MARIANA ISLANDS (UNITED STATES)
Saipan

Guam (U.S.)

PALAU
Melekeok

Yap Islands
Truk Islands
Palikir
FEDERATED STATES OF MICRONESIA
CAROLINE ISLANDS

MARSHALL ISLANDS
Bikini Atoll
Ratak Chain
Ralik Chain
Majuro

Tarawa
Gilbert Islands

NAURU
Yaren

Palmyra Atoll (U.S.)
Kingman Reef (U.S.)
Kiritimati
Jarvis I. (U.S.)
Howland Island (U.S.)
Baker Island (U.S.)
Phoenix Islands

KIRIBATI

TUVALU
Funafuti

Tokelau (N.Z.)

SAMOA
Apia
AMERICAN SAMOA (U.S.)
Pago Pago

Niue (N.Z.)
Nuku'alofa
TONGA

Marquesas Islands

Papeete
Society Is.
FRENCH POLYNESIA (FRANCE)
Austral Islands

COOK ISLANDS (NEW ZEALAND)
Avarua

Pitcairn Island (UNITED KINGDOM)

Îles Wallis (FRANCE)
Îles de Horne
Suva
FIJI ISLANDS

VANUATU
Port Vila
NEW CALEDONIA (FRANCE)
Nouméa

SOLOMON ISLANDS
Honiara
Santa Cruz Islands
Solomon Islands

PAPUA NEW GUINEA
Port Moresby
New Guinea

CORAL SEA ISLANDS TERRITORY (AUSTRALIA)

Norfolk Island (AUSTRALIA)
Lord Howe Island (AUSTRALIA)

Kermadec Islands (NEW ZEALAND)

Chatham Islands (NEW ZEALAND)

Wellington
Auckland
Christchurch

Brisbane
Sydney
Canberra
Melbourne
Adelaide
Hobart
Tasmania
Darwin
Perth

SCALE AT THE EQUATOR
1,000 miles
1,000 kilometers
Mercator Projection

Australia,
New Zealand, & Oceania
WORLDS APART

⇧ AUSTRALIAN TEDDY BEAR. Koalas, which are not bears at all, are native to the eucalyptus forests of eastern Australia.

This vast region includes Australia—the world's smallest continent—New Zealand, and a fleet of mostly tiny island worlds scattered across the Pacific Ocean. Apart from Australia, New Zealand, and Papua New Guinea, Oceania's other 11 independent countries cover about 25,000 square miles (65,000 sq km), an area only slightly larger than half of New Zealand's North Island. Twenty-one other island groups are dependencies of the United States, France, Australia, New Zealand, or the United Kingdom. Long isolation has allowed the growth of diverse marine communities such as Australia's Great Barrier Reef and the evolution of platypuses, kangaroos, and other land animals that live nowhere else on the planet.

⇦ ANCIENT VOYAGERS. The Maoris are believed to have sailed to New Zealand from islands far to the northeast. Maori warriors traditionally adorned themselves with elaborate tattoos to frighten enemies.

⇓ PLACE OF LEGENDS. Sacred to native Aborigines, Uluru, also known as Ayers Rock, glows a deep red in the rays of the setting sun. Uluru is the tip of a massive sandstone block—part of an ancient seabed exposed by erosion.

⇐ TROPICAL HABITAT. Brilliantly colored fish swim among branching corals in the warm waters of the Vatuira Channel in the Fiji Islands. The waters around Fiji have some of the richest and most diverse fish populations in the world.

⇒ NATIVE COWBOYS. Competition is fierce during a rodeo in Hope Vale, an Aboriginal community on Australia's Cape York Peninsula. Hope Vale is home to several Aboriginal clan groups.

more about
AUSTRALIA, NEW ZEALAND & OCEANIA

⇧ BIG JUMPER. The red kangaroo, largest living marsupial—an animal that carries its young in a pouch—is at home on the dry inland plains of Australia. It can cover 30 feet (9 m) in a single hop.

⇦ HOT SPOT. This geothermal pool at Waiotapu, on New Zealand's North Island, is evidence of ongoing volcanic activity. Minerals dissolved in superheated water give the pool its vivid colors.

⇦ FESTIVAL DRESS. Women of Tanna Island, in Vanuatu, wear face paint and ceremonial clothes in preparation for a festival. Traditional festivals often involve an elaborate exchange of gifts, such as pigs, mats, and baskets, between villages to gain social status.

⇩ A WATER WORLD. Located just 7 degrees north of the Equator in the western Pacific Ocean, the islands of the Republic of Palau were a United Nations Trust Territory until 1994, when they gained independence.

WHERE THE PICTURES ARE

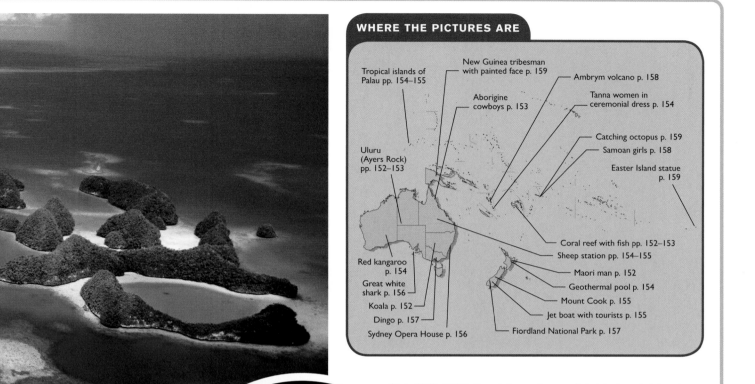

Tropical islands of Palau pp. 154–155

New Guinea tribesman with painted face p. 159

Ambrym volcano p. 158

Aborigine cowboys p. 153

Tanna women in ceremonial dress p. 154

Uluru (Ayers Rock) pp. 152–153

Catching octopus p. 159

Samoan girls p. 158

Easter Island statue p. 159

Red kangaroo p. 154

Coral reef with fish pp. 152–153

Sheep station pp. 154–155

Maori man p. 152

Great white shark p. 156

Geothermal pool p. 154

Koala p. 152

Mount Cook p. 155

Dingo p. 157

Jet boat with tourists p. 155

Sydney Opera House p. 156

Fiordland National Park p. 157

⇦ A WET RIDE. Tourists go for a wild ride in a jet boat on the roaring waters of New Zealand's Shotover River.

⇩ SNOWY PEAK. New Zealand's Mount Cook rises above the clouds. Legend says the peak is a frozen Maori warrior.

⇩ A SEA OF SHEEP. Sheep outnumber people in Australia and New Zealand. Wool production is an important part of the economy of these two countries.

THE REGION:
AUSTRALIA,
NEW ZEALAND, & OCEANIA

THE BASICS

STATS

Largest country
**Australia 2,969,906 sq mi
(7,692,024 sq km)**

Smallest country
**New Zealand 104,454 sq mi
(270,534 sq km)**

Most populous country
Australia 21,852,000

Least populous country
New Zealand 4,317,000

Predominant languages
English, Maori

Predominant religion
Christianity

Highest GDP per capita
Australia $39,400

Lowest GDP per capita
New Zealand $27,700

Highest life expectancy
Australia 82 years

Highest literacy rate
**Australia, New Zealand
99%**

GEO WHIZ

Australian Aborigines use a small tree trunk hollowed out by termites to make a musical instrument called a didgeridoo.

One-fourth of New Zealand's population lives in Auckland, on North Island, making it the largest city in Polynesia.

Lake Eyre is Australia's largest lake, but it is very shallow—not quite 20 feet (6 m) deep when full. Most of the rivers that flow into it dry up before they reach the lake. During the last 150 years, it has filled to capacity only three times.

Australia's location south of the Equator earned it the nickname Land Down Under.

The ceilings of grottoes in New Zealand's Waitomo Caves look like starry night skies thanks to the light given off by thousands of glowworms.

The Tasmanian devil is a meat-eating marsupial that lives only in Tasmania. Its high-pitched screeches can be heard at night when the animal is most active. This protected species is the symbol of the Tasmanian National Parks and Wildlife Service.

AUSTRALIA & NEW ZEALAND

Most people in Australia live along the coast, far from the country's dry interior, known as the Outback. The most populous cities and the best croplands are in the southeast. This "Land Down Under" is increasingly linked by trade to Asian countries and to 4 million "neighbors" in New Zealand. Twelve hundred miles (1,930 km) across the Tasman Sea, New Zealand is cooler, wetter, and more mountainous than Australia. It is geologically active and has ecosystems ranging from subtropical forests on North Island to snowy peaks on South Island. Both countries enjoy high standards of living and strong agricultural and mining outputs, including wool, wines, gold, coal, and iron ore.

⇐ KILLER OF THE DEEP. Great white sharks inhabit the warm waters off the coast of southern Australia. These warm-blooded marine predators can grow up to 20 feet (6 m) in length.

⇒ SAILS AT SUNSET. Reminiscent of a ship in full sail, the Sydney Opera House, in Sydney Harbor, has become a symbol of Australia that is recognized around the world.

⇐ DOG OF THE OUTBACK. The dingo is a wild dog found throughout Australia except for Tasmania. Unlike most domestic dogs, the dingo does not bark, although it howls. Aborigines sometimes use dingos as hunting companions or guard dogs.

⇧ SOUTHERN FIORDLAND. Partially hidden behind a cloud, Mitre Peak rises more than 5,500 feet (1,676 m) above Milford Sound on the southwest coast of New Zealand's South Island.

Map Key

● Country capital
◉ State capital
• City or town
— Boundary

ANIMAL MAJORITY

□ Australia ☐ New Zealand

	Sheep	Cattle	People
Australia	76.9*	27.3	21.9
New Zealand	32.4	5.8	4.3

Figures in millions, 2009 data

Sheep, raised for wool and meat, far outnumber people in both Australia and New Zealand. Beef and dairy cattle also surpass human population numbers.

200 miles

200 kilometers

Oblique Mercator Projection

THE BASICS

STATS

Largest country
Papua New Guinea
178,703 sq mi (462,840 sq km)

Smallest country
Nauru 8 sq mi (21 sq km)

Most populous country
Papua New Guinea 6,610,000

Least populous country
Nauru 10,000

Predominant languages
English, various indigenous
languages and dialects

Predominant religion
Christianity, various indigenous
beliefs

Highest GDP per capita
Palau $8,100

Lowest GDP per capita
Solomon Islands $1,600

Highest life expectancy
Samoa 74 years

Highest literacy rate
Samoa
100%

GEO WHIZ

Tuvalu's highest point is roughly 16 feet (5 m) above sea level. Predictions that rising sea levels due to global warming could drown the island within the next 50 years have caused some of its people to emigrate to New Zealand and other countries with higher elevations.

For centuries in Fiji, tribal officials would bring out their best utensils for special people—not to serve them, but to eat them. Cannibalism in the islands ended in the late 1800s, when Christianity was adopted.

Only 36 of Tonga's 170 islands are inhabited. It was in Tongan waters that the infamous mutiny aboard the British ship HMAV *Bounty* took place in 1789.

The interior highland region of Papua New Guinea is so mountainous and forested that it wasn't explored by outsiders until the 1930s. Europeans were surprised to find people living there whose cultures hadn't changed since the Stone Age.

Kennedy Island, in the Solomon Islands, is named for U.S. President John F. Kennedy. During World War II he and some of his crew swam to this island—known as Plum Pudding at the time—after their PT boat was rammed by a Japanese destroyer.

⇨ LIVING EARTH.
Ambrym volcano, in Vanuatu, is one of the most active volcanoes in Oceania. First observed by Captain Cook in 1774, Ambrym continues to erupt regularly, adding to the island's black sand beaches.

OCEANIA

Although in its broadest sense Oceania includes Australia and New Zealand, more commonly it refers to some 25,000 islands that make up three large cultural regions in the Pacific Ocean. Melanesia, which extends from Papua New Guinea to Fiji, is closest to Australia. Micronesia lies mostly north of the Equator and includes Palau and the Federated States of Micronesia. New Zealand, Hawai'i, and Rapa Nui (Easter Island) mark the western, northern, and eastern limits of Polynesia, with Tahiti, Samoa, and Tonga near its heart. Oceania's people often face problems of limited living space and fresh water. Plantation agriculture, fishing, tourism, or mining form the economic base for most of the islands in this region.

⇧ SUNDAY SERVICES. These Samoan girls are dressed for church. The London Missionary Society brought Christianity to Samoa in the mid-1800s. The eastern islands became a U.S. territory in 1900.

⇐ UNSOLVED MYSTERY. Carved from volcanic rock, the giant stone heads of Rapa Nui, also known as Easter Island, remain a mystery. Although culturally Polynesian, the island belongs to Chile, 2,400 miles (3,862 km) to the east (see page 44).

⇓ LONG ARMS. Octopuses live on coral reefs in the warm tropical waters of the South Pacific Ocean. They use the suckers on their tentacles to move around and to catch crustaceans and small fish.

Midway Islands (U.S.)

TROPIC OF CANCER

H A W A I ' I (UNITED STATES)

Honolulu ⊙ O'ahu
● Hilo
Hawai'i

Wake Island (U.S.)

Johnston Atoll (U.S.)

P A C I F I C   O C E A N

kini oll

Ratak Chain

MARSHALL ISLANDS

y Chain S

★ Majuro

Kingman Reef (U.S.)
Palmyra Atoll (U.S.)

AURU
n★

Gilbert Islands

★ Tarawa

Howland Island (U.S.)
Baker Island (U.S.)

Kiritimati (Christmas I.)

Jarvis Island (U.S.)

EQUATOR

K I R I B A T I

L I N E   I S L A N D S

Malden Island

Starbuck Island

Phoenix Islands

TUVALU
● Funafuti

TOKELAU (NEW ZEALAND)

Vostok Island

Caroline Island

Flint Island

MARQUESAS ISLANDS (FRANCE)

N ISLANDS

Santa Cruz Is.

Rotuma

Îles (FRANCE) Wallis
Îles de Horne

SAMOA
Apia ★⊙
⊙ Pago Pago

AMERICAN SAMOA (U.S.)

Samoa Islands

Cook Islands (NEW ZEALAND)

TUAMOTU ARCHIPELAGO

ANUATU

Vanua Levu

Port Vila ● Éfaté

FIJI

Viti Levu

★ Suva

ISLANDS

Society Islands

Tahiti
● Papeete

FRENCH POLYNESIA (FRANCE)

t. Panié 341 ft 1,628 m
●Nouméa

TONGA
★ Nuku'alofa

Austral Islands

TROPIC OF CAPRICORN

Henderson Island (UNITED KINGDOM)

Caledonia
ANCE

S O U T H   P A C I F I C   O C E A N

Pitcairn Island (U.K.)

Ducie Island (U.K.)

Sala-y-Gómez (CHILE)

ALIA) Norfolk Island
Phillip Island

Kermadec Islands (NEW ZEALAND)

Isla de Pascua (Easter Island) (CHILE)

NEW ZEALAND

Map Key

- ★ Country capital
- ⊙ State or province capital
- ●●● City or town
- ...... Boundary

SCALE AT THE EQUATOR

0 — 1,000 miles

0 — 1,000 kilometers

Mercator Projection

⇐ MELANESIAN CUSTOM.
In the Huli culture of Papua New Guinea's Eastern Highlands, men adorn themselves with colorful paints, feathers, and grasses in preparation for a festival.

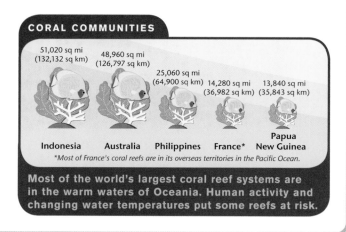

CORAL COMMUNITIES

Indonesia	Australia	Philippines	France*	Papua New Guinea
51,020 sq mi (132,132 sq km)	48,960 sq mi (126,797 sq km)	25,060 sq mi (64,900 sq km)	14,280 sq mi (36,982 sq km)	13,840 sq mi (35,843 sq km)

*Most of France's coral reefs are in its overseas territories in the Pacific Ocean.

Most of the world's largest coral reef systems are in the warm waters of Oceania. Human activity and changing water temperatures put some reefs at risk.

THE CONTINENT:
ANTARCTICA

PHYSICAL

Land area
5,100,000 sq mi (13,209,000 sq km)

Highest point
Vinson Massif
16,067 ft (4,897 m)

Lowest point
Bentley Subglacial Trench
-8,383 ft (-2,555 m)

Coldest place
Plateau Station
Annual average temperature
−70°F (-56.7°C)

**Average precipitation
on the polar plateau**
Less than 2 in (5 cm)
per year

POLITICAL

Population
There are no indigenous
inhabitants, but there
are both permanent and
summer-only staffed
research stations.

**Number of independent
countries**
0

**Number of countries
claiming land**
7

**Number of countries
operating year-round
research stations**
19

**Number of year-round
research stations**
45

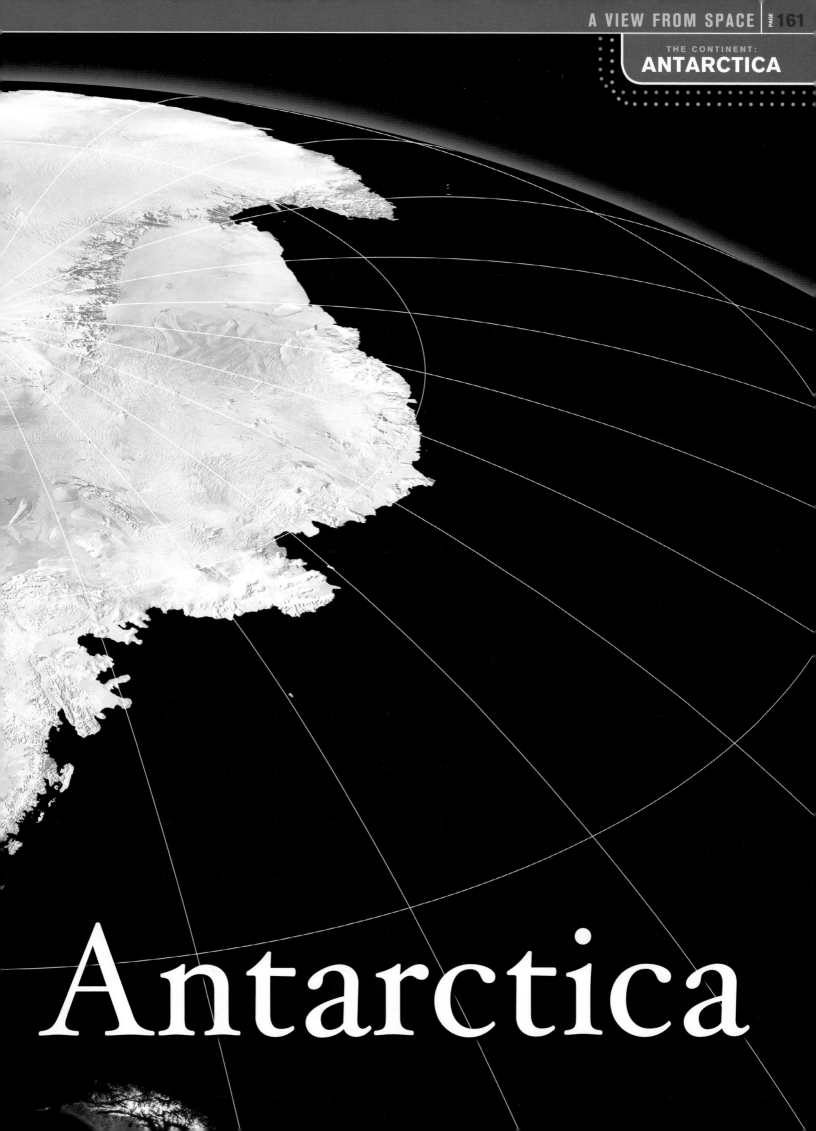

Antarctica

THE CONTINENT:
ANTARCTICA

ANTARCTICA

THE BASICS

Antarctica is the only continent that has no sovereign boundaries and no economy or permanent population. Seven countries claim portions of the landmass (see map below), but according to the Antarctic Treaty, which preserves the continent for peaceful use and scientific study, no country rules the continent.

GEO WHIZ

In winter, sea ice averaging 6 feet (2 m) deep more than doubles the size of the continent as it forms a belt ranging from 300 miles (483 km) to more than 1,000 miles (1,620 km) wide.

The Antarctic Convergence, an area where the waters of the Pacific, Atlantic, and Indian Oceans meet the cold Antarctic Circumpolar Current, is one of Earth's richest marine ecosystems.

The largest iceberg ever spotted in Antarctic waters measured 208 miles (335 km) long by 60 miles (97 km) wide, making it slightly larger than Belgium.

 Krill, a tiny shrimplike creature that thrives in the waters around the continent of Antarctica, is important in the Antarctic food chain. Whales, seals, and penguins are among the creatures that depend on it for survival.

A small insect known as the wingless midge is Antarctica's largest land animal.

 Five species of penguins live on the continent and nearby islands. The Emperor penguin is the only one that breeds during the winter.

Fierce, bitter cold winds batter the coast at speeds of as much as 180 miles per hour (300 km/h).

Mount Erebus is the world's southernmost volcano. Polar explorer James Clark Ross named it after one of his ships.

The Antarctic Treaty was signed in 1959 by 12 countries. To date, 47 countries have signed the document, agreeing to cooperate in scientific research and forbidding military action, nuclear tests, and the dumping of radioactive waste on the continent and in its waters.

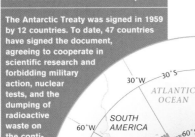

⇧ SOUTHERN HEIGHTS. Standing on the rocky summit of Mount Bearskin, named for a member of the team that established the 1956–57 IGY (International Geophysical Year) South Pole Station, a climber looks out across a vast snowfield.

Antarctica is the coldest, windiest, and even the driest continent. Though its immense ice cap holds 70 percent of the world's fresh water, its interior averages less than 2 inches (5 cm) of precipitation per year. Hidden beneath the ice is a continent of valleys, mountains, and lakes, but less than 2 percent of the land breaks through the ice cover. Reaching toward South America is the Antarctic Peninsula, the most visited of Antarctic regions. Though it is remote and mostly inhospitable, issues of human impact abound: fishing in rich but fragile waters that are sometimes called the Southern Ocean, future mining rights, and concern about the impact of global warming on the ice sheet.

South Orkney Islands

South Shetland Islands

Joinvi

Alexander Island

Bellingshausen

PACI

Thu Is

In color are shown 7 nations' territorial claims recognized by the Antarctic Treaty.

0 — 2,000 mi
0 — 2,000 km

Azimuthal Equidistant Projection

0°
30°W   30°S   AFRICA   30°E
ATLANTIC OCEAN
SOUTH AMERICA   60°W   60°S   60°E
UNITED KINGDOM   ARGENTINA   CHILE   NORWAY   AUSTRALIA
90°W   90°E   INDIAN OCEAN
UNCLAIMED   AUSTRALIA
FRANCE
NEW ZEALAND
120°W   PACIFIC OCEAN   120°E
AUSTRALIA
150°W   New Zealand   150°E
180°

← STANDING GUARD. Even while resting, this leopard seal is alert to danger. Although penguins are their main food, leopard seals also eat other species of seals and have even been known to attack humans.

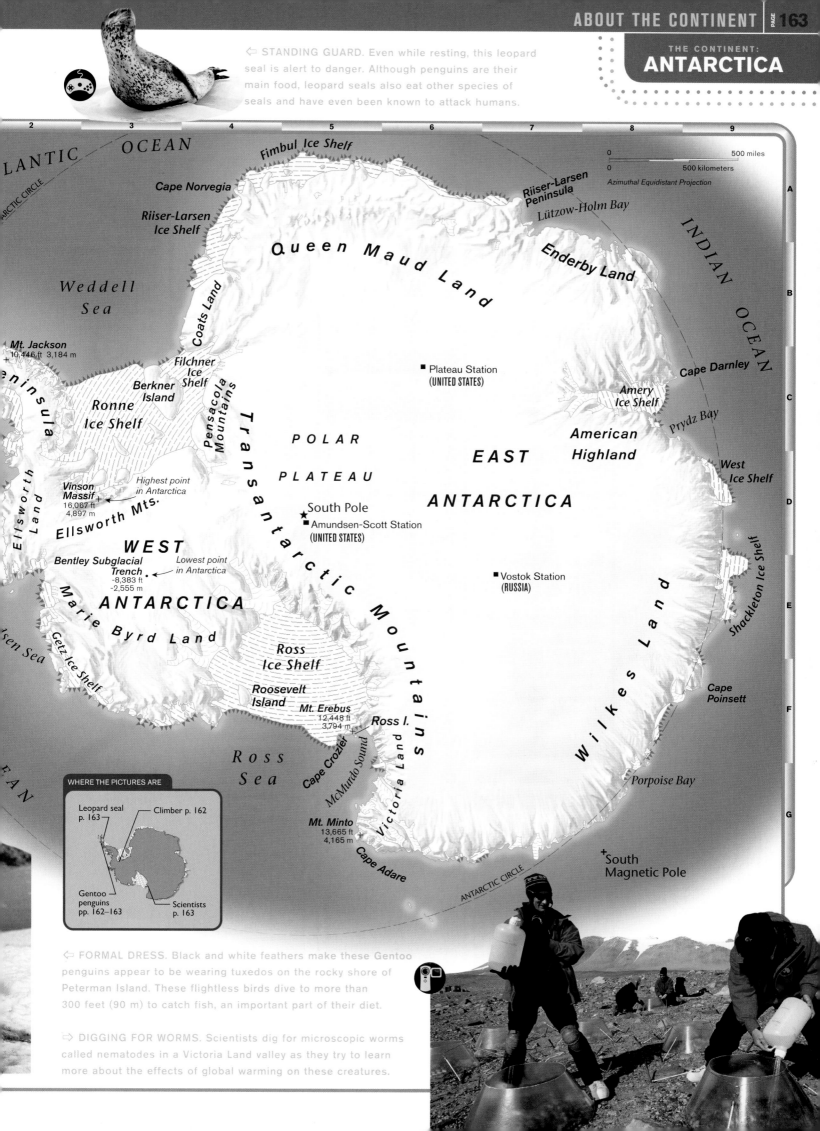

ATLANTIC OCEAN

ARCTIC CIRCLE

Fimbul Ice Shelf

Cape Norvegia

Riiser-Larsen Peninsula

Lützow-Holm Bay

Riiser-Larsen Ice Shelf

Queen Maud Land

Enderby Land

INDIAN OCEAN

Weddell Sea

Cape Darnley

Coats Land

Mt. Jackson
10,446 ft 3,184 m

Amery Ice Shelf

Filchner Ice Shelf

Berkner Island

Pensacola Mountains

Plateau Station
(UNITED STATES)

Ronne Ice Shelf

POLAR PLATEAU

American Highland

Prydz Bay

EAST ANTARCTICA

West Ice Shelf

Peninsula

Ellsworth Land

Vinson Massif
16,067 ft
4,897 m

Highest point in Antarctica

Transantarctic Mountains

South Pole

Amundsen-Scott Station
(UNITED STATES)

Ellsworth Mts.

WEST ANTARCTICA

Bentley Subglacial Trench
-8,383 ft
-2,555 m

Lowest point in Antarctica

Vostok Station
(RUSSIA)

Shackleton Ice Shelf

Marie Byrd Land

Getz Ice Shelf

Wilkes Land

Ross Ice Shelf

Cape Poinsett

Roosevelt Island

Mt. Erebus
12,448 ft
3,794 m

Ross I.

...sen Sea

...E A N

Ross Sea

Cape Crozier

McMurdo Sound

Victoria Land

Porpoise Bay

Mt. Minto
13,665 ft
4,165 m

Cape Adare

ANTARCTIC CIRCLE

+South Magnetic Pole

0   500 miles
0   500 kilometers
Azimuthal Equidistant Projection

WHERE THE PICTURES ARE

Leopard seal p. 163
Climber p. 162
Gentoo penguins pp. 162-163
Scientists p. 163

← FORMAL DRESS. Black and white feathers make these Gentoo penguins appear to be wearing tuxedos on the rocky shore of Peterman Island. These flightless birds dive to more than 300 feet (90 m) to catch fish, an important part of their diet.

→ DIGGING FOR WORMS. Scientists dig for microscopic worms called nematodes in a Victoria Land valley as they try to learn more about the effects of global warming on these creatures.

FLAGS & STATS

These flags and fact boxes represent the world's 194 independent countries—those with national governments that are recognized as having the highest legal authority over the land and people within their boundaries. The flags shown are national flags recognized by the United Nations. Area figures include land plus surface areas for inland bodies of water. Population figures are for mid-2009 as provided by the Population Reference Bureau of the United States. The languages listed are either the ones most commonly spoken within a country or official languages of a country.

NORTH AMERICA

Antigua and Barbuda
Area: 171 sq mi
(442 sq km)
Population: 88,000
Capital: St. John's
Languages: English (official), local dialects

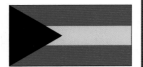

Bahamas
Area: 5,382 sq mi
(13,939 sq km)
Population: 341,000
Capital: Nassau
Languages: English (official), Creole

Barbados
Area: 166 sq mi
(430 sq km)
Population: 281,000
Capital: Bridgetown
Language: English

Belize
Area: 8,867 sq mi
(22,965 sq km)
Population: 329,000
Capital: Belmopan
Languages: Spanish, Creole, Mayan dialects, English, Garifuna (Carib), German

Canada
Area: 3,855,101 sq mi
(9,984,670 sq km)
Population: 33,707,000
Capital: Ottawa
Languages: English, French (both official)

Costa Rica
Area: 19,730 sq mi
(51,100 sq km)
Population: 4,509,000
Capital: San José
Languages: Spanish (official), English

Cuba
Area: 42,803 sq mi
(110,860 sq km)
Population: 11,225,000
Capital: Havana
Language: Spanish

Dominica
Area: 290 sq mi
(751 sq km)
Population: 72,000
Capital: Roseau
Languages: English (official), French patois

Dominican Republic
Area: 18,704 sq mi
(48,442 sq km)
Population: 10,090,000
Capital: Santo Domingo
Language: Spanish

El Salvador
Area: 8,124 sq mi
(21,041 sq km)
Population: 7,339,000
Capital: San Salvador
Languages: Spanish, Nahua

Grenada
Area: 133 sq mi
(344 sq km)
Population: 106,000
Capital: St. George's
Languages: English (official), French patois

Guatemala
Area: 42,042 sq mi
(108,889 sq km)
Population: 14,027,000
Capital: Guatemala City
Languages: Spanish, 23 Amerindian languages

Haiti
Area: 10,714 sq mi
(27,750 sq km)
Population: 9,242,000
Capital: Port-au-Prince
Languages: French, Creole (both official)

Honduras
Area: 43,433 sq mi
(112,492 sq km)
Population: 7,466,000
Capital: Tegucigalpa
Languages: Spanish, Amerindian dialects

Jamaica
Area: 4,244 sq mi
(10,991 sq km)
Population: 2,702,000
Capital: Kingston
Languages: English, patois English

México
Area: 758,449 sq mi
(1,964,375 sq km)
Population: 109,610,000
Capital: México City
Languages: Spanish, Maya, Nahuatl, other indigenous languages

Nicaragua
Area: 50,193 sq mi
(130,000 sq km)
Population: 5,669,000
Capital: Managua
Languages: Spanish (official), English, indigenous languages

Panama
Area: 29,157 sq mi
(75,517 sq km)
Population: 3,454,000
Capital: Panama City
Languages: Spanish (official), English

St. Kitts and Nevis
Area: 104 sq mi
(269 sq km)
Population: 50,000
Capital: Basseterre
Language: English

St. Lucia
Area: 238 sq mi
(616 sq km)
Population: 172,000
Capital: Castries
Languages: English (official), French patois

St. Vincent and the Grenadines
Area: 150 sq mi
(389 sq km)
Population: 110,000
Capital: Kingstown
Languages: English, French patois

Trinidad and Tobago
Area: 1,980 sq mi
(5,128 sq km)
Population: 1,333,000
Capital: Port of Spain
Languages: English (official), Caribbean Hindustani, French, Spanish, Chinese

United States
Area: 3,794,083 sq mi
(9,826,630 sq km)
Population: 306,805,000
Capital: Washington, D.C.
Languages: English, Spanish

SOUTH AMERICA

Argentina
Area: 1,073,518 sq mi
(2,780,400 sq km)
Population: 40,276,000
Capital: Buenos Aires
Languages: Spanish (official),
English, Italian, German, French

Bolivia
Area: 424,164 sq mi
(1,098,581 sq km)
Population: 9,863,000
Capitals: La Paz, Sucre
Languages: Spanish,
Quechua, Aymara (all official)

Brazil
Area: 3,300,171 sq mi
(8,547,403 sq km)
Population: 191,481,000
Capital: Brasília
Language: Portuguese (official)

Chile
Area: 291,930 sq mi
(756,096 sq km)
Population: 16,970,000
Capital: Santiago
Language: Spanish

Colombia
Area: 440,831 sq mi
(1,141,748 sq km)
Population: 46,065,000
Capital: Bogotá
Language: Spanish

Ecuador
Area: 109,483 sq mi
(283,560 sq km)
Population: 13,625,000
Capital: Quito
Languages: Spanish (official),
Quechua, other Amerindian
languages

Guyana
Area: 83,000 sq mi
(214,969 sq km)
Population: 773,000
Capital: Georgetown
Languages: English,
Amerindian dialects, Creole,
Hindi, Urdu

Paraguay
Area: 157,048 sq mi
(406,752 sq km)
Population: 6,349,000
Capital: Asunción
Languages: Spanish, Guaraní
(both official)

Peru
Area: 496,224 sq mi
(1,285,216 sq km)
Population: 29,165,000
Capital: Lima
Languages: Spanish, Quechua
(both official), Aymara, minor
Amazonian languages

Suriname
Area: 63,037 sq mi
(163,265 sq km)
Population: 502,000
Capital: Paramaribo
Languages: Dutch (official),
English, Sranang Tongo (Taki-
Taki), Hindustani, Javanese

Uruguay
Area: 68,037 sq mi
(176,215 sq km)
Population: 3,364,000
Capital: Montevideo
Languages: Spanish, Portunol,
Brazilero

Venezuela
Area: 352,144 sq mi
(912,050 sq km)
Population: 28,368,000
Capital: Caracas
Languages: Spanish
(official), many indigenous
languages

EUROPE

Albania
Area: 11,100 sq mi
(28,748 sq km)
Population: 3,196,000
Capital: Tirana
Languages: Albanian
(official), Greek, Vlach,
Romani, Slavic dialects

Andorra
Area: 181 sq mi
(468 sq km)
Population: 86,000
Capital: Andorra la Vella
Languages: Catalan
(official), French, Castilian,
Portuguese

Austria
Area: 32,378 sq mi
(83,858 sq km)
Population: 8,374,000
Capital: Vienna
Languages: German (official),
Slovene, Croatian, Hungarian

Belarus
Area: 80,153 sq mi
(207,595 sq km)
Population: 9,662,000
Capital: Minsk
Languages: Belarusian, Russian

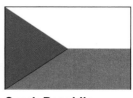

Belgium
Area: 11,787 sq mi
(30,528 sq km)
Population: 10,792,000
Capital: Brussels
Languages: Flemish (Dutch),
French, German (all official)

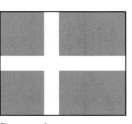

Bosnia and
Herzegovina
Area: 19,741 sq mi
(51,129 sq km)
Population: 3,843,000
Capital: Sarajevo
Languages: Croatian, Serbian,
Bosnian

Bulgaria
Area: 42,855 sq mi
(110,994 sq km)
Population: 7,590,000
Capital: Sofia
Languages: Bulgarian, Turkish,
Roma

Croatia
Area: 21,831 sq mi
(56,542 sq km)
Population: 4,433,000
Capital: Zagreb
Language: Croatian

Cyprus
Area: 3,572 sq mi
(9,251 sq km)
Population: 1,072,000
Capital: Nicosia
Languages: Greek, Turkish,
English

Czech Republic
Area: 30,450 sq mi
(78,866 sq km)
Population: 10,511,000
Capital: Prague
Language: Czech

Denmark
Area: 16,640 sq mi
(43,098 sq km)
Population: 5,529,000
Capital: Copenhagen
Languages: Danish, Faroese,
Greenlandic, German

Estonia
Area: 17,462 sq mi
(45,227 sq km)
Population: 1,340,000
Capital: Tallinn
Languages: Estonian (official),
Russian

FLAGS & STATS

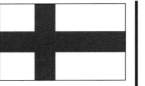

Finland
Area: 130,558 sq mi
(338,145 sq km)
Population: 5,339,000
Capital: Helsinki
Languages: Finnish, Swedish
(both official)

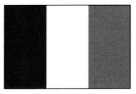

France
Area: 210,026 sq mi
(543,965 sq km)
Population: 62,621,000
Capital: Paris
Language: French

Germany
Area: 137,847 sq mi
(357,022 sq km)
Population: 81,980,000
Capital: Berlin
Language: German

Greece
Area: 50,949 sq mi
(131,957 sq km)
Population: 11,227,000
Capital: Athens
Language: Greek, English,
French

Hungary
Area: 35,919 sq mi
(93,030 sq km)
Population: 10,024,000
Capital: Budapest
Language: Hungarian

Iceland
Area: 39,769 sq mi
(103,000 sq km)
Population: 321,000
Capital: Reykjavik
Languages: Icelandic, English,
Nordic languages, German

Ireland
Area: 27,133 sq mi
(70,273 sq km)
Population: 4,528,000
Capital: Dublin
Languages: Irish (Gaelic),
English

Italy
Area: 116,345 sq mi
(301,333 sq km)
Population: 60,274,000
Capital: Rome
Languages: Italian (official),
German, French, Slovene

Kosovo
Area: 4,203 sq mi
(10,887 sq km)
Population: 2,191,000
Capital: Pristina
Languages: Albanian, Serbian,
Bosnian, Turkish, Roma

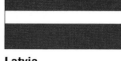

Latvia
Area: 24,938 sq mi
(64,589 sq km)
Population: 2,256,000
Capital: Riga
Languages: Latvian (official),
Russian, Lithuanian

Liechtenstein
Area: 62 sq mi
(160 sq km)
Population: 40,000
Capital: Vaduz
Language: German (official),
Alemannic dialect

Lithuania
Area: 25,212 sq mi
(65,300 sq km)
Population: 3,339,000
Capital: Vilnius
Languages: Lithuanian
(official), Polish, Russian

Luxembourg
Area: 998 sq mi
(2,586 sq km)
Population: 498,000
Capital: Luxembourg
Languages: Luxembourgish
(official), German, French

Macedonia
Area: 9,928 sq mi
(25,713 sq km)
Population: 2,049,000
Capital: Skopje
Languages: Macedonian,
Albanian, Turkish

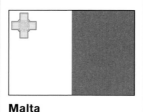

Malta
Area: 122 sq mi
(316 sq km)
Population: 414,000
Capital: Valletta
Languages: Maltese, English
(both official)

Moldova
Area: 13,050 sq mi
(33,800 sq km)
Population: 4,133,000
Capital: Chişinău
Languages: Moldovan
(official), Russian, Gagauz

Monaco
Area: 0.8 sq mi
(2 sq km)
Population: 35,000
Capital: Monaco
Languages: French (official),
English, Italian, Monegasque

Montenegro
Area: 5,415 sq mi
(14,026 sq km)
Population: 628,000
Capital: Podgorica
Languages: Serbian (official),
Bosnian, Albanian, Croatian

Netherlands
Area: 16,034 sq mi
(41,528 sq km)
Population: 16,527,000
Capital: Amsterdam
Languages: Dutch, Frisian
(both official)

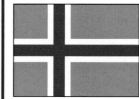

Norway
Area: 125,004 sq mi
(323,758 sq km)
Population: 4,827,000
Capital: Oslo
Language: Norwegian (official)

Poland
Area: 120,728 sq mi
(312,685 sq km)
Population: 38,146,000
Capital: Warsaw
Language: Polish

Portugal
Area: 35,655 sq mi
(92,345 sq km)
Population: 10,639,000
Capital: Lisbon
Languages: Portuguese,
Mirandese (both official)

Romania
Area: 92,043 sq mi
(238,391 sq km)
Population: 21,474,000
Capital: Bucharest
Languages: Romanian (official),
Hungarian, German

Russia
Area: 6,592,850 sq mi
(17,075,400 sq km)
Population: 141,839,000
Capital: Moscow
Languages: Russian, many
minority languages

San Marino
Area: 24 sq mi
(61 sq km)
Population: 31,000
Capital: San Marino
Language: Italian

Serbia
Area: 29,913 sq mi
(77,474 sq km)
Population: 7,322,000
Capital: Belgrade
Languages: Serbian (official),
Romanian, Hungarian, Slovak,
Croatian

Slovakia
Area: 18,932 sq mi
(49,035 km)
Population: 5,417,000
Capital: Bratislava
Languages: Slovak (official),
Hungarian

Slovenia
Area: 7,827 sq mi
(20,273 sq km)
Population: 2,043,000
Capital: Ljubljana
Languages: Slovene, Serbo-
Croatian

Spain
Area: 195,363 sq mi
(505,988 sq km)
Population: 46,916,000
Capital: Madrid
Languages: Castilian Spanish
(official), Catalan, Galician,
Basque

Sweden
Area: 173,732 sq mi
(449,964 sq km)
Population: 9,288,000
Capital: Stockholm
Language: Swedish, Sami,
Finnish

Switzerland
Area: 15,940 sq mi
(41,284 sq km)
Population: 7,754,000
Capital: Bern
Languages: German,
French, Italian (all official),
Romansch

Ukraine
Area: 233,090 sq mi
(603,700 sq km)
Population: 46,030,000
Capital: Kiev
Languages: Ukrainian (official),
Russian

United Kingdom
Area: 93,788 sq mi
(242,910 sq km)
Population: 61,823,000
Capital: London
Languages: English, Welsh,
Scottish form of Gaelic

Vatican City
Area: 0.2 sq mi
(0.4 sq km)
Population: 798
Languages: Italian, Latin,
French

ASIA

Afghanistan
Area: 251,773 sq mi
(652,090 sq km)
Population: 28,396,000
Capital: Kabul
Languages: Afghan Persian
(Dari), Pashtu (both official),
Turkic languages

Armenia
Area: 11,484 sq mi
(29,743 sq km)
Population: 3,097,000
Capital: Yerevan
Language: Armenian

Azerbaijan
Area: 33,436 sq mi
(86,600 sq km)
Population: 8,781,000
Capital: Baku
Language: Azerbaijani (Azeri)

Bahrain
Area: 277 sq mi
(717 sq km)
Population: 1,217,000
Capital: Manama
Languages: Arabic, English,
Farsi, Urdu

Bangladesh
Area: 56,977 sq mi
(147,570 sq km)
Population: 162,221,000
Capital: Dhaka
Languages: Bangla (Bengali)
(official), English

Bhutan
Area: 17,954 sq mi
(46,500 sq km)
Population: 683,000
Capital: Thimphu
Languages: Dzongkha
(official), Tibetan dialects,
Nepali dialects

Brunei
Area: 2,226 sq mi
(5,765 sq km)
Population: 383,000
Capital: Bandar Seri Begawan
Languages: Malay (official),
English, Chinese

Cambodia
Area: 69,898 sq mi
(181,035 sq km)
Population: 14,805,000
Capital: Phnom Penh
Language: Khmer (official)

China
Area: 3,705,405 sq mi
(9,596,960 sq km)
Population: 1,362,069,000
Capital: Beijing
Languages: Standard Chinese
(Mandarin), Yue, Wu, Minbei,
other dialects and minority
languages

Timor-Leste
(East Timor)
Area: 5,640 sq mi
(14,609 sq km)
Population: 1,134,000
Capital: Dili
Languages: Tetum, Portuguese
(official), Indonesian, English

Georgia
Area: 26,911 sq mi
(69,700 sq km)
Population: 4,611,000
Capital: T'bilisi
Languages: Georgian (offi-
cial), Russian, Armenian, Azeri,
Abkhaz

India
Area: 1,171,221 sq mi
(3,287,270 sq km)
Population: 1,171,000,000
Capital: New Delhi
Languages: Hindi, English
(both official), 21 other official
languages

Indonesia
Area: 742,308 sq mi
(1,922,570 sq km)
Population: 243,306,000
Capital: Jakarta
Languages: Bahasa Indonesian
(official), English, Dutch, Javanese

Iran
Area: 636,296 sq mi
(1,648,000 sq km)
Population: 73,244,000
Capital: Tehran
Languages: Farsi (modern-day
Persian), Turkic, Kurdish

Iraq
Area: 168,754 sq mi
(437,072 sq km)
Population: 30,047,000
Capital: Baghdad
Languages: Arabic, Kurdish,
Assyrian, Armenian

FLAGS & STATS

Israel
Area: 8,550 sq mi
(22,145 sq km)
Population: 7,634,000
Capital: Jerusalem
Languages: Hebrew (official),
Arabic, English

Japan
Area: 145,902 sq mi
(377,887 sq km)
Population: 127,568,000
Capital: Tokyo
Language: Japanese

Jordan
Area: 34,495 sq mi
(89,342 sq km)
Population: 5,915,000
Capital: Amman
Languages: Arabic (official),
English

Kazakhstan
Area: 1,049,155 sq mi
(2,717,300 sq km)
Population: 15,880,000
Capital: Astana
Languages: Kazakh (Qazaq),
Russian (official)

Korea, North
Area: 46,540 sq mi
(120,538 sq km)
Population: 22,665,000
Capital: Pyongyang
Language: Korean

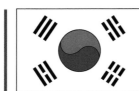

Korea, South
Area: 38,321 sq mi
(99,250 sq km)
Population: 48,747,000
Capital: Seoul
Languages: Korean,
English widely taught

Kuwait
Area: 6,880 sq mi
(17,818 sq km)
Population: 2,985,000
Capital: Kuwait
Languages: Arabic (official),
English

Kyrgyzstan
Area: 77,182 sq mi
(199,900 sq km)
Population: 5,304,000
Capital: Bishkek
Languages: Kyrgyz, Russian
(both official)

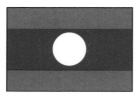

Laos
Area: 91,429 sq mi
(236,800 sq km)
Population: 6,320,000
Languages: Lao (official),
French, English, various ethnic
languages

Lebanon
Area: 4,036 sq mi
(10,452 sq km)
Population: 3,876,000
Capital: Beirut
Languages: Arabic (official),
French, English, Armenian

Malaysia
Area: 127,355 sq mi
(329,847 sq km)
Population: 28,985,000
Capital: Kuala Lumpur
Languages: Bahasa Melayu
(official), English, Chinese
dialects, Tamil, Telugu,
indigenous languages

Maldives
Area: 115 sq mi
(298 sq km)
Population: 315,000
Capital: Male
Languages: Maldivian Dhivehi,
English

Mongolia
Area: 603,909 sq mi
(1,564,116 sq km)
Population: 2,708,000
Capital: Ulaanbaatar
Languages: Khalkha Mongol,
Turkic, Russian

Myanmar (Burma)
Area: 261,218 sq mi
(676,552 sq km)
Population: 50,020,000
Capitals: Nay Pyi Taw,
Yangon (Rangoon)
Languages: Burmese, minority
ethnic languages

Nepal
Area: 56,827 sq mi
(147,181 sq km)
Population: 27,504,000
Capital: Kathmandu
Languages: Nepali, Maithali,
Bhojpuri, Tharu, Tamang,
English

Oman
Area: 119,500 sq mi
(309,500 sq km)
Population: 3,108,000
Capital: Muscat
Languages: Arabic (official),
English, Baluchi, Urdu, Indian
dialects

Pakistan
Area: 307,374 sq mi
(796,095 sq km)
Population: 180,808,000
Capital: Islamabad
Languages: Urdu, English
(both official), Punjabi, Sindhi,
Siraiki, Pashtu

Philippines
Area: 115,831 sq mi
(300,000 sq km)
Population: 92,227,000
Capital: Manila
Languages: Filipino (based on
Tagalog), English (both official),
8 major dialects

Qatar
Area: 4,448 sq mi
(11,521 sq km)
Population: 1,409,000
Capital: Doha
Languages: Arabic (official),
English

Saudi Arabia
Area: 756,985 sq mi
(1,960,582 sq km)
Population: 28,687,000
Capital: Riyadh
Language: Arabic

Singapore
Area: 255 sq mi
(660 sq km)
Population: 5,113,000
Capital: Singapore
Languages: Mandarin, English,
Malay, Hokkien

Sri Lanka
Area: 25,299 sq mi
(65,525 sq km)
Population: 20,502,000
Capital: Colombo
Languages: Sinhala
(official), Tamil, English

Syria
Area: 71,498 sq mi
(185,180 sq km)
Population: 21,906,000
Capital: Damascus
Languages: Arabic (official),
Kurdish, Armenian, Aramaic,
Circassian

Tajikistan
Area: 55,251 sq mi
(143,100 sq km)
Population: 7,450,000
Capital: Dushanbe
Languages: Tajik (official),
Russian

Thailand
Area: 198,115 sq mi
(513,115 sq km)
Population: 67,764,000
Capital: Bangkok (Krung Thep)
Languages: Thai, English,
ethnic and regional dialects

Turkey
Area: 300,948 sq mi
(779,452 sq km)
Population: 74,816,000
Capital: Ankara
Languages: Turkish (official),
Kurdish, Arabic, Armenian,
Greek

Turkmenistan
Area: 188,300 sq mi
(488,100 sq km)
Population: 5,110,000
Capital: Ashgabat
Languages: Turkmen, Russian,
Uzbek

United Arab Emirates
Area: 30,000 sq mi
(77,700 sq km)
Population: 4,900,000
Capital: Abu Dhabi
Languages: Arabic (official),
Persian, English, Hindi, Urdu

Uzbekistan
Area: 172,742 sq mi
(447,400 sq km)
Population: 27,562,000
Capital: Tashkent
Languages: Uzbek, Russian

Vietnam
Area: 127,844 sq mi
(331,114 sq km)
Population: 84,263,000
Capital: Hanoi
Languages: Vietnamese
(official), English, French,
Chinese, Khmer

Yemen
Area: 207,286 sq mi
(536,869 sq km)
Population: 22,880,000
Capital: Sanaa
Language: Arabic

AFRICA

Algeria
Area: 919,595 sq mi
(2,381,741 sq km)
Population: 33,370,000
Capital: Algiers
Languages: Arabic (official),
French, Berber dialects

Angola
Area: 481,354 sq mi
(1,246,700 sq km)
Population: 17,074,000
Capital: Luanda
Languages: Portuguese
(official), Bantu, other African
languages

Benin
Area: 43,484 sq mi
(112,622 sq km)
Population: 8,935,000
Capitals: Porto-Novo,
Cotonou
Languages: French (official),
Fon, Yoruba, tribal languages

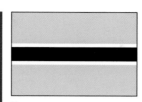

Botswana
Area: 224,607 sq mi
(581,730 sq km)
Population: 1,991,000
Capital: Gaborone
Languages: English (official),
Setswana, Kalanga, Sekgalgadi

Burkina Faso
Area: 105,869 sq mi
(274,200 sq km)
Population: 15,757,000
Capital: Ouagadougou
Languages: French (official),
indigenous languages

Burundi
Area: 10,747 sq mi
(27,834 sq km)
Population: 8,303,000
Capital: Bujumbura
Languages: Kirundi, French
(both official), Swahili

Cameroon
Area: 183,569 sq mi
(475,442 sq km)
Population: 18,879,000
Capital: Yaoundé
Languages: French, English
(both official), 24 major African
language groups

Cape Verde
Area: 1,558 sq mi
(4,036 sq km)
Population: 509,000
Capital: Praia
Languages: Portuguese,
Crioulo

**Central African
Republic**
Area: 240,535 sq mi
(622,984 sq km)
Population: 4,511,000
Capital: Bangui
Languages: French (official),
Sangho, tribal languages

Chad
Area: 495,755 sq mi
(1,284,000 sq km)
Population: 10,329,000
Capital: N'Djamena
Languages: French, Arabic
(both official), Sara, more
than 120 other languages
and dialects

Comoros
Area: 719 sq mi
(1,862 sq km)
Population: 676,000
Capital: Moroni
Languages: Arabic, French
(both official), Shikomoro

Congo
Area: 132,047 sq mi
(342,000 sq km)
Population: 3,683,000
Capital: Brazzaville
Languages: French (official),
Lingala, Monokutuba,
many local languages
and dialects

**Congo, Democratic
Republic of the**
Area: 905,365 sq mi
(2,344,885 sq km)
Population: 68,693,000
Capital: Kinshasa
Languages: French (official),
Lingala, Kingwana, Kikongo,
Tshiluba

Côte d'Ivoire
Area: 124,503 sq mi
(322,462 sq km)
Population: 21,395,000
Capitals: Abidjan, Yamoussoukro
Languages: French (official),
Dioula, 60 native dialects

Djibouti
Area: 8,958 sq mi
(23,200 sq km)
Population: 864,000
Capital: Djibouti
Languages: French, Arabic
(both official), Somali, Afar

Egypt
Area: 386,874 sq mi
(1,002,000 sq km)
Population: 78,629,000
Capital: Cairo
Languages: Arabic (official),
English, French

Equatorial Guinea
Area: 10,831 sq mi
(28,051 sq km)
Population: 676,000
Capital: Malabo
Languages: Spanish, French
(both official), pidgin English,
Fang, Bubi, Ibo

FLAGS & STATS

Eritrea
Area: 46,774 sq mi
(121,144 sq km)
Population: 5,073,000
Capital: Asmara
Languages: Afar, Arabic,
Tigre, Kunama, Tigrinya, other
Cushitic languages

Ethiopia
Area: 437,600 sq mi
(1,133,380 sq km)
Population: 82,825,000
Capital: Addis Ababa
Languages: Amharic, Tigrinya,
Oromigna, Guaragigna, Somali

Gabon
Area: 103,347 sq mi
(267,667 sq km)
Population: 1,475,000
Capital: Libreville
Languages: French (official),
Fang, Myene, Nzebi,
Bapounou/Eschira

Gambia
Area: 4,361 sq mi
(11,295 sq km)
Population: 1,609,000
Capital: Banjul
Languages: English (official),
Mandinka, Wolof, Fula

Ghana
Area: 92,100 sq mi
(238,537 sq km)
Population: 23,837,000
Capital: Accra
Languages: English (official),
Akan, Moshi-Dagomba, Ewe, Ga

Guinea
Area: 94,926 sq mi
(245,857 sq km)
Population: 10,058,000
Capital: Conakry
Languages: French (official),
indigenous languages

Guinea-Bissau
Area: 13,948 sq mi
(36,125 sq km)
Population: 1,611,000
Capital: Bissau
Languages: Portuguese
(official), Crioulo, indigenous
languages

Kenya
Area: 224,081 sq mi
(580,367 sq km)
Population: 39,070,000
Capital: Nairobi
Languages: English, Kiswahili
(both official), indigenous
languages

Lesotho
Area: 11,720 sq mi
(30,355 sq km)
Population: 2,135,000
Capital: Maseru
Languages: Sesotho, English
(official), Zulu, Xhosa

Liberia
Area: 43,000 sq mi
(111,370 sq km)
Population: 3,955,000
Capital: Monrovia
Languages: English (official),
20 ethnic group languages

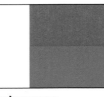

Libya
Area: 679,362 sq mi
(1,759,540 sq km)
Population: 6,283,000
Capital: Tripoli
Languages: Arabic, Italian,
English

Madagascar
Area: 226,658 sq mi
(587,041 sq km)
Population: 19,464,000
Capital: Antananarivo
Languages: French, Malagasy
(both official), English

Malawi
Area: 45,747 sq mi
(118,484 sq km)
Population: 14,214,000
Capital: Lilongwe
Languages: Chichewa (official),
Chinyanja, Chiyao, Chitumbuka

Mali
Area: 478,841 sq mi
(1,240,192 sq km)
Population: 13,010,000
Capital: Bamako
Languages: French, Bambara
(both official), numerous
African languages

Mauritania
Area: 397,955 sq mi
(1,030,700 sq km)
Population: 3,291,000
Capital: Nouakchott
Languages: Arabic (official), Pulaar,
Soninke, French, Hassaniya, Wolof

Mauritius
Area: 788 sq mi
(2,040 sq km)
Population: 1,276,000
Capital: Port Louis
Languages: Creole, Bhojpuri,
French (official)

Morocco
Area: 274,461 sq mi
(710,850 sq km)
Population: 31,495,000
Capital: Rabat
Languages: Arabic (official),
Berber dialects, French

Mozambique
Area: 308,642 sq mi
(799,380 sq km)
Population: 21,971,000
Capital: Maputo
Languages: Emakhuwa,
Xichangana, Portuguese (official),
Elomwe, Cisena, Echuwabo

Namibia
Area: 318,261 sq mi
(824,292 sq km)
Population: 2,171,000
Capital: Windhoek
Languages: English (official),
Afrikaans, German, indigenous
languages

Niger
Area: 489,191 sq mi
(1,267,000 sq km)
Population: 15,290,000
Capital: Niamey
Languages: French (official),
Hausa, Djerma

Nigeria
Area: 356,669 sq mi
(923,768 sq km)
Population: 152,616,000
Capital: Abuja
Languages: English (official),
Hausa, Yoruba, Igbo (Ibo), Fulani

Rwanda
Area: 10,169 sq mi
(26,338 sq km)
Population: 9,877,000
Capital: Kigali
Languages: Kinyarwanda,
French, English (all official),
Kiswahili

São Tomé and Principe
Area: 386 sq mi
(1,001 sq km)
Population: 163,000
Capital: São Tomé
Language: Portuguese
(official)

Senegal
Area: 75,955 sq mi
(196,722 sq km)
Population: 12,534,000
Capital: Dakar
Languages: French (official),
Wolof, Pulaar, Jola, Mandinka

Seychelles
Area: 176 sq mi
(455 sq km)
Population: 87,000
Capital: Victoria
Languages: English (official),
Creole

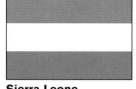

Sierra Leone
Area: 27,699 sq mi
(71,740 sq km)
Population: 5,696,000
Capital: Freetown
Languages: English (official),
Mende, Temne, Krio

Somalia
Area: 246,201 sq mi
(637,657 sq km)
Population: 9,133,000
Capital: Mogadishu
Languages: Somali (official),
Arabic, Italian, English

South Africa
Area: 470,693 sq mi
(1,219,090 sq km)
Population: 50,674,000
Capitals: Pretoria (Tshwane),
Cape Town, Bloemfontein
Languages: IsiZulu, IsiXhosa,
Afrikaans, Sepedi, English,
Setswana

Sudan
Area: 967,500 sq mi
(2,505,813 sq km)
Population: 42,272,000
Capital: Khartoum
Languages: Arabic (official),
Nubian, Ta Bedawie, many
local dialects

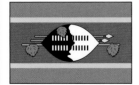

Swaziland
Area: 6,704 sq mi
(17,363 sq km)
Population: 1,185,000
Capitals: Mbabane, Lobamba
Languages: English, siSwati
(both official)

Tanzania
Area: 364,900 sq mi
(945,087 sq km)
Population: 43,739,000
Capitals: Dar es Salaam, Dodoma
Languages: Swahili, English
(both official), Arabic, many local
languages

Togo
Area: 21,925 sq mi
(56,785 sq km)
Population: 6,619,000
Capital: Lomé
Languages: French (official),
Ewe, Mina, Kabye, Dagomba

Tunisia
Area: 63,170 sq mi
(163,610 sq km)
Population: 10,429,000
Capital: Tunis
Languages: Arabic (official),
French

Uganda
Area: 93,104 sq mi
(241,139 sq km)
Population: 30,700,000
Capital: Kampala
Languages: English (official),
Ganda or Luganda, many local
languages

Zambia
Area: 290,586 sq mi
(752,614 sq km)
Population: 12,555,000
Capital: Lusaka
Languages: English (official),
75 indigenous languages

Zimbabwe
Area: 150,872 sq mi
(390,757 sq km)
Population: 12,523,000
Capital: Harare
Languages: English (official),
Shona, Sindebele, tribal dialects

AUSTRALIA, NEW ZEALAND, & OCEANIA

Australia
Area: 2,969,906 sq mi
(7,692,024 sq km)
Population: 21,852,000
Capital: Canberra
Language: English

Fiji Islands
Area: 7,095 sq mi
(18,376 sq km)
Population: 844,000
Capital: Suva
Languages: English (official),
Fijian, Hindustani

Kiribati
Area: 313 sq mi
(811 sq km)
Population: 99,000
Capital: Tarawa
Languages: English (official),
I-Kiribati

Marshall Islands
Area: 70 sq mi
(181 sq km)
Population: 54,000
Capital: Majuro
Languages: Marshallese
(official), English

Micronesia
Population: 271 sq mi
(702 sq km)
Population: 111,000
Capital: Palikir
Languages: English (official),
Trukese, Pohnpeian, Yapese,
Kosrean

Nauru
Area: 8 sq mi
(21 sq km)
Population: 10,000
Capital: Yaren
Languages: Nauruan
(official), English

New Zealand
Area: 104,454 sq mi
(270,534 sq km)
Population: 4,371,000
Capital: Wellington
Languages: English, Maori
(both official)

Palau
Area: 189 sq mi
(489 sq km)
Population: 21,000
Capital: Melekeok
Languages: Palauan, Filipino,
English, Chinese

Papua New Guinea
Area: 178,703 sq mi
(462,840 sq km)
Population: 6,610,000
Capital: Port Moresby
Languages: Melanesian pidgin,
715 indigenous languages

Samoa
Area: 1,093 sq mi
(2,831 sq km)
Population: 190,000
Capital: Apia
Languages: Samoan
(Polynesian), English

Solomon Islands
Area: 10,954 sq mi
(28,370 sq km)
Population: 519,000
Capital: Honiara
Languages: Melanesian pidgin,
120 indigenous languages

Tonga
Area: 289 sq mi
(748 sq km)
Population: 103,000
Capital: Nuku'alofa
Languages: Tongan, English

Tuvalu
Area: 10 sq mi
(26 sq km)
Population: 11,000
Capital: Funafuti
Languages: Tuvaluan, English,
Samoan, Kiribati

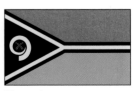

Vanuatu
Area: 4,707 sq mi
(12,190 sq km)
Population: 239,000
Capital: Port Vila
Languages: over 100 local
languages, pidgin (Bislama or
Bichelama)

GLOSSARY

acid rain precipitation containing acid droplets resulting from the mixture of moisture in the air with carbon dioxide, nitrogen oxide, sulfur dioxide, and hydrocarbons released by factories and motor vehicles

archipelago a group or chain of islands

bathymetry measurement of depth at various places in the ocean or other body of water

bay a body of water, usually smaller than a gulf, that is partially surrounded by land

biomass the total volume of organic material in a certain area or ecosystem that can be used as a renewable energy source

border the area on either side of a boundary

boundary most commonly, a line that has been established by people to mark the limit of one political unit, such as a country or state, and the beginning of another; geographical features such as mountains sometimes act as boundaries

breakwater a structure, such as a wall, that protects a harbor or beach from pounding waves

caloric supply a measure of the amount of food available to a particular person, household, or community

canal a human-made waterway that is used by ships or to carry water for irrigation

canyon a deep, narrow valley that has steep sides

cape a point of land that extends into an ocean, a lake, or a river

carat a unit of weight for precious stones equal to 200 milligrams

cataract a steplike series of waterfalls or rapids such as occur on the Nile River

cliff a very steep rock face, usually along a coast but also on the side of a mountain

continent one of the seven main landmasses on Earth's surface

country a territory whose government is the highest legal authority over the land and people within its boundaries

delta lowland formed by silt, sand, and gravel deposited by a river at its mouth

desert a hot or cold region that receives 10 inches (25 cm) or less of rain or other kinds of precipitation a year

desertification the spread of desertlike conditions in semiarid regions resulting from climatic changes and increasing human pressures, such as overgrazing, removal of natural vegetation, and cultivation of land

dialect a regional variation of a language

divide an elevated area drained by different river systems flowing in different directions

elevation distance above sea level, usually measured in feet or meters

escarpment a cliff that separates two nearly flat land areas that lie at different elevations

fault a break in Earth's crust along which movement up, down, or sideways occurs

fork in a river, the place where two streams come together

geographic pole 90°N, 90°S latitude; location of the ends of Earth's axis

geomagnetic pole point where the axis of Earth's magnetic field intersects Earth's surface; compass needles align with Earth's magnetic field so that one end points to the magnetic north pole, the other to the magnetic south pole

glacier a large, slow-moving mass of ice

global warming a theory explaining that the recent increase in Earth's average global temperature is due to a buildup of greenhouse gases, such as carbon dioxide and methane, in excess of natural levels due mainly to human activities

greenhouse gases atmospheric gases, such as carbon dioxide and methane, in excess of natural levels due mainly to human activities

gross domestic product (GDP) the total market value of goods and services produced by a country's economy in a year

gulf a portion of the ocean that cuts into the land; usually larger than a bay

harbor a body of water, sheltered by natural or artificial barriers, that is deep enough for ships

hemisphere literally half a sphere; Earth has four hemispheres: Northern, Southern, Eastern, and Western

highlands an elevated area or the more mountainous region of a country

hybrid car a car that is powered by gasoline and electricity

hydrothermal vent a crack in the ocean floor that releases mineral-rich, superheated water

inlet a narrow opening in the land that is filled with water flowing from an ocean, a lake, or a river

island a landmass, smaller than a continent, that is completely surrounded by water

isthmus a narrow strip of land that connects two larger landmasses and has water on two sides

lagoon a shallow body of water that is open to the sea but also protected from it by a reef or sandbar

lake a body of water that is surrounded by land; large lakes are sometimes called seas

landform a physical feature that is shaped by tectonic activity and weathering and erosion; the four major kinds on earth are plains, mountains, plateaus, and hills

landmass a large area of Earth's crust that lies above sea level, such as a continent

large-scale map a map, such as a street map, that shows a small area in great detail

Latin America cultural region generally considered to include Mexico, Central America, South America, and the West Indies; Portuguese and Spanish are the priniciple languages

latitude distance north and south of the Equator, which is 0° latitude

leeward the side away from or sheltered from the wind

lingua franca a language not native to the local population but that is used as a common or commercial language

longitude distance east and west of the prime meridian, which is 0° longitude

magma molten rock in Earth's mantle

mesa an eroded plateau, broader than it is high, that is found in arid or semiarid regions

metropolitan area a city and its surrounding suburbs or communities

Middle East term commonly used for the countries of Southwest Asia but can also include northern Africa from Morocco to Somalia

molten liquefied by heat; melted

mountain a landform, higher than a hill, that rises at least 1,000 feet (300 m) above the surrounding land and is wider at its base than at its top, or peak; a series of mountains is called a range

nation people who share a common culture; often used as another word for "country," although people within a country may be of many cultures

ocean the large body of saltwater that surrounds the continents and covers more than two-thirds of Earth's surface

peninsula a piece of land that is almost completely surrounded by water

permafrost a permanently frozen sub-surface soil in frigid regions

plain a large area of relatively flat land that is often covered with grasses

plateau a relatively flat area, larger than a mesa, that rises above the surrounding landscape

poaching the illegal killing or taking of animals from their natural habitats

point a narrow piece of land smaller than a cape that extends into a body of water

population density in a country, the number of people living on each square mile or square kilometer of land (calculated by dividing population by land area)

Prairie Provinces popular name for the Canadian provinces of Manitoba, Saskatchewan, and Alberta

prime meridian an imaginary line that runs through Greenwich, England, and is accepted as the line of 0° longitude

projection the process of representing the round Earth on a flat surface, such as a map

rain shadow the dry region on the leeward side of a mountain range

reef an offshore ridge made of coral, rocks, or sand

renewable resources resources that are replenished naturally, but the supply of which can be endangered by overuse and pollution

Sahel a semiarid grassland in Africa along the Sahara's southern border

savanna a tropical grassland with scattered trees

scale on a map, a means of explaining the relationship between distances on the map and actual distances on Earth's surface

sea the ocean or a partially enclosed body of saltwater that is connected to the ocean; completely enclosed bodies of saltwater, such as the Dead Sea, are really lakes

slot canyon a very narrow, deep canyon formed by water and wind erosion

small-scale map a map, such as a country map, that shows a large area without much detail

sound a long, broad inlet of the ocean that lies parallel to the coast and often separates an island and the mainland

Soviet Union shortened name for the Union of Soviet Socialist Republics (U.S.S.R.), a former Communist republic (1920–1991) in eastern Europe and northern and central Asia that was made up of 15 republics of which Russia was the largest

spit a long, narrow strip of land, often of sand or silt, extending into a body of water from the land

staple a chief ingredient of a people's diet

steppe a Slavic word referring to relatively flat, mostly treeless temperate grasslands that stretch across much of central Europe and central Asia

strait a narrow passage of water that connects two larger bodies of water

territory land that is under the jurisdiction of a country but that is not a state or a province

tributary a stream that flows into a larger river

tropics region lying within 23 1/2° north and south of the Equator that experiences warm temperatures year-round

topography the relief features that are evident on a planet's surface

upwelling process by which nutrient-rich water rises from ocean depths to the surface

valley a long depression, usually created by a river, that is bordered by higher land

virgin forest a forest made up of trees that have never been cut down by humans

volcano an opening in Earth's crust through which molten rock erupts

windward the unsheltered side toward which the wind blows

GEO FACTS & FIGURES

PLANET EARTH

Mass: 6,583,348,000,000,000,000,000 tons
(5,974,000,000,000,000,000,000 metric tons)
Distance around the Equator: 24,901 mi
(40,073 km)
Area: 196,938,000 sq mi (510,066,000 sq km)
Land area: 57,393,000 sq mi (148,647,000 sq km)
Water area: 139,545,000 sq mi
(361,419,000 sq km)

The Continents

Asia: 17,208,000 sq mi (44,570,000 sq km)
Africa: 11,608,000 sq mi (30,065,000 sq km)
North America: 9,449,000 sq mi
(24,474,000 sq km)
South America: 6,880,000 sq mi
(17,819,000 sq km)
Antarctica: 5,100,000 sq mi (13,209,000 sq km)
Europe: 3,841,000 sq mi (9,947,000 sq km)
Australia: 2,968,000 sq mi (7,687,000 sq km)

Highest Mountain on Each Continent

Everest, Asia: 29,035 ft (8,850 m)
Aconcagua, South America: 22,834 ft (6,960 m)
McKinley (Denali), North America:
20,320 ft (6,194 m)
Kilimanjaro, Africa: 19,340 ft (5,895 m)
El'brus, Europe: 18,510 ft (5,642 m)
Vinson Massif, Antarctica: 16,067 ft (4,897 m)
Kosciuszko, Australia: 7,310 ft (2,228 m)

Lowest Point on Each Continent

Bentley Subglacial Trench, Antarctica: −8,383 ft
(−2,555 m)
Dead Sea, Asia: −1,385 ft (−422 m)
Lake Assal, Africa: −512 ft (−156 m)
Death Valley, North America: −282 ft (−86 m)
Laguna del Carbón, South America: −344 ft
(−105 m)
Caspian Sea, Europe: −92 ft (−28 m)
Lake Eyre, Australia: −52 ft (−16 m)

Longest Rivers

Nile, Africa: 4,241 mi (6,825 km)
Amazon, South America: 4,000 mi (6,437 km)
Yangtze (Chang), Asia: 3,964 mi (6,380 km)
Mississippi-Missouri, North America: 3,710 mi
(5,971 km)
Yenisey-Angara, Asia: 3,440 mi (5,536 km)
Yellow (Huang), Asia: 3,395 mi (5,464 km)
Ob-Irtysh, Asia: 3,362 mi (5,410 km)
Congo (Zaire), Africa: 2,715 mi (4,370 km)
Amur, Asia: 2,744 mi (4,416 km)
Lena, Asia: 2,734 mi (4,400 km)

Largest Islands

Greenland: 836,000 sq mi (2,166,000 sq km)
New Guinea: 306,000 sq mi (792,500 sq km)
Borneo: 280,100 sq mi (725,500 sq km)
Madagascar: 226,600 sq mi (587,000 sq km)
Baffin: 196,000 sq mi (507,500 sq km)
Sumatra: 165,000 sq mi (427,300 sq km)
Honshu: 87,800 sq mi (227,400 sq km)
Great Britain: 84,200 sq mi (218,100 sq km)
Victoria: 83,900 sq mi (217,300 sq km)
Ellesmere: 75,800 sq mi (196,200 sq km)

Largest Lakes (by area)

Caspian Sea, Europe-Asia: 143,200 sq mi
(371,000 sq km)
Superior, North America: 31,700 sq mi
(82,100 sq km)
Victoria, Africa: 26,800 sq mi (69,500 sq km)
Huron, North America: 23,000 sq mi
(59,600 sq km)
Michigan, North America: 22,300 sq mi
(57,800 sq km)
Tanganyika, Africa: 12,600 sq mi (32,600 sq km)
Baikal, Asia: 12,200 sq mi (31,500 sq km)
Great Bear, North America: 12,100 sq mi
(31,300 sq km)
Malawi, Africa: 11,200 sq mi (28,900 sq km)
Great Slave Lake, Canada: 11,000 sq mi
(28,600 sq km)

Oceans

Pacific: 65,436,200 sq mi (169,479,000 sq km)
Atlantic: 35,338,500 sq mi (91,526,400 sq km)
Indian: 28,839,800 sq mi (74,694,800 sq km)
Arctic: 5,390,000 sq mi (13,960,100 sq km)

Largest Seas (by area)

Coral: 1,615,260 sq mi (4,183,510 sq km)
South China: 1,388,570 sq mi (3,596,390 sq km)
Caribbean: 1,094,330 sq mi (2,834,290 sq km)
Bering: 972,810 sq mi (2,519,580 sq km)
Mediterranean: 953,320 sq mi (2,469,100 sq km)
Sea of Okhotsk: 627,490 sq mi (1,625,190 sq km)
Gulf of Mexico: 591,430 sq mi (1,531,810 sq km)
Norwegian: 550,300 sq mi (1,425,280 sq km)
Greenland: 447,050 sq mi (1,157,850 sq km)
Sea of Japan: 389,290 sq mi (1,008,260 sq km)

Geographic Extremes

Highest Mountain

Everest, China/Nepal:
29,035 ft (8,850 m)

Deepest Point in the Ocean

Challenger Deep, Mariana Trench, Pacific:
-35,827 ft (-10,920 m)

Hottest Place

Dalol, Danakil Depression, Ethiopia:
annual average temperature 93° F (34° C)

Coldest Place

Plateau Station, Antarctica:
annual average temperature -70° F (-56.7° C)

Wettest Place

Mawsynram, Assam, India: annual average rainfall
467 in (1,187 cm)

Driest Place

Arica, Atacama Desert, Chile: barely measurable
rainfall

Largest Hot Desert

Sahara, Africa: 3,475,000 sq mi (9,000,000 sq km)

Largest Cold Desert

Antarctica: 5,100,000 sq mi (13,209,000 sq km)

People

Most People by Continent

Asia: 4,117,435,000

Least People by Continent

Antarctica: 2,000 (transient)
Australia: 21,852,000

Most Densely Populated Country

Monaco: 45,455 people per sq mi/17,500 per sq km

Least Densely Populated Country

Mongolia: 4 people per sq mi/1.5 per sq km

Biggest Metropolitan Areas

Tokyo, Japan: 36,094,000
Mumbai (Bombay), India: 20,072,000
São Paulo, Brazil: 19,582,000
México City, México: 19,485,000
New York, United States: 19,441,000
Delhi, India: 17,015,000
Shanghai, China: 15,789,000
Kolkata (Calcutta), India: 15,577,000
Dhaka, Bangladesh: 14,796,000
Buenos Aires, Argentina: 13,089,000

Countries with the Highest Life Expectancy

Andorra: 82.15 years
Japan: 82.12 years
Singapore: 81.98 years
Hong Kong: 81.86 years
Australia: 81.63 years
Canada: 81.23 years
France: 80.98 years

Countries with the Lowest Life Expectancy

Angola: 38.20 years
Zambia: 38.63 years
Lesotho: 40.38 years
Mozambique: 41.18 years
Zimbabwe: 37 years
Liberia: 41.84 years
Afghanistan: 44.40 years

Countries with the Highest Annual Income per Person

Liechtenstein: $122,100
Qatar: $121,400
Luxembourg: $77,600
Bermuda: $69,900
Norway: $59,300

Countries with the Lowest Annual Income per Person

Zimbabwe: $200
Democratic Republic of the Congo: $300
Burundi: $300
Liberia: $500
Somalia: $600

OUTSIDE WEB SITES

The following Web sites will provide you with additional valuable information about various topics discussed in this atlas. You can find direct links to each by going to the atlas URL (www.nationalgeographic.com/kids-world-atlas) and clicking on "Other Stuff."

Antarctic wildlife:
http://www.antarcticconnection.com/antarctic/wildlife/index.shtml

Biomes:
http://www.blueplanetbiomes.org

Currency converter:
http://www.xe.com/ucc

Earth's climates:
http://www.worldclimate.com

Earth's geologic history:
Earthquakes: http://earthquake.usgs.gov/
Tsunamis: http://www.tsunami.noaa.gov
Volcanoes: http://www.geo.mtu.edu/volcanoes/

Extreme facts about the world:
http://www.extremescience.com

Flags of the world:
http://www.fotw.us/flags/index.html

Languages of the world:
http://www.ipl.org/div/hello/

Mapping sites:
http://earth.google.com/
http://www.skylineglobe.com/

National anthems:
http://www.nationalanthems.info

Political world (lots of statistics):
https://www.cia.gov/library/publications/the-world-factbook/index.html

Religions of the world:
http://www.adherents.com/Religions_By_Adherents.html

Solar system:
http://solarsystem.nasa.gov/planets

Time differences between places:
http://www.worldtimeserver.com

Time zone map:
http://www.worldtimezone.com

Tracking Quakes (page 33)
http://www.iris.edu/seismon

Weather around the world right now:
http://www.weather.com

World heritage sites:
(important historic places around the world):
http://whc.unesco.org/en/list

INDEX

Map references are in bold-face (**50**) type. Letters and numbers following in lightface (D12) locate the place-names using the map grid. (Refer to page 7 for more details.)

PLACE-NAMES

Anadyr — Bitola

Ciudad del Este — England

English Channel — Guinea, Gulf of

Guinea-Bissau — Kansas

Lord Howe Island — Moroni

Osijek — Rangitata

Severn — The Hague

Wau — Cape Verde Plain

OCEAN FEATURES

Cargados Carajos Bank — Lau Ridge

Lesser Sunda Islands — Somerset Island

South Australian Basin — Zhokhova

Illustrations Credits

Abbreviations for terms appearing below: lo = lower; NGS = National Geographic Society.

All continent opening spreads (60–61, 76–77, 90–91, 108–109, 132–133, 148–149, 160–161) Blue Marble: Next Generation was produced by Reto Stöckli, NASA Earth Observatory (NASA Goddard Space Flight Center) http://earthobservatory.nasa.gov/Newsroom/BlueMarble/. The satellite imagery was captured for the month of May.

All graphic illustrations by Stuart Armstrong unless otherwise noted.

All locator globes created by Theophilus Britt Griswold and NGS.

Front cover globe, Premium Stock/Corbis; front cover photos, (left to right), Ron Kimball Stock, Jose Fuste Raga/Corbis, Sexh, Brand X; back cover photos (top to bottom), Richard Nowitz/NGS, Roy Toft/NGS, Roy Toft/NGS, Arthur ThÉvenart/Corbis.

Front of the Book
1, Premium Stock/Corbis; 2 up, Premium Stock/Corbis; 2 lo (left to right), Roy Toft/NGS, Tom Murphy/NGS, Cary Wolinsky/NGS, Richard Nowitz/NGS; 3 (left to right), far left, Ron Kimball Stock, Jose Fuste Raga/Corbis, Sexh, Brand X; 4 left, Raymond Gehman/NGS; 4 up right, Todd Gipstein/NGS; 4 lo right, Cary Wolinsky/NGS; 5 left, Richard Nowitz/NGS; 5 center up, Frans Lanting/NGS; 5 center lo, Justin Guariglia/NGS; 5 up right, Gordon Wiltsie/NGS.

Understanding Maps
10 (all), 3D Globe visualizations provided by SkylineGlobe (www.skylineglobe.com); 12 lo left (art) Shusei Nagaoka; 12 lo right, Mark Thiessen/NGS; 12 lo left (art), Lockheed Martin; 14–15 (art), Shusei Nagaoka.

Planet Earth
16 lo (art), Shusei Nagaoka; 16–17 (art), David Aguillar; 17 lo (art), Robert Hynes; 18 up right (art), Tibor G. Tóth/NGS; 18 lo (all art), Christopher R. Scotese/PALEOMAP Project, University of Texas, Arlington; 19 lo (all art), NGS.

Physical World
22 far left, Maria Stenzel/NGS; 22 left, Bill Hatcher/NGS; 22 right, Carsten Peter/NGS; 22 far right, Carsten Peter/NGS; 22–23 (ART), Shusei Nagaoka; 23 far left, Gordon Wiltsie/NGS; 23 left, James P. Blair/NGS; 23 right, Thomas J. Abercrombie/NGS; 23 far right, Anne Keiser/NGS; 27 up right, Kevin Rivoli/Associated Press; 27, up left, O. Brown, R. Evans, and M. Carle, University of Miami Rosenstiel School of Marine and Atmospheric Science, Miami, Florida; 27 lo right (both), Weiss and Overpeck, The University of Arizona; 26–27 (art), NGS. 28 far left, Raymond Gehman/NGS; 28 left, George F. Mobley/NGS; 28 right, Paul Nicklen/NGS; 28 far right, Raymond Gehman/NGS; 29 far left, Annie Griffiths Belt/NGS; 29 left, Beverly Joubert/NGS; 29 right, Michael Melford/NGS; 29 far right, Maria Stenzel/NGS; 30 left a, George Grall/NGS; 30 left b, Nicole Duplaix/NGS; 30 left c, Michael Nichols/NGS; 30 left d, William Albert Allard/NGS; 30 left e, Michael Nichols/NGS; 30 left f, Paul Sutherland/NGS; 30 right, James P. Blair/NGS; 31 left, William Thompson/NGS; 31 center, Steve McCurry/NGS; 31 right, Peter Essick/NGS; 32 up, NSSL/NOAA Photo Librry; 32 lo, Getty Images; 33 up, Dave Harlow/USGS; 33 lo left, The Seismic Monitor is an online product of the IRIS Consortium and displays earthquake locations from the U.S. Geological Survey; 33 lo right, Mario Tama/Getty Images.

The Oceans
35 lo left, Scripps Institute of Oceanography; 35 up right, NOAA; 35 lo right, NASA; 36 up, Wolcott Henry/NGS; 36 lo, Karen Kasmauski/NGS; 38 up, Tom Murphy/NGS; 38 lo left, Emory Kristof/NGS; 38 lo right, John Eastcott and Yva Momatiuk/NGS; 40, Hans Fricke/NGS; 42 up, Norbet Rosing/NGS; 42 lo, Paul Nicklen/NGS.

Political World
47, Justin Guariglia/NGS; 48, Maria Stenzel/NGS; 49 left, Justin Guariglia/NGS; 49 right, Phillipe Lissac/Godong/Corbis; 50 left, Martin Gray/NGS; 50 center, Randy Olson/NGS; 50 right, Amit Dave/Reuters/Corbis; 51 left, Reza/NGS; 51 right, Richard Nowitz/NGS; 52, Justin Guariglia/NGS; 53 left, George F. Mobley/NGS; 53 right, Phil Schermeister/NGS; 54, Jodi Cobb/NGS; 55 lo (art), NGS 57 left, James P. Blair/NGS; 57 up right, Stephen St. John/NGS; 57 center right, Joel Sartore/NGS; 57 lo right, Michael Nichols/NGS; 58 lo (art), NGS; 59 far left, Walter Rawlings/Robert Harding World Imagery/Corbis; 59 left, Richard Nowitz/NGS; 59 right, Sarah Leen/NGS; 59 far right, Priit Vesilind/NGS.

North America
64 up, Raymond Gehman/NGS; 64 lo, Tomas Tomaszewski/NGS; 64–65 up, Michael Melford/NGS; 64–55 lo, Rex Stucky/NGS; 65 lo, Jeff Vanuga/Corbis; 66 up left, Ira Block/NGS; 66 up right, NGS; 66 lo left, George F. Mobley/NGS; 66 lo right, Martin Gray/NGS; 67 up, David Doubilet/NGS; 67 lo left, Mark Cosslett/NGS; 67 lo right, Glen Allison/Stone/Getty Images; 68 center, William Albert Allard/NGS; 68 lo left, Michael S. Yamashita/NGS; 68 lo right, Richard Nowitz/NGS; 69 up, Tim Laman/NGS; 69 right, William Albert Allard/NGS; 70 up, NASA; 70 lo left, Todd Gipstein/NGS; 70 lo right, Norbet Rosing/NGS; 71 up, Brooks Walker/NGS; 72 up, Kenneth Garrett/NGS; 72 lo, Kenneth Garrett/NGS; 73up left, MacDuff Everton/NGS; 73 up right, Steve Winter/NGS; 73 lo, Roy Toft/NGS; 74 up, Pablo Corral Vega/Corbis; 74 lo left, Steve Raymer/NGS; 74-75 lo, Bill Curtsinger/NGS; 75 up, Michael Melford/NGS; 75 lo right, Jose Fuste Raga/Corbis.

(Continued on page 192)

Published by the National Geographic Society

John M. Fahey, Jr.,
President and Chief Executive Officer

Gilbert M. Grosvenor, *Chairman of the Board*

Tim T. Kelly, *President, Global Media Group*

John Q. Griffin, *Executive Vice President; President, Publishing*

Nina D. Hoffman,
Executive Vice President; President, Book Publishing Group

Melina Gerosa Bellows,
Executive Vice President, Children's Publishing

Prepared by the Book Division

Nancy Laties Feresten,
Vice President, Editor in Chief, Children's Books

Jonathan Halling,
Design Director, Children's Publishing

Jennifer Emmett,
Executive Editor, Reference and Solo, Children's Books

Carl Mehler, *Director of Maps*

R. Gary Colbert, *Production Director*

Jennifer A. Thornton, *Managing Editor*

Staff for this book

Suzanne Patrick Fonda, *Project Editor*

Priyanka Lamichhane, *Associate Editor*

Lori Epstein, *Illustrations Editor*

David M. Seager, *Art Director*

Bea Jackson, *Designer*

Ruthie Thompson, Nancy Sabato, *Production Design*

Thomas L. Gray, Nicholas P. Rosenbach, *Map Editors*
Matt Chwastyk, Sven M. Dolling, Steven D. Gardner,
Michael McNey, Gregory Ugiansky, Mapping Specialists, and
XNR Productions, *Map Research and Production*

Tibor G. Tóth, *Map Relief*

Martha B. Sharma, *Consultant*

Mark H. Bockenhauer, Martha B. Sharma, *Writers*

Stuart Armstrong, *Graphics Illustrator*

Kate Olesin, *Editorial Assistant*

Grace Hill, *Associate Managing Editor*

Lewis R. Bassford, *Production Manager*

Susan Borke, *Legal and Business Affairs*

Manufacturing and Quality Management

Christopher A. Liedel, *Chief Financial Officer*

Phillip L. Schlosser, *Vice President*

Chris Brown, *Technical Director*

Nicole Elliott, *Manager*

Rachel Faulise, *Manager*

Founded in 1888, the National Geographic Society is one of the largest nonprofit scientific and educational organizations in the world. It reaches more than 285 million people worldwide each month through its official journal, NATIONAL GEOGRAPHIC, and its four other magazines; the National Geographic Channel; television documentaries; radio programs; films; books; videos and DVDs; maps; and interactive media. National Geographic has funded more than 8,000 scientific research projects and supports an education program combating geographic illiteracy.

For more information, please call 1-800-NGS LINE (647-5463) or write to the following address:

NATIONAL GEOGRAPHIC SOCIETY
1145 17th Street N.W., Washington, D.C. 20036-4688 U.S.A.

Visit us online at www.nationalgeographic.com/books

For information about special discounts for bulk purchases, please contact National Geographic Books Special Sales: ngspecsales@ngs.org

For rights or permissions inquiries, please contact National Geographic Books Subsidiary Rights: ngbookrights@ngs.org

(Continued from page 191)

South America

80 up, Tim Laman/NGS; 80 lo left, Pablo Corral Vega/NGS; 80-81 up, Stephanie Maze/NGS; 81 lo left, Anne Keiser/NGS; 81 lo right, Todd Gipstein/NGS; 82 up left, Jimmy Chin/NGS; 82 up right, Kenneth Garrett/NGS; 82 lo left, Pablo Corral Vega/NGS; 82 lo right, Ed George/NGS; 83 up, Richard Nowitz/NGS; 83 lo left, Joel Sartore/NGS; 83 lo right, Melissa Farlow/NGS; 84 up, William Albert Allard/NGS; 84 lo left, Pablo Corral Vega/NGS; 84 lo right, Meredith Davenport/NGS; 85 up, O. Louis Mazzatenta/NGS; 86 up, Priit Vesilind/NGS; 86 lo left, MacDuff Everton/NGS; 86–87 lo, James L. Amos/NGS; 87 up, Joel Sartore/NGS; 88 up, O. Louis Mazzatenta/NGS; 88–89 lo, Skip Brown/NGS; 89 up, Maria Stenzel/NGS; 89 center, Joel Sartore/NGS.

Europe

94 up, Richard Nowitz/NGS; 94 lo left, Priit Vesilind/NGS; 94–95 up, Melissa Farlow/NGS; 94–95 lo, Richard Nowitz/NGS; 95 up right, Richard Nowitz/NGS; 96 up left, Taylor S. Kennedy/NGS; 96 lo left, Steve McCurry/NGS; 96 lo right, Sisse Brimberg/NGS; 96–97 up, Richard Nowitz/NGS; 97 lo left, Richard Nowitz/NGS; 97 center, Nicole Duplaix/NGS; 97 lo right, James P. Blair/NGS; 98 up, Sisse Brimberg & Cotton Coulson, Keepress/NGS; 98 lo left, Karen Kasmauski/NGS; 98 lo right, Priit Vesilind/NGS; 99 up, The Art Archive/Corbis; 100 up, Cees Van Leeuwen; Cordaiy Photo Library Ltd./Corbis; 100 lo left, Jim Richardson/NGS; 100 lo right, Richard Nowitz/NGS; 101 up, Richard Nowitz/NGS; 102 up, Catherine Karnow/NGS; 102 lo, Catherine Karnow/NGS; 103 up left, Sisse Brimberg/NGS; 103 right, Sisse Brimberg/NGS; 104 up, James P. Blair/NGS; 104 lo left, James P. Blair/NGS; 104 lo right, Todd Gipstein/NGS; 105 up, James L. Stanfield/NGS; 106 up, Steve Raymer/NGS; 106 lo, Steve Raymer/NGS 107 up, Richard Nowitz/NGS.

Asia

112 up, Taylor S. Kennedy/NGS; 112 lo left, Steve McCurry/NGS; 112–113 up, Steve Raymer/NGS; 112–113 lo, Justin Guariglia/NGS; 113 lo right, David Edwards/NGS; 114 up left, Fred de Noyelle/Godong/Corbis; 114 lo right, Jodi Cobb/NGS; 114 lo right, Justin Guariglia/NGS; 114–115 up, Todd Gipstein/NGS; 115 lo left, Michael Nichols/NGS; 115 lo right, Justin Guariglia/NGS; 116 up, Maria Stenzel/NGS; 116 lo, Steve Winter/NGS; 117 up, Steve Raymer/NGS; 117 lo, Cary Wolinsky/NGS; 118 up, Medford Taylor/NGS; 118 lo, Gordon Wiltsie/NGS; 119 up, David Edwards/NGS; 119 lo, Dean Conger/NGS; 120 up, H. Kim/NGS; 120–121 lo, Justin Guariglia/NGS; 121 up, O. Louis Mazzatenta/NGS; 121 lo, Roy Toft/NGS; 122 up, James L. Stanfield/NGS; 122 lo, Alex Webb/NGS; 123 up, Martin Gray/NGS; 123 lo, Priit Vesilind/NGS; 124 up left, Morteza Nikoubazl/Reuters/Corbis; 124 up right, Arthur Thèvenart/Corbis; 124 lo, Robb Kendrick/NGS; 125 up, Bill Lyons/NGS; 126 up, Ed George/NGS; 126 lo, Bobby Model/NGS; 127 up, Jason Horowitz/zefa/Corbis; 127 lo, James P. Blair/NGS; 128 up left, Paul Chesley/NGS; 128 up right, MacDuff Everton/NGS; 128 lo, Paul Chesley/NGS; 129 up, Jack Fields/Corbis; 129 lo, Steve Raymer/NGS; 130 up, Reuters/Corbis; 130 lo, Richard Nowitz/NGS; 131 up left, Paul Chesley/NGS; 131 up right, Tim Laman/NGS; 131 lo, Tim Laman/NGS.

Africa

136 up, George F. Mobley/NGS; 136 lo left, Michael Nichols/NGS 136-137 up, Skip Brown/NGS; 136-137 lo, Kenneth Garrett/NGS; 137 lo left, Bill Curtsinger/NGS; 137 lo right, Cary Wolinsky/NGS; 138 up, Georg Gerster/NGS; 138 lo left, Digital Vision/Getty Images; 138 lo right, Kenneth Garrett/NGS; 139 up, Cary Wolinsky NGS; 139 lo left, Bill Curtsinger/NGS; 139 lo right, Michael Nichols/NGS 140 up, W. Robert Moore/NGS; 140 lo left, Sarah Leen/NGS; 140–141 lo, NGS; 141 up, James L. Stanfield/NGS; 142 up, Randy Olson/NGS; 142 lo left, Michael Lewis/NGS; 142 lo right, Richard Nowitz/NGS; 143 up left, Kenneth Garrett/NGS; 143 up right, Bobby Haas/NGS; 144 up, George Steinmetz/NGS; 144 lo, Michael Nichols/NGS; 145 up, Werner Forman/Corbis; 145 up right, Michael Nichols/NGS; 146 up, George F. Mobley/NGS; 146 lo, Tim Laman/NGS; 147 up, Kenneth Garrett/NGS; 147 lo, Bob Krist/Corbis.

Australia, New Zealand, and Oceania

152 up, Nicole Duplaix/NGS; 152 lo left, Frans Lanting/NGS; 152–153 up, Art Wolfe/NGS; 152–153 lo, Tim Laman/NGS; 153 lo right, Nicole Duplaix/NGS; 154 up left, Medford Taylor/NGS; 154 lo left, Carsten Peter/NGS; 154 center, Frans Lanting/NGS 154–155 up, Tim Laman/NGS; 154–155 lo, Winfield Parks/NGS; 155 center, Paul Chesley/NGS; 155 lo right, Mark Cosslett/NGS; 156 lo left, Bill Curtsinger/NGS; 156 lo right, Sam Abell/NGS; 157 up left, Jason Edwards/NGS; 157 up right, Paul Chesley NGS; 158 up, Randy Olson/NGS; 158 lo, Carsten Peter/NGS; 159 up left, Martin Gray/NGS; 159 up right, Randy Olson/NGS; 159 lo, Jodi Cobb/NGS.

Antarctica

162 up, Gordon Wiltsie/NGS; 162 lo, Gordon Wiltsie/NGS; 163 up, Paul Nicklen/NGS; 163 lo, Maria Stenzel/NGS.

ISBN 978-1-4263-0687-7

This book is an updated edition of the *National Geographic World Atlas for Young Explorers, Third Edition*, published in 2007 (ISBN 978-1-4263-0088-2).

Printed in U.S.A.
10/RRDW/1